THE AMERICAN WOMEN'S ALMANAC

THE AMERICAN WOMEN'S ALMANAC

An Inspiring and Irreverent Women's History

Louise Bernikow

in association with the
National Women's History Project

Developed by The Philip Lief Group, Inc.

BERKLEY BOOKS, NEW YORK

THE AMERICAN WOMEN'S ALMANAC

A Berkley Book
Published by The Berkley Publishing Group
200 Madison Avenue, New York, New York 10016

The Putnam Berkley World Wide Web site address is http://www.berkley.com/berkley
First edition: March 1997

Library of Congress Cataloging-in-Publication Data
Bernikow, Louise, 1940–
    The American women's almanac : an inspiring and irreverent women's
history / Louise Bernikow ; in association with the National Women's
History Project.
        p.   cm
    Includes bibliographical references and index.
    ISBN 0-425-15686-9. — ISBN 0-425-15616-8 (trade)
    1. Women—United States—History—Miscellanea. 2. Women—United
States—Biography.   I. National Women's History Project.
II. Title.
HQ1410.B47   1997
305.4'0973—dc21   96-50917
                                                                          CIP

Printed in the United States of America

10 9 8 7 6 5 4 3 2 1

In memory of my mother, Rita, the reader

Contents

Introduction
The Shoulders We Stand On

This is a book about vision, courage, and stamina. Plus a few quirks. It celebrates the women who made the United States of America—all kinds of women in all kinds of situations doing all kinds of unimaginable things. Twenty-five years ago, this would have been an impossible undertaking.

Women were invisible then in accounts of the American past, with the exception of a few stereotypes—a mom here, a woman sewing a flag there, a bitch, a helpmeet. There were no African-American women, except an occasional slave, no Native Americans except white versions of Pocahontas and Sacajawea, no Hispanics, no Asian-Americans, no Jews. If there were lesbians, they weren't identified as such. Or, like most other women, they didn't matter.

This book is only possible because of the feminist work in women's history over the past quarter century. It stands on the shoulders of scholars, editors, writers, women's studies students, and researchers who have been finding the lost women and unearthing what has been left out of the story. They have been great detectives, hunting for documents in musty archives, traveling around with tape recorders to preserve the oral histories of women disdained by conventional scholarship. They have rescued papers, memoirs, correspondence, notebooks, and sketchbooks from families anxious to protect a relative's reputation and keep her hidden. Respecting what used to be called marginal, women in every field have saved what others, disrespectful of women's importance, were ready to throw away.

We owe the feminist historians everything we know. But women's history, as it is evolving, not only fills in gaps but changes the picture. Like everyone else, I have been taught by the new historians to see the record of history as a construct and to ask, who's in, who's out, and what are the criteria? Why is Betsy Ross, who stayed home sewing, so famous? Why does every schoolchild know of Paul Revere's ride, but not the stirring story of Molly Tynes, who rode forty miles over treacherous mountain roads (on a horse called Fashion) warning her Virginia neighbors that "The Yankees are coming, the Yankees are coming"? Having a place in history is clearly a political event.

With women at the center of the story, as they are here, the whole account of the American past and its connection to the present changes. The sense of good times and bad times shifts radically. The American Revolution, a time men were proud of and saw as progressive, took away freedoms and powers some women had established in the growing country. The devastations of the fratricidal Civil War were, paradoxically, occasions for some women to do things they had been prevented from doing for decades. Wars, perversely, were generally "good" for women.

Actually, nothing was good for women unless women made it so, seizing or creating an opportunity. The new women's history not only alters the facts and emphasis we learned in the past, but gives them a different attitude, restoring women's agency. The truth is not that Congress gave women the vote, but that women won the right to vote. The walls keeping women out of medicine and law did not suddenly crumble, and unequal wages did not suddenly become equal, but women, acting together, with a few good men, over the long haul, broke the barriers down. They are still doing so.

It is now possible to look at the enormous opposition to female progress, the ferocious attempts to contain female people in a category designated "women," and ask questions about the category. If "women" were not meant to work or study because it would endanger their delicate childbearing apparatus, as many people believed in the nineteenth century and might continue to believe today, what, then, of the female people slaving in the fields or losing their eyesight in the needle trades? Who decides which people fit the category called "women"?

So here is a new common history, full of charmers and cranks, visionaries, misguided souls, oddballs, and heroes. It displays the extraordinary acts by which women have challenged injustice and sees their wily and subversive strategies of resistance as important as overt acts of derring-do.

But single heroics and isolated great women are misleading. For every famous woman, there are hundreds who weren't and aren't. The networks are what is important, the connections among women, the ways they inspired or provided or loved each other enough to change the world. These links are perhaps the most missing part of what we know as our history.

Maybe someday we'll have the story right. Here is a way to begin piecing it together. Here is a celebration of many struggles, the implication being that not only does the long road from the past to the present, with its alternations of progress and repression, lend itself to dramatic and often witty tales, but that we can learn from it. It is alive to us today. And we deserve to have its record.

THE AMERICAN WOMEN'S ALMANAC

"

Nearly all the opportunities, educational and political, that woman has acquired have been gained by a march of conquest with a skirmish at every post. . . . We must make ourselves so aggressive a political factor that our natural protectors can no longer deny us a voice.

"

Helen Keller, 1915

Women's Action Coalition (WAC) demonstration, New York City, July 1992

CHAPTER 1

Politics

*D*o not put such unlimited power into the hands of the Husbands. Remember all Men would be tyrants if they could.
Abigail Adams to John Adams, 1776

Women should forget tender appeals to man's chivalry and instead sing hallelujas to single women, rebukes for spaniel wives, and reasonable denunciations for all flesh in male form.
Elizabeth Cady Stanton

I am prepared to sacrifice every so-called privilege I possess in order to have a few rights.
Inez Milholland, 1909

Wonderful girl. I'm glad she's gone.
Vassar College president, 1909, on the graduation of Inez Milholland, who, barred from holding a suffrage rally on campus, had assembled forty women in a nearby cemetery

The first thing I would do is run home. Then I'd call Bess Truman up and apologize profusely.
Maine Senator Margaret Chase Smith, during Harry Truman's presidency, responding to a question about what she would do if she woke up to find herself in the White House

Women are not more moral, we are only less corrupted by power. But we haven't been culturally trained to feel our identity depends on money, manipulative power, or a gun.
Gloria Steinem, 1971

Marisol, Women's Equality, lithograph of Elizabeth Cady Stanton and Lucretia P. Mott, 1975

Probably a portrait of Cheyenne warrior Yellow-Haired Woman, who fought at the 1868 Battle of Beecher's Island, drawn by Yellow Nose, 1880s

*I*n the beginning was blindness. The first white settlers encountered Native American cultures where the right to decide whether a war captive should be killed or adopted into the tribe was exclusively female, where women proven brave in battle sat on the warriors' council, and where "ordinary" women could veto a declaration of war by withholding the labor needed to carry it out.

The settlers neither saw nor cared what "savages" arranged. No women sat on the councils of the Great White Fathers. When women fought in battles, as they did, they hid female bodies in men's clothes. The rules of the New World for white women meant obedience to husbands, hard domestic labor, risky childbirth, inability to own or inherit property, and severe prohibitions about participating in public life.

Women always broke the rules. In the 1630s, Anne Hutchinson threatened the established order by preaching in public and encouraging other women, Massachusetts authorities said, "to be rather a husband than a wife." Branded a heretic and a leper, she was banished from the colony. In Maryland, Margaret Brent didn't get the message. In 1648, she went to the colony's legislature demanding the vote, only to be turned down.

As resistance to British authority grew in the eighteenth century, women organized effective boycotts of East India tea and other taxed goods before anyone dumped tea into Boston Harbor. Mercy Warren wrote political pamphlets and witty dramas mocking colonial overseers. When the battles began, women kept the troops alive with "women's work" like laundry and cooking, while some put on men's clothes and took up arms.

Female ingenuity took many forms: as British troops approached, a New Jersey woman took her horse into her home and kept it there for six weeks, until the danger was past.

"Independent" America did not reward its female patriots. Abigail Adams threatened her husband in 1776 that: "If perticular care and attention is not paid to the Ladies, we are determined to forment a Rebellion and will not hold ourselves bound by any Laws in which we have no voice, or Representation."

The rebellion was a long time coming.

Enslaved African women waged their own war. Some, like Harriet Tubman, Harriet Jacobs, and Ellen Craft, defied the system by escaping and carrying on the struggle once they were free—

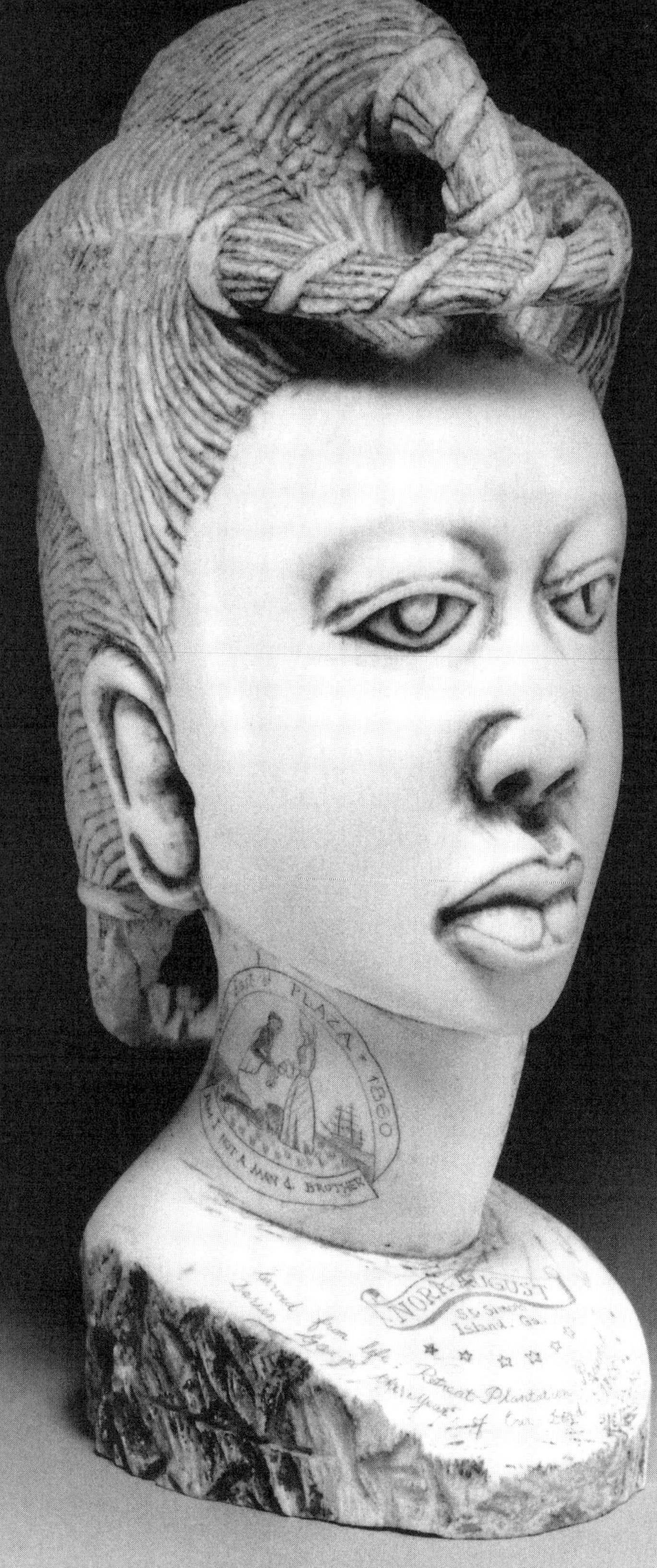

Bust of freed Georgia slave Nora August with the abolitionist symbol on her neck, by David Gaione, 1865

Tubman by returning to free more slaves, Jacobs by writing, Craft by appearing on abolitionist platforms in the North. Many led uprisings or helped the men who did. Others resisted by defending themselves against the "acceptable" practice of rape by their white owners or by aborting themselves rather than having children born as chattel.

Prayer meetings and revivalist waves in the 1820s and 1830s brought women into public in large numbers for the first time. Crusading white women, out to eradicate male drunkenness and the attendant violence against women were the first to travel unchaperoned and to challenge the ideals of female passivity and silence so central to the "civilization" America was constructing. These speakers and the mostly female

Shary Fenniken, Betsy Ross, from Wimmen's Comix, 1975

audiences who came to hear them formed, they believed, a morally superior sisterhood against the vices of a man's world, an idea that would run through women's movements in the years to come.

When women like Angelina and Sarah Grimké, white Southerners opposed to slavery, spoke out in public, at "promiscuous" assemblies of both men and women, the opposition was vicious. Speaking against slavery meant putting your life on the line.

Yet speak they did. Racial justice and gender justice were on the table together in the middle of the nineteenth century. They were seen as linked, as mirrors: no husband should own his wife; no person should own a slave. "I expect to plead not for the slave only, but for suffering humanity everywhere," Lucy Stone wrote to her mother in 1846, during her last year at Oberlin College. "Especially," she added, "do I mean to labor for the elevation of my sex."

Fighting for abolition prepared women to fight for themselves. The Civil War expanded the arena women were contesting. To the speaker's platform and the ballot box, add the battlefield where, it is rumored, 400 women fought as men. Clara Barton, abolitionist and femi-

THE GREAT REPUBLICAN REFORM PARTY,
Calling on their Candidate.
For Sale at No. 2 Spruce St. N.Y.
1856

Louis Maurer cartoon satirizing the radicalism of the newly formed Republican party and its candidate, John C. Fremont, 1856

nist, braved smoke, fire, and 23,000 wounded or dying soldiers to nurse at Antietam. Dr. Mary Walker, assistant surgeon in the Union army, wearing her usual men's clothes, was captured and eventually exchanged for a man of equal rank. Large numbers of women on both sides were spies, blockade runners, and saboteurs.

For the next sixty years, a women's movement struggled for equality against men who refused to relinquish power and women who clung to the status quo, "spaniel wives," as Elizabeth Stanton called them. Remembered now as frumps in black dresses and lace collars, cookie-cutter "ladies," bland and boring, mostly racist, the women of feminism's first wave were actually firebrands and revolutionaries. The mere act of organizing politically, acquiring the tools of the master's house, defied all gender constraints. The struggle for women's freedom built on those skills and expanded them.

The most sophisticated questions of our own time were first addressed in theirs. They questioned not only a woman's place, but all the customs and institutions that enforced it: church, state, courts, law enforcement, schools, marriages, divorce, and birth control. Stanton was eventually shunned in the movement for taking on the church by rewriting the Bible. Flamboyant Victoria Woodhull, banker, publisher, and intended candidate for the presidency in 1872, known to her many opponents as "Mrs. Satan," was ostracized by "respectable" feminists for her beliefs in "free love," but embraced by Stanton and Anthony.

The first movement battled over race and gender, especially the question of whether exclusions based on race and gender should be fought together or separately. Stanton and Anthony put women first and were not polite about it. Former slave Sojourner Truth agreed with them. Refusing to endorse the fifteenth constitutional amendment that extended the vote to Negro men but not to any women, Stanton and Anthony splintered lifetime friendships with former allies among the abolitionists.

The generation coming into the women's movement toward the end of the nineteenth century narrowed the agenda to winning the vote. After decades of debate, both conversation and persuasion seemed fruitless. Instead of ideology, attention shifted to tactics. Harriot Blatch, Stanton's daughter, recruited radical trade union women to the fight and, with Alice Paul, made it a fight again. Paul, a young Quaker, had learned militant disobedience from English suffragists, particularly Emmeline Pankhurst, whose motto was "Deeds, not words."

In 1912, the monumental parades began. Thousands marched in uniform rows, with military discipline, in New York, where windows displayed suffrage slogans on placards: 20,000 "voiceless speeches," they were called. In the capital the next year, Inez Milholland in Grecian robes on a white horse led off. Contingents came from every state, artists marching together, college students under their school banners, factory workers, farm women and, after some division in the ranks, black women from the black club movement and from Howard University. The marchers were heckled and grabbed by onlookers, including local police. The cavalry was called in to keep order. There were no arrests, but there was a Votes for Women ball.

As the country moved toward a world war, the movement warred with itself. Previously, women's politics had taken a backseat in wartime. Not now. Defying the women's rights mainstream that called her tactics "suicidal" for the movement, Paul organized pickets in 1917. High society ladies and working women stood silently in front of the White House six days a week, holding banners demanding the vote. The country cried treason. President Wilson offered them tea. Over two militant years, five hundred women were arrested.

In January 1918, the House of Representatives passed the Nineteenth Amendment, guaranteeing women's suffrage, by one vote. When Southern senators tried to attach a rider allowing individual states to exclude black women, Carrie Chapman Catt, directing the national suffrage organization, was willing to go along, but was dissuaded. In June 1919, the riderless amendment passed the Senate. The measure crept through the states for ratification. On August 18, 1920, the youngest member of the Tennessee state legislature, after reading aloud a letter from his mother urging him to do the right thing, cast the vote that, legally, made all women full American citizens.

It would be nice to say everyone lived happily ever after, but we know they didn't. Although popular perception in the 1920s was that women's freedom and equality had arrived, many feminists thought otherwise. Some turned their energies to the Equal Rights Amendment, introduced in Congress in 1923—and yet to be ratified—while others remained active through the 1930s and the 1940s in emerging struggles for labor rights, birth control, peace, education, and an end to economic exploitation.

By the 1950s, while middle-class white women were being manipulated into believing that bliss was a suburban tract house and a shining kitchen floor, black women like Mary Church Terrell were integrating eating establishments in Washington, D.C., and Rosa Parks was refusing to ride in the back of the bus in Montgomery, Alabama. Fannie Lou Hamer came out of the Mississippi Delta to risk her life registering voters and to shake up the entire Democratic party structure. Black women with political vision—including singer Berenice Johnson Reagon and Children's Defense Fund head Marian Wright Edelman—first learned about organizing and building power bases for social change in the civil rights movement.

All the liberation struggles of the sixties—civil rights, the student movement, the Black Panthers, the Young Lords, the new left, the gay rights movement—left a generation of women asking, as though it had never been asked before: What about our liberation? The question coincided with a battle already undertaken by the older generation of white women shunted into domesticity that Betty Friedan described in *The Feminine Mystique* in 1963.

From commissions on the status of women to the founding of the National Organization for Women in 1966, a new push for equality grew. Alongside what became an essentially inside-the-walls drive for removing discrimination against women was a women's liberation movement whose goals were far-reaching social change. The movement was far more fluid than any description suggests. Women joined NOW, left NOW, or ignored NOW. In numbers impossible to record, many women simply did feminist work without joining organizations.

Feminist structures and consciousness survived, however assaulted, through the 1970s and 1980s. Still, some women believed that they lived in "postfeminist" America. By 1992, however, it was clear that feminist organizing and protest was still necessary. The double whammy of watching "the trial of Anita Hill," as some called the spectacle of law professor Hill's testimony before a white male Senate committee considering the Supreme Court nomination of Clarence Thomas, and fearing the erosion of reproductive freedom, including the potential repeal of the 1973 court decision in *Roe v. Wade*, a new generation of women took to the streets.

Pocahontas

America's first Native American heroine is a symbol of assimilation. Her story, the first sanctioned racial intermarriage in America, is surrounded by myth and legend. Pocahontas certainly lived and was a chief's daughter. Pictured everywhere—in history texts and on the silver screen—she is an object of conjecture and fantasy; there are no authentic likenesses of her. A teenager, she was known to run naked through the young Jamestown colony, and at one point she was imprisoned on a British ship for a year. She probably didn't save John Smith's life; he told the same story about other women in other circumstances. No part of the tale, apparently, had much to do with love. Her marriage to colonist John Rolfe was probably a political union. She dressed in English clothes and was baptized a Christian. When they sailed to England in 1616, the point was to show her off at court and raise money for the colony. She died on that journey and is buried in an English churchyard.

Crimes against the State: Ann Hutchinson

Hutchinson, who arrived in Boston from England in 1634, believed women could understand God's word as well as men could. Women could not be inferior to men, she said, because only God was superior. She held "subversive" meetings with other women for three years, until, eventually, the Bay Colony ministers demanded a hearing. The year was 1637. She was forty-seven years old. Her crime, one minister said, was to have "stepped out of your place. You have rather been a husband than a wife." Although Hutchinson was married and had fifteen children, her refusal to keep her place led to her exile from the colony.

Hannah Lee Corbin and the Politics of Desire

A few years before the colonists declared themselves independent of England, Virginia widow Hannah Lee Corbin declared her own independence. Loudly and publicly, she protested being taxed for her land when she had no voice in making the laws. Corbin also insisted on her right to live in a romantic relationship of her own choosing and without penalty. Since her husband's will required the thirty-four-year-old widow to forfeit her land if she remarried, Hannah Lee Corbin simply invited her lover to move in with her. They had two children and lived for fifteen years as respected members of the community.

Deborah Sampson: Cross-Dressing for the Revolution

In 1782, a strapping indentured servant who stood five feet nine inches enlisted in the Continental army under her brother's name. In men's clothes, her breasts tightly bound, she served for a year and a half at West Point, defending the Hudson River Valley. Wounded and afraid of discovery, she removed the musket ball herself. When she came down with a severe fever, the doctor who treated her discovered her secret.

After the war, she married, had three children, and made money lecturing about her experience. She received back pay from the army and a disability pension, which Paul Revere helped her to get.

Angelina Grimké in Philadelphia, 1838

The "promiscuous assembly" of antislavery activists took place in Philadelphia's Pennsylvania Hall, a splendid, gaslit building with the motto "Virtue, Liberty, Independence" in gold letters over the stage. The audience was made up of men and women, black and white.

On the second day of the convention, the fiery speaker Abigail Kelley Foster announced that she refused to pay taxes on her farm because she was being taxed without representation. The next day, Angelina Grimké, a white Southerner who had denounced slavery, came to the platform.

A mob of angry white men formed in the streets, made up, observers said, of "strangers from the South" and Southern students attending Philadelphia's medical college. The howling mob surrounded the building.

"Do you ask," Grimké shouted, "what has the North to do with slavery? Hear it, hear it! Those voices without tell us that the spirit of slavery is here . . ."

Suddenly, there were cries of "fire." People ran. Heavy stones thudded against the windows. Angelina Grimké kept speaking.

The Truth about Sojourner Truth

In 1827, a slave named Isabella Baumfree, freed after forty years' bondage to a Dutch farmer in upstate New York, had the audacity to act publicly against slavery's devastating sundering of families. With the help of local Quakers, she sued to recover a son illegally sold to a Southerner. She won and retrieved the boy. Some years later, Isabella changed her name to Sojourner Truth, becoming one of the most famous and most mythologized speakers in the abolitionist and women's rights movements.

Sojourner Truth's carte-de-visite, sold to support herself.

I Sell the Shadow to Support the Substance.

SOJOURNER TRUTH.

Most of what we know about this fiery, illiterate preacher comes mediated by white women and influenced not only by their points of view, but by the political relationships between them. Olive Gilbert, a New England feminist abolitionist, took down *The Narrative of Sojourner Truth: A Bondswoman of Olden Time*, which was published in Boston in 1850. For two decades, Truth sold copies of this narrative to support herself. When she spoke at the women's rights convention in Akron, Ohio, in 1851, the only black woman present, the record of what happened was written by the meeting's chair, Frances Dana Gage, a white woman. Gage's version, in which Truth rises to speak in an atmosphere of opposition, misrepresented the tenor of the meeting, actually attended by many antislavery people and women willing to speak up.

Novelist Harriet Beecher Stowe, author of *Uncle Tom's Cabin*, wrote an essay called "Sojourner Truth, the Libyan Sibyl" in 1863. Stowe emphasized Truth's evangelical religion and barely mentioned feminism. In response, now twelve years after the event, Frances Dana Gage wrote her account of the Ohio meeting. Eager to restore Truth's feminism, according to historian Nell Irvin Painter, Gage invented the "Ain't I a Woman" speech, which has "defined Truth's persona in the twentieth century" and "become the main means of perpetuating the figure of Sojourner Truth in American memory."

Attacking the Slave System: Lydia Maria Child

After white abolitionist John Brown was caught raiding an arsenal in Harper's Ferry, Virginia, Northern writer Lydia Maria Child offered to go care for him in prison. The outraged wife of Virginia Senator James M. Mason, author of the 1850 Fugitive Slave Act, which made recovery of escaped slaves legal, attacked Child. Three hundred thousand copies of the exchange between the women, printed as a pamphlet, flooded the North.

To Mrs. Mason's boast that Southern ladies were kind to their slave women when they gave birth, Child responded that in New England, "the pangs of maternity meet with the requisite assistance; and here at the north, after we have helped the mothers, *we do not sell the babies.*"

Birth of a Movement: Seneca Falls

In 1848, Lucretia Mott, whose Quaker religion encouraged her to stand for justice and to speak her conscience, with Elizabeth Cady Stanton, daughter of a judge and wife of an abolitionist, gathered 300 women in Seneca Falls, New York for a women's rights convention. The group eventually agreed on the need for better divorce laws, education, and property rights, but balked at Stanton's radical demand for the vote. In the end, the Seneca Falls Declaration, modeled on the Declaration of Independence, was supported by progressive people of all genders and colors, the first document in American history reflecting the ideals of men and women, white and black.

Images of Female Power: Harriet Jacobs

[My grandmother] was a woman of a high spirit. I had been told that she once chased a white gentleman with a loaded pistol, because he insulted one of her daughters. . . . Though she had been a slave, Dr. Flint was afraid of her. He dreaded her scorching rebukes.

. . . One woman begged me to get a newspaper and read it over. She said her husband told her that the black people had sent word to the Queen of 'Merica that they were all slaves; that she didn't believe it, and went to Washington city to see the President about it. They quarreled; she drew her sword upon him, and swore that he should help her to make them all free.

That poor, ignorant woman thought that America was governed by a Queen, to whom the President was subordinate. I wish the President was subordinate to Queen Justice.

For most of the century since it was published in 1861, scholars believed that Lydia Maria Child was the real author of *Incidents in the Life of a Slave Girl, Written by Herself* and that the work was fiction. In fact, Child edited the narrative of escaped slave Harriet Jacobs. Its authenticity was finally established beyond any doubt by historian Jean Fagan Yellin.

Harriet Tubman: The General

Except for a ragged edge of sea islands, South Carolina was in Confederate hands on June 2, 1863, when three Union gunboats headed up the Combahee River into enemy territory. Their holds were empty and their gear stripped down. Beside Colonel James Montgomery stood Harriet Tubman, ex-slave.

With nine former slaves from the plantations along the river, she had scouted every house and camp and mapped every twist in the river. The map was in her head, since she could not write.

When the boats stopped, Tubman disappeared, followed by four black male scouts and forty-eight black soldiers. An hour later, the nearest plantation on fire behind them, the party returned with close to two hundred slaves. It was said that Tubman carried a pistol and threatened to shoot any slave who would not go with her.

Harriet Tubman with freed slaves, 1850s

The official Confederate report on the incident said: "A parcel of Negro wretches, calling themselves soldiers, with a few degraded whites made a few unsuccessful forays within our lines."

Tubman was the most successful conductor on the Underground Railroad, by which slaves escaped to the North. In addition to carrying hundreds to freedom and acting as an intelligence agent for the Union army during the Civil War, she allegedly helped plan John Brown's raid on the arsenal at Harper's Ferry.

Civil War Spies

Women make "natural" spies because their comings and goings are easily overlooked. The odd thing about the subversive women of the Civil War is that they are all described by male chroniclers as beautiful and alluring. Allowing for the male gaze and changing standards of beauty, the observation remains peculiar. Apparently unable to conceive of female ingenuity, those who reported on the spies assumed that they got what they did because of their allure.

✁ *Rose O'Neal Greenhow,* "The Rebel Rose," was a Virginian married to a State Department official. After his death in 1854, she remained in the capital, charming and well-connected. She sent secret troop information in code by courier to the general in command at Manassas, resulting in an early Southern victory. The courier, "Pretty" Betty Duvall, stopped to change her peasant dress into a formal riding habit before handing information over. Letting down her hair—"the longest and most beautiful roll of hair I have ever seen," recalled the general—she removed the secret message wrapped in a silver-dollar-sized package sewn up in a silk pouch as black as her hair.

Rose Greenhow was caught and imprisoned in the Old Capitol Prison, the window of her room nailed shut to prevent her from passing messages to couriers outside. After nearly a year, she was "banished" to Richmond, Virginia, where Jefferson Davis rewarded her with praise and money. In 1864, returning from England, where she had published her prison diary and gathered support for the Confederate cause, she drowned in a storm off the coast of North Carolina.

✃ *Belle Boyd,* "The Siren of the South," lived in Martinsburg, Virginia, a Union stronghold, but she proudly wore a Confederate sash and flew the rebel flag. At seventeen, she shot a Union soldier for insulting her mother.

Boyd, too, was said to have had "a way with men." With Confederate allies, she spied on Union soldiers and troop movements and sent messages to the battlefields. One of her most famous achievements shows how useful the things women know can be for espionage. A Union officer who occupied her aunt's house held a war council there before marching against Andrew Jackson. Boyd knew there was a hole in the floor of a bedroom closet above the drawing room. She hid there, listening, then passed on the information. Imprisoned several times, she was eventually deported to Europe.

✁ *Elizabeth Van Lew,* "Crazy Bet," went around the streets of Richmond, Virginia, in strange clothes, muttering to herself. Her behavior was likely a mask and a good one at that. No one took her seriously as a threat. A lifelong abolitionist, she helped Union soldiers escape from the local hospital and smuggled Mary Elisabeth Bowser, a slave she had freed years before, into the home of Jefferson Davis, president of the Confederacy. From what she heard at dinner table conversations, Bowser reported to Van Lew, who wrote messages on onion skin, slipped them through pinpricks into hollowed-out eggs, and often carried the innocuous looking baskets of produce to Union officers herself. She also hid messages in her servants' shoes and in cut flowers from her garden. General Grant, camped on the outskirts of town, waited for her inside intelligence. After the war, he made her Richmond's postmaster.

✃ *Pauline Cushman,* an actress of Creole descent, was "expelled" from Nashville as a dangerous secessionist, but was actually a double agent, her expulsion staged to ingratiate her with the rebels. She managed to steal military maps and drawings of fortifications from a Confederate engineer, smuggling them out in the handles of butcher knives and stuffed into the craw of a chicken, all carried across the lines by a female farmer. In the last year of the war,

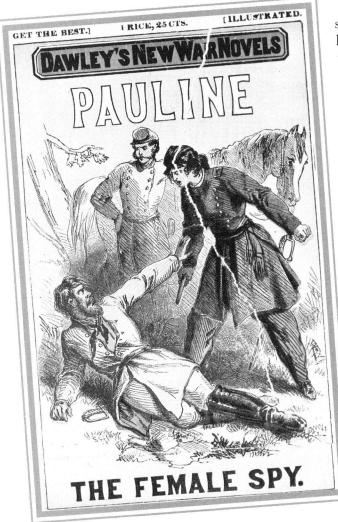

Dawley's New War Novels/Pauline the Female Spy—*dime novel about Civil War spy Pauline Cushman, 1870s*

she was caught and sentenced to be hanged, but federal troops arrived in time to save her.

Blockade Runner: 1864

Mary Louisa Walder of Philadelphia, Confederate supporter and nurse in Richmond, Virginia, agonized over watching men die because of inadequate medical supplies and decided to act. In 1864, she went to Canada, appealing for money and medicine. Remarkably successful, she loaded the hospital supplies on sleds and took them down the frozen St. Lawrence River. Transferring to a ship that took her and the cargo to Havana, Walder saw the supplies placed on a blockade runner to be carried into Galveston, Texas, then distributed.

Crimes against the State: Mary Suratt

Mary Suratt, the first woman hanged in America, was a mother. Her son was second in command to John Wilkes Booth, who assassinated Abraham Lincoln in 1865. Suratt, a forty-one-year-old Washington, D.C., boardinghouse keeper, had supported three children during the war. Although her boardinghouse was a regular meeting place for the Booth conspirators, there is no evidence of how much she participated. President Andrew Johnson said she owned the nest where the egg was hatched. The trial judge linked her to all women spies in the Civil War who had never been caught, and she was hanged on July 7, 1865.

Not Just the Vote: Defending Hester Vaughan

Stanton and Anthony made connections across class lines. Working women's exploitation, they said, was possible because of the lack of political rights. They not only went after the vote, but agitated for equal pay for equal work and eight-hour workdays.

In 1869, they used their newspaper, *The Revolution*, to defend a young woman accused of infanticide. Hester Vaughan had immigrated from England only to find her husband married to another woman. Deserted and alone, she did what poor girls did, hiring out as a servant and dairy maid. "Overcome by brute force"—raped, that is—presumably by her employer, pregnant, she ran away to Philadelphia and barely supported herself with odd jobs. Often living without food or fire, sick and dazed, she gave birth and dragged herself to her door, calling for help. The infant died, and the police charged her with infanticide.

Stanton and Anthony not only believed that Vaughan hadn't killed her child, but that the rape and her subsequent trauma were crucial to what happened. They recruited women doctors to examine Vaughan in prison, raised money, and hired lawyers. Nonetheless, Vaughan was convicted and sentenced to death.

The state's governor told Stanton that because the crime of infanticide was increasing at an alarming rate, an example had to be made of the prisoner . Stanton and Anthony set an example of their own, using their newspaper and their organizations to stir up a mass protest. Feminist pressure forced the governor to pardon Hester Vaughan, who returned to England.

Race and the Women's Movement

The council-tent is our Congress, and anybody can speak who has anything to say, women and all. . . . If women could go into your Congress, I think justice would soon be done to the Indians.

Sara Winnemucca, Paiute activist, writer and lecturer, who exposed corrupt Indian Bureau agents and officials by writing and lecturing, 1883

White women in the early women's movement looked to Native Americans for mod-

Sara Winnemucca, Paiute
writer and activist, 1871

els and rhetoric. Stanton and Anthony were well acquainted with the Iroquois in New York State. Many other Native American tribes in the Northeast, Southeast, and Southwest were matrilineal: a child received his or her identity from the mother's family, inheriting personal property and the right to hold office through her. Women had authority over property. The female-centered Iroquois and Cherokee had clan mothers who nominated and deposed chiefs and subchiefs. Mothers of those slain in battle and clan mothers were in charge of prisoners.

> Not only does the woman (under our white nation) lose her independent hold on her property and herself, but there are offenses and injuries which would be avenged and punished by relatives under tribal law, but which have no penalty or recognition under our laws. . . .
>
> . . . As I have tried to explain our statutes to Indian women, I have met with one response. They have said, "As an Indian woman, I was free. I owned my home, my person, the work of my hands, and my children would never forget me. I was better as an Indian woman than under white law."
>
> *Alice Fletcher, ethnologist, friend of Susan B. Anthony and Elizabeth Cady Stanton, 1888*

The Great Vote-in of 1872

On election day, 1872, in spite of the law, hundreds of women went to the polls demanding to vote. Dr. Mary Walker, dressed in men's clothes, her Congressional medal on her lapel, was turned away in Oswego, New York. Sojourner Truth tried to vote in Battle Creek, Michigan. Susan B. Anthony, who had registered at her local polling place, a barbershop, was arrested at her home on Thanksgiving Day. Refusing to go in the patrol wagon, she and her guards took a streetcar to downtown police headquarters.

It amazed everyone that Anthony was actually brought to trial, but the authorities thought they could stop the movement by prosecuting her. Anthony and friends used the upcoming trial to launch an educational campaign, intensifying their lectures on women's rights, hoping to reach the town's citizens who would be on the jury. When the state moved the trial to a small town farther upstate, the suffragists began canvassing there. Matilda Jocelyn Gage's speech was called "That the United States Is on Trial, Not Susan B. Anthony."

In June 1873, Susan B. Anthony was brought to trial before a male judge who had written his decision in advance and an all-male jury. Anthony, "incompetent" to testify under the law because she was a woman, was not allowed to speak. Without deliberation, the jury found her guilty.

Finally asked if she had anything to say, she began, constantly interrupted by the judge, "Resistance to tyranny is obedience to God." Her punishment was a $100 fine and court costs.

"The Prairie Joan of Arc": Mary Elizabeth Lease

What you farmers need to do is raise less corn and more Hell!
Mary Elizabeth Lease, campaigning for the Populist party, 1890

Mrs. Lease should raise more children and less hell.
Atchinson, Kansas Globe *newspaper, 1890*

I used to be radical and vindictive. I am still radical, but I am not vindictive. Time has mellowed me.
Mary Elizabeth Lease, 1931

Scarcely more than a child, Mary Elizabeth taught school in the 1870s and started a movement to demand better pay for female teachers. She moved to the Kansas prairie, and at nineteen, she married, tried farming with her husband, and failed. An early convert to the temperance movement, which meant public speaking, she also took in washing to support her family. Like Abraham Lincoln, she passed the Illinois bar by "reading law," often pasting passages to study on the wall near her washtubs. As farmers began rebelling against grain merchants and railroad operators—"the bloodhounds of money," she called them—Lease became their most stirring speaker. In 1890, on behalf of the new Populist party, she made 160 speeches in Kansas alone. When the party won control of the state government, people clamored to elect Mary Lease its senator. Suffrage leaders rallied to her, but the populist men weren't ready for so radical a step. Eventually, Joseph Pulitzer hired her as a reporter for his New York *World*. In her last years, she ran a small law clinic offering free legal advice to the poor.

Ida B. Wells

A former schoolteacher, Wells wrote for the *Memphis Free Speech* newspaper, where her investigative reporting on lynching was the first light shed on a taboo. Her analysis challenged the myths of white female purity and black male rapaciousness. Many lynchings of black men, she found, were related to interracial love affairs; the Southern rape complex ignored the fact that most actual rape was intraracial. Lynchings were not based on sexual crimes, real or alleged, but on economics. In 1892, Wells charged white merchants with lynching three black grocery store owners to eliminate competition and urged fellow black citizens to leave a city that condoned such barbarity. Hundreds sold property and moved west; those staying behind boycotted streetcars and stayed away from work.

One of the most prominent black women to organize for suffrage, she founded the first black women's suffrage group, the Alpha Suffrage Club, whose 200 members registered thousands of women to vote in local and state elections and formed the National Association of Colored Women at the turn of the century. When she tried to march with the white Illinois delegation in the 1913 suffrage parade, she was sent to the black contingent at the rear. As the parade stepped out, there was Ida B. Wells with the Illinois contingent. Among the 8,000 marchers were some rather perturbed Southern ladies.

Friend of Susan B. Anthony, ally of W. E. B. Du Bois, she was branded a "dangerous radical" by the government and an inspiration by those she touched in a long activist career.

Josephine St. Pierre Ruffin

Ruffin worked with the Sanitary Commission during the Civil War and, afterward, started the Kansas Relief Association to help former slaves in trouble in the West. A political ally of Elizabeth Cady Stanton and Susan B. Anthony, she became a charter member of the Massachusetts Suffrage Association in 1870. When a white Missouri newspaper editor maligned Ida B. Wells, sending a letter to sponsors of her lecture tour that not only attacked Wells but called all African-American women blatantly immoral, Ruffin responded. The meeting she called in Boston in 1895 brought women from thirty-six clubs in twelve states together to create the National Federation of Afro-American Women.

Should Women Vote?

Men are too emotional to vote. Their conduct at baseball games and political conventions shows this, while their innate tendency to appeal to force renders them particularly unfit for the task of government.
Alice Duer Miller, 1915

Would-Be Voters, *November 14, 1885. The caption reads: "A bevy of strong-minded Amazons make a sensation at a New York uptown polling place."*

The woman who thinks that the keeping of the home is beneath her sex is not fit to vote and is not fit for anything else. . . . There are some differences between men and women that were ordained by the Almighty and that all the cranks and agitators of earth can never remove.

Missouri senator James Reed, on the Senate floor, 1918

How can this Congress, which voted for war to make the world safe for democracy, not allow women this small measure of democracy?

Montana Representative Jeannette Rankin, in the House of Representatives, 1918

You gentlemen say we should not vote because we'll mingle at the polls with horrid men, but these are the same horrid men we live with the rest of the year.

Anna Howard Shaw, minister and president of the National Woman Suffrage Association

Women were working in the foundries, stripped to the waist because of the heat, but he said nothing about their losing their charm. Nor had he mentioned the women in laundries who stood for thirteen and fourteen hours a day in terrible heat and steam with their hands in hot starch. I asked him if he thought they would lose more of their beauty and charm by putting a ballot in the ballot box than standing around all day in foundries or laundries.

Garment industry organizer Rose Schneiderman on her conversation with a New York State senator opposed to suffrage

Winning the West

We may stay out of the Union a hundred years, but we will come in with our women.

Wyoming state legislature to the U.S. Congress, 1889, as its application for statehood was questioned because women could vote there

In 1874, with sixty other women, veteran black abolitionist Mary Ann Shadd Cary tried to vote in Washington, D.C. In 1878, she shared the podium with Elizabeth Cady Stanton and Susan B. Anthony at the National Woman Suffrage Association convention. Testifying on behalf of women's suffrage before the Judiciary Committee of the House of Representatives, she demanded that the word *male* be expunged from the Constitution.

Suffrage parade,
Washington, D.C., 1913

WE DEMAND AN AMENDMENT TO THE CONSTITUTION OF THE UNITED STATES ENFRANCHISING THE WOMEN OF THIS COUNTRY

Chicago Tribune *cartoon celebrating the passage of women's suffrage in Illinois, 1913*

⋙ The first city entirely governed by women was Oskaloosa, Kansas. In 1887, a municipal suffrage law was enacted in Kansas, "the great experimental ground of the nation." The female slate was elected in Oskaloosa that year and reelected in 1889, when there were also completely female governments in Cottonwood Falls and Rossville.

⋙ Suffrage circuit riders traveled by rail, stage, wagon, and buckboard through storm and mountain cold to organize suffrage clubs in the 1890s. A huge suffrage convention was held in Helena, Montana, in 1895. President of the state's suffrage association, Ella Knowles, had come to Montana for a health cure and stayed to get a law passed permitting women to practice law. Nearly thirty years later, in September 1914, hundreds of women marched, dressed in suffrage yellow, led by Anna Howard Shaw, Jeannette Rankin, and an Indian woman representing Indian guide Sacajawea as "Montana's first suffragist." On November 14, women won the right to vote there by fewer than 4,000 votes.

⋖ The first dozen states to grant women suffrage were all in the West. By 1914, New Mexico was the only Western state where women could not vote.

Abigail Scott Duniway in Oregon

She went West in a wagon train across Kansas, to Fort Laramie in Wyoming, through Plains Indian country, an unending sea of grass and prairie storms. In the fourth week, cholera killed twelve people, including her mother. By winter, the survivors crossed the Great Divide. In the spring of 1852, they crested the Blue Mountains, entering Oregon. Abigail Scott was seventeen years old.

She married quickly, had five sons and a daughter, was a farmer's wife. When her husband became an invalid, she taught school, opened a millinery shop, and published *The New Northwest*, a weekly women's rights newspaper, writing sketches of women's lives on the frontier and an advice column about everything from honeymoons to drunken husbands. In 1871, she managed Susan B. Anthony's campaign through the Pacific Northwest.

"It's odd," she would say, "that men feel they must protect women, since for the most part they must be protected from men."

Once, while Duniway spoke in a church, the women's choir began singing. The louder she spoke, the louder they sang, but she wore the choir out.

She lived to see Oregon pass laws permitting women to own land in their own names and have businesses as their own property. In 1912, at age seventy-eight, she was the first woman to cast a vote in her state.

Mary White Ovington and the NAACP: 1909

In 1904, settlement worker Mary White Ovington, raised in an abolitionist family and a Radcliffe College graduate, began to study Manhattan's black population. Living for a time as the only white person in a black tenement, she saw housing and employment as the most important issues and came to see class as important as race. Her work brought her in contact with black leaders, especially W. E. B. Du Bois, and she joined his radical Niagara Movement.

In 1908, following a violent race riot in Springfield, Illinois, she and two white men (socialist William English Walling and labor reformer Dr. Henry Moscowitz) formed what they intended as a biracial protest group to fight racial discrimination and push for civil rights, including the vote. DuBois was the only black member. For almost forty years, Ovington worked with the National Association for the Advancement of Colored People, chairing its board for a time, although she believed black people should lead the organization. She pressured suffragists to fight for black women as well as white, opposed U.S. participation in World War I, and helped remove D. W. Griffith's racist film, *Birth of a Nation*, from circulation.

The First Women's Peace March

The United States entered the First World War on August 7, 1914. On August 12, feminist Lillian Wald told the Women's Peace March organizing committee:

> It may seem a mockery to call the women together to protest; but there is among many of us an imperative demand for expression at this time—when the horrifying spectacle of a world engaged in slaughter fairly unhinges reason . . . women more than men can strip war of its glamour and its out-of-date heroisms and patriotisms, and see it as a demon of destruction and hideous wrong.

Before August was over, fifteen hundred women were marching down New York's Fifth Avenue in protest, dressed in black or in white with black armbands. They came not only from the United States, but from the warring nations of France, Germany, England, and Austria. Among the prominent Americans were longtime peace, suffrage, and civil rights activists Fannie Garrison Villard and Lillian Wald, who brought a contingent of nurses from her Henry Street Settlement.

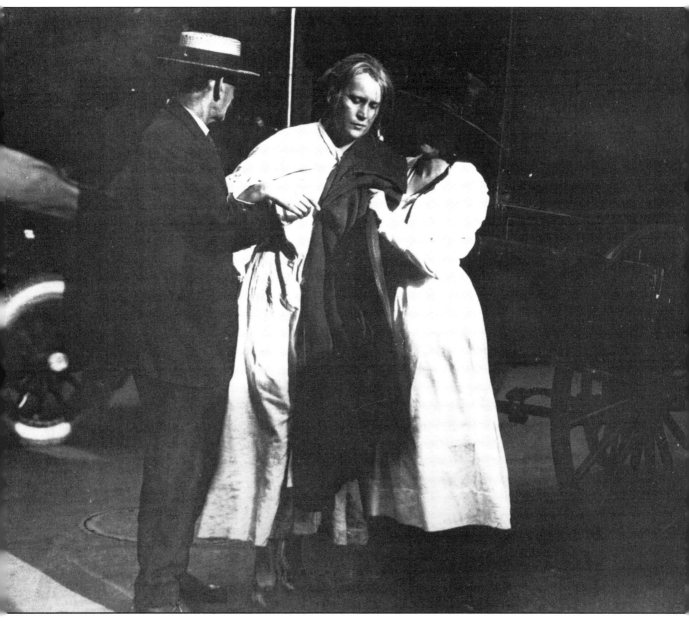

Suffragist Mrs. Lawrence (Dora) Lewis, released from jail after a hunger strike, 1917

Picketing the White House

As World War I escalated, the suffrage pickets remained in place, weathering insults, physical attacks, and criticism from less radical women in the movement. Among those on the line were women like art patron Louisine Havemeyer, whose husband had made a fortune in the sugar trade and who became the first American to buy a Degas and to promote painter Mary Cassatt, and Allison Turnbull Hopkins, wife of one of President Wilson's advisors, who had often dined at the White House.

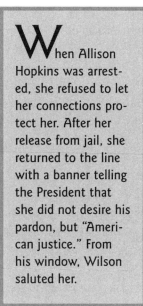

When Allison Hopkins was arrested, she refused to let her connections protect her. After her release from jail, she returned to the line with a banner telling the President that she did not desire his pardon, but "American justice." From his window, Wilson saluted her.

Ada Davenport Kendall, a fifty-year-old journalist, came to observe the action outside the White House in 1917 and joined the line. For her Buffalo newspaper, she wrote, "There is nothing hysterical or violent in their method. Although men have thought it glorious to slay their brothers and raze cities for liberty, these women have raised neither hand nor voice."

Police arrested ten women in the first sweep, then sixteen. They became the second group of women in the country jailed for advocating women's rights; birth control advocates were serving time in New York.

The arrests brought more protests, the protests brought more arrests: five hundred over two militant years. Alice Paul was kept in solitary confinement for five weeks, and a psychiatrist was called in to evaluate her sanity. Much to the dismay of the authorities, he found her sane.

Held in a former men's workhouse in a swamp that had been declared unfit for habitation since 1909, the prisoners called hunger strikes and were gruesomely force-fed. Their resistance gave them the nickname, "The Iron Jawed Angels."

Prison radicalized many. Released, Paul organized a "Prison Train," traveling across the country with women who had survived imprisonment, stopping to make speeches in favor of the Nineteenth Amendment. Outside the White House, the militants burned Wilson's speeches, mocking what he said of freedom and setting fire to an effigy of the President. The prison terms got longer, the forced feeding more violent.

Mother's Day: An Activist and Pacifist Holiday

Many actions led to the establishment of Mother's Day as a national holiday in 1915. Whichever story of origins carries the most weight, the decision to honor mothers came at the highest point of militant suffrage activism, as pickets outside Wilson's White House were being hauled off to jail. Woodrow Wilson intended the holiday as a bone thrown to women, perhaps, or a distraction. The connections between motherhood and pacifism so inherent in its beginnings have been lost in the evolution of Mother's Day.

Version 1. Anna M. Jarvis of West Virginia established a Mother's Friendship Day in 1868 to ease tensions between North and South after the Civil War. Some say the Mother's Work Days began earlier, to improve community sanitation, a task that was continued through women's brigades during the Civil War. In 1907, two years after she died, her daughter, also named Anna Jarvis, a single woman with no children, organized 400 people to attend a church service honoring hers and other mothers in the church where Mother Jarvis had taught. She distributed white carnations, symbols of purity, which have become symbols of the holiday. With the patronage of department store impresario John Wanamaker, she ran the Mother's Day International Association, eventually convincing Congress and the President to dedicate the second Sunday in May to mothers.

Version 2. In 1870, horrified by the Civil War and what she heard of the carnage of the Franco-Prussian War, Julia Ward Howe, who had written "The Battle Hymn of the Republic," called for an international gathering of women to abolish war. In London, denied permission to speak at a major peace conference because she was a woman, she rented a theater and called her own meeting. From the stage, she said, "The ambition of rulers has been allowed to barter the dear interests of domestic life for the bloody exchange of the battlefield. . . . From the bosom of the devastated earth a voice goes up with our own. It says, 'Disarm, Disarm.'"

Back in the United States, she organized Mothers' Peace Day celebrations every June 2nd in Boston. City after city adopted the tradition until President Woodrow Wilson declared it a national holiday.

Nina Otero-Warren: Pushing New Mexico over the Line

Nina Otero's father was killed in a land grant dispute with Eastern millionaire James Whitney. Her cousin was the state's first native-born territorial governor. She grew up a firebrand, agitating for better pay for teachers and for bilingual education. After a two-year marriage to a cavalry officer, she left him and declared herself "widowed," which allowed her to campaign for suffrage, run for public office, and homestead land. In 1918, defeating a male opponent, she was elected superintendent of public schools, the youngest in the county.

Her moment of glory came in 1920, as the process of ratifying the Nineteenth Amendment moved through the states. When thirty-one of the necessary thirty-six had passed it, antisuffrage forces concentrated on New Mexico. "Suffrage Totters on Edge of Defeat by

Winning the Vote: A Time Line

1776–1807: Women have the vote under New Jersey's state constitution, only to lose it.

1838: Kentucky widows with children in school win "school suffrage," the right to vote in school board elections.

July 19–20 1848: First convention to discuss women's rights is held in Seneca Falls, New York.

October 23–24, 1850: First National Women's Rights Convention, planned by Lucy Stone, Lucretia Mott, and Abby Kelley, draws one thousand people. Annual national conferences are held through 1860 (except 1857).

1866: Suffragists present petitions bearing 10,000 signatures to Congress for an amendment prohibiting disenfranchisement on the basis of sex.

May 1, 1866: The American Equal Rights Association is formed to work toward suffrage for both women and Negroes.

1867: Kansas puts woman suffrage on the ballot. It loses.

1868: The Fourteenth Amendment is ratified; the word *male* defines a citizen.

December 1868: The federal women's suffrage amendment is introduced in Congress.

1869: Women win voting rights in the Wyoming Territory.

May 1869: The National Woman Suffrage Association is founded by Susan B. Anthony and Elizabeth Cady Stanton to get the vote through a Congressional amendment and to address other women's rights issues.

November 18, 1869: The American Woman Suffrage Association is formed by Lucy Stone, Henry Blackwell, and others to work exclusively for woman suffrage by amending individual state constitutions.

1871: Wives of prominent men, including many Civil War generals, start the Anti-Suffrage Party.

1878: Senator A. A. Sargent of California introduces a woman suffrage amendment in Congress; the wording remains unchanged until it is finally passed in 1919.

1890: The American Federation of Labor supports a woman suffrage amendment. The South Dakota campaign for woman suffrage loses.

July 23, 1890: Wyoming, the first state since New Jersey to grant women full enfranchisement, is admitted to the Union.

1893: Colorado adopts woman suffrage.

1894: At the New York State Constitutional Convention, 600,000 signatures are presented in an effort to bring a woman suffrage amendment to the voters. The effort fails.

1896: Utah joins the Union, granting women full suffrage. Idaho adopts woman suffrage. Washington State adopts woman suffrage. The first large suffrage parade in New York City is organized by the Women's Political Union.

November 1911: The most elaborate suffrage campaign ever mounted succeeds in California by only 3,587 votes, an average of a single vote in every precinct in the state.

1912: Twenty thousand suffrage supporters join a New York City parade, with a half million onlookers. Oregon, Kansas, and Arizona adopt woman suffrage.

1913: The Congressional Union is formed by Alice Paul and Lucy Burns to secure passage of a federal amendment. Their efforts revive the issue on a national level.

March 3, 1913: The day preceding President Wilson's inauguration, thousands of suffragists organized by Alice Paul parade in Washington, D.C., and are mobbed by abusive crowds along the way.

May 10, 1913: The largest suffrage parade to date, including perhaps 500 men, marches down Fifth Avenue in New York City.

1914: Montana and Nevada adopt woman suffrage.

1915: A transcontinental tour by suffragists gathers over a half million signatures on petitions to Congress. Forty thousand march in New York City. Woman suffrage measures are defeated in Pennsylvania, New York, and Massachusetts.

JUNE 6, 1916: Alice Paul creates the National Woman's Party.

1917: New York State adopts woman suffrage.

JANUARY 10, 1917: The National Woman's Party picketers appear in front of the White House, remaining there in spite of bad weather and violent public response.

APRIL 2, 1917: Jeannette Rankin of Montana is seated in the U.S. House of Representatives, the first woman elected to Congress.

JUNE 22, 1917: Arrests of White House picketers on charges of obstructing traffic begin. Sentenced to up to six months in jail, their inhumane treatment in jail creates martyrs for the suffrage cause.

NOVEMBER 27–28, 1917: In response to public outcry and jailers' inability to stop the picketers' hunger strikes, the government unconditionally releases them.

1918: Michigan, South Dakota, and Oklahoma adopt woman suffrage.

JANUARY 9, 1918: President Wilson publicly supports the federal woman suffrage amendment.

JANUARY 6, 1919: Directly in line with the White House front door, the National Woman's Party builds a perpetual "watchfire for freedom" in which they burn the words of every speech President Wilson gives about democracy.

SPRING 1919: Released from jail, protesters tour the country on a train called the Prison Special.

MAY 21, 1919: The House of Representatives passes the federal woman suffrage amendment.

JUNE 4, 1919: The Senate passes the Nineteenth Amendment with just two votes to spare.

FEBRUARY 14, 1920: The League of Women Voters is founded. Thirty-three states have ratified the suffrage amendment, but final victory is still three states away.

AUGUST 18, 1920: Tennessee becomes the thirty-sixth state to ratify the amendment.

AUGUST 26, 1920: The Nineteenth Amendment is quietly signed into law by Secretary of State Bainbridge Colby, granting women the right to vote.

Chronology compiled by Mary Ruthsdotter; reprinted from the National Women's History Project

Alice Paul toasting victory in front of a National Woman's Party suffrage banner, 1920

> Let us review the incidents of our long struggle together before they are laid away with other buried memories. Let us honor our pioneers. Let us tell the world of the ever-buoyant hope, born of the assurance of the justice and inevitability of our cause, which has given our army of workers the unswerving courage and determination that at last have overcome every obstacle and attained their aim.
> *Call to the Victory Convention of the National American Woman Suffrage Association, February 1920*

Pledge-Breakers," read the local newspaper headline. On February 18, Otero-Warren spoke to lawmakers for three hours. The next day, suffrage passed.

Good Guys

≪ *William Lloyd Garrison* insisted that women, the backbone of antislavery societies, be allowed to hold office in the national organization. In 1840, Abby Kelley, Lucretia Mott, and Lydia Maria Child were elected. Conservative men walked out. The next year, the World Anti-Slavery Convention in London rejected the credentials of the seven women in the American delegation. Garrison refused to take his seat, watching the proceedings from the gallery with the women.

≫ *James Mott,* Quaker businessman, accompanied his wife Lucretia Mott to Seneca Falls and chaired the first women's rights meeting.

≪ *Parker Pillsbury,* antislavery editor, worked on their newspaper, *The Revolution,* with Susan B. Anthony and Elizabeth Cady Stanton.

≫ *Robert Purvis and Frederick Douglass,* prominent black antislavery leaders, were lifelong suffrage allies.

≪ *Henry Blackwell,* constant agitator for women's rights, helped publish *The Woman's Journal* with his wife, Lucy Stone, and their daughter, Alice Stone Blackwell.

Eleanor Roosevelt

She would rather light candles than curse the darkness, and her glow has warmed the world.
Adlai Stevenson

There had never been a First Lady like her, and there hasn't been one since. Beginning with volunteer work in a settlement house on the Lower East Side, Eleanor Roosevelt had developed a strong political vision of her own. Franklin's first visit to the University Settlement was his introduction to the concept of slums and poverty. Eleanor's role in FDR's political life would remain the role of conscience.

Her own political life would set precedents for American women and have enormous

*Eleanor Roosevelt and
Marion Anderson at
NAACP awards,
Richmond, Virginia,
July 2, 1937*

Running for Office

Victoria Woodhull, known to her opponents, who were many, as "Mrs. Satan" and to her political sisters as an eccentric, attacked constraints on female sexuality. A successful banker and financial advisor to J. P. Morgan, Woodhull created her own party advocating freedom to divorce and the right to birth control. In 1872, she declared her candidacy for the presidency of the United States. On election day, however, she was in jail for her "free love" advocacy, accused of sending obscenity through the mail.

Belva Lockwood was a teacher first, founding an early coeducational school in Washington, D.C., before she became a lawyer and the first woman permitted to practice before the Supreme Court. A year later, she sponsored the first Southern black man's appearance before the Supreme Court. In 1872, she made speeches on Victoria Woodhull's behalf. In 1884, Lockwood herself ran for president on the National Equal Rights party ticket and was loudly ridiculed in the press. She ran again in 1888.

Jeannette Rankin, suffragist from Missoula, Montana, where women won the vote in 1914, was elected the nation's first congresswoman in 1916. "I felt at the time that the first woman should take the first stand, that the first time the first woman had a chance to say no to war she should say it," she said, explaining her shocking solitary vote against World War I. Rankin distinguished herself by voting against every war that came before Congress. In 1968, at age eighty-eight, she not only said no to the Vietnam War, but led the Jeannette Rankin Brigade on a protest march to the capital.

Margaret Chase Smith, too poor for college, worked in Maine as a maid, telephone operator, basketball coach, and executive secretary to Clyde Smith, who she married. Clyde Smith was elected to the House of Representatives in 1936. When he died four years later, she won a special election for his seat and then a Senate seat of her own in 1948. She immediately helped pass legislation providing equal pay, privileges, and rank for women in the military. In 1950, she stood up to and denounced fellow Republican, Red-baiting Joseph R. McCarthy. In 1972, she lost her bid for a fifth term because of her age. Throughout her political career, she never took a poll, never did television advertising, and never accepted campaign contributions. She also never appeared in public dressed in anything but a dress or suit with pearls and high heels.

Shirley Chisholm, the first black woman elected to Congress, in 1969, was one of the first black female leaders to speak against sexism and to support reproductive and abortion rights. "As a black person, I am no stranger to race prejudice. But the truth is that in the political world I have been far oftener discriminated against because I am a woman than because I am black," she said in 1969, introducing the Equal Rights Amendment on the House floor. Her autobiography is called *Unbossed and Unbought*, which is what she was. In 1972, Chisholm campaigned for the Democratic presidential nomination, a move seen by some as serious, others as quixotic, and by most as symbolic of the new political power women had.

Geraldine Ferraro, New York congresswoman, ran for the vice presidency in 1984 on the Democratic ticket. She said that being in the Congress turned her into a feminist: "I realized my definition of feminism was really all wrong." From sister congresswoman Bella Abzug, she learned that women's issues went beyond the Equal Rights Amendment and reproductive choice: "War and peace is a woman's issue, the environment is a woman's issue, economic equality is a woman's issue." Barbara Bush, whose husband won the election, said Ferraro was "something that rhymed with rich."

Elaine Noble became the first "out" gay person elected to a state legislature in 1974, running against the owner of a "swinging singles" bar in a Boston, Massachusetts, working-class district. Successful on local issues like street lighting and rent control and national issues like the Equal Rights Amendment, she was reelected in 1976. But a homophobic campaign started by conservative Anita Bryant led the gay community to pressure her to fight back against Bryant and focus her political agenda entirely on gay rights. Saying, "Any politician has to have a series of issues, and once you're pigeon-holed with one issue, it is sort of a death knell," she did not run again in 1978.

Barbara Jordan went to Congress from Texas in 1972, the first African-American to do so since Reconstruction. Two years later, she became a national celebrity, eloquently defending the U.S. Constitution and calling for Richard Nixon's impeachment for his role in the Watergate scandal. In 1976, she gave a historic keynote address at the Democratic National Convention and many believed she might become the first black president. Instead, she retired from national politics and took up academic life in 1977. She died in 1996.

The Year of the Woman: 1992. The number of women in the U.S. Senate tripled after the November elections—from two to six. In the House, twenty-nine female representatives became forty-eight. Women were elected governors in Texas, New Jersey, Oregon, and Kansas. Most observers attributed these gains to female anger and political passion after the televised hearings on Clarence Thomas's nomination to the Supreme Court and the increasing willingness of women to support female candidates with money. Emily's List, founded by philanthropist Ellen Malcolm a decade earlier, raised six million dollars for female candidates, making it the largest political action committee in the country.

Senator Barbara Boxer and other elected women officials running up Capitol steps to protest the treatment of witness Anita Hill by a Senate committee considering Supreme Court nominee Clarence Thomas, October 9, 1991

impact on the life of the country. She came to the White House with feminist principles, experience, and friends. Before FDR took office in 1932, only twelve women had held presidential appointments. Under FDR, their numbers were legion. Eleanor Roosevelt used her public platform to speak out and act for social and racial justice and, with her newspaper columns and radio talks, she earned her own money.

She also earned her own place in international politics. After FDR's death in 1945, she went on to help found the United Nations. Her links to the modern women's movement lie in her relentless feminism and antiracism, the role model she provided, her tireless activism, and the extraordinary number of women she attracted to and supported in government. She was the first chair of President Kennedy's Commission on the Status of Women in 1961.

Eleanor Roosevelt's Women's Cabinet

The door might not be opened to a woman again for a long, long time and I had a kind of duty to other women to walk in and sit down on the chair that was offered, and so establish the right of others long hence and far distant in geography to sit in the high seats.
Frances Perkins to Carrie Chapman Catt

Molly Dewson, America's first woman political boss, known as "More Women Dewson" for her insistence on important political and government jobs for women, was a Wellesley graduate, veteran of the suffrage movement and the National Consumer's League. She organized women within the Democratic party, especially for Franklin Roosevelt's campaigns for governor of New York in 1930, president in 1932, and again in 1936.

Josephine Roche, Assistant Secretary of the Treasury, had a social work degree from Columbia University. In Denver, Colorado, where her father owned a coal company, she had been a controversial social reformer. In 1928, she took over her father's business and ran it with unprecedented progressive measures, inviting the savage animosity of barons like John D. Rockefeller, Jr. After losing a race for the governorship of Colorado, she served in Washington for three years, battling Depression poverty, but resigned to try to salvage her faltering family business.

Did You Know?

Frances Perkins, Secretary of Labor, was the first female cabinet member in American history. A Mount Holyoke graduate who worked at Hull House in Chicago, she had been a marcher and speaker for the suffrage cause and a crusader against sweatshops with the National Consumer's League. She was a crucial part of the labor program of Roosevelt's New Deal.

Mary McLeod Bethune, the first black person with a high federal position, a close friend of Eleanor Roosevelt, was head of the Office of Minority Affairs at the National Youth Administration. A lifetime's activism in the black club movement, fighting against school segregation and for prison reform, had led to this appointment. Her real influence came from the informal "black cabinet" she organized, which met in her house, advocating black interests to a government that essentially did not respond until World War II. She was present at the founding conference for the United Nations in 1945, representing the National Council of Negro Women. In 1974, the first statue to honor any black woman leader in a public park was erected to her in Washington, D.C.

> If those talented white women were working at such responsible jobs in a time of crisis, I could do the same thing. I visualized dozens of women coming after me, filling positions of high trust and strategic importance.
> Mary McLeod Bethune

Crimes against the State: Lolita Lebron

On March 1, 1954, sewing machine operator and Puerto Rican nationalist Lolita Lebron and three men walked into the gallery of the House of Representatives, waved a Puerto Rican flag, and opened fire. Five congressmen were wounded. Lebron and the others were sentenced to seventy-five years in jail, but President Jimmy Carter commuted their sentences in 1979.

Contesting Public Space

⤜ In 1864, *Sojourner Truth* helped integrate the streetcars in Washington, D.C.

⤜ In 1866, San Francisco millionaire boardinghouse owner and gold speculator **Mary Ellen Pleasant** was returning from shopping with two friends. Because of their dark skin, Pleasant and one friend were not allowed to board a streetcar, while the lighter-skinned friend did ride. Pleasant sued the trolley company and collected minimal damages.

⤜ **Ida B. Wells** refused to move to the "colored" cars on a Tennessee train and was forcibly ejected. She sued but eventually lost before the state Supreme Court in 1887.

⤜ In 1955, **Rosa Parks** refused to move to the "colored" seats in the back of a Montgomery, Alabama, bus. Her action and its consequences sparked a citywide boycott and is one of the precipitating events of the Civil Rights movement.

Lolita Lebron under arrest, Washington, D.C., March 1954

The Civil Rights Movement

> The qualitative change in the struggle for Negro freedom is that we are not, any of us, remotely interested in the all-insulting concept of the 'exceptional Negro.'
> *Lorraine Hansberry*

> It was women going door to door, speaking with their neighbors, meeting in voter registration classes together, organizing through their churches, that gave the vital momentum and energy to the movement, that made it a mass movement. Hundreds of women took leadership in the movement and from it learned the lessons that inspired the women's movement.
> *Andrew Young at Fannie Lou Hamer's funeral, 1978*

◄ In 1951, playwright **Lorraine Hansberry,** writing for *Freedom* magazine, published by Paul Robeson, covered a protest against the Korean War and racial discrimination by 132 black women who called themselves Sojourners for Truth. A strong supporter of the civil rights movement a decade later, she wrote the text for a book about the Student Nonviolent Coordinating Committee, an organization formed by black college students to fight segregation in the South, in 1964.

◄ **Rosa Parks** grew up in Tuskegee, Alabama, with a grandfather who stood up to the Ku Klux Klan. By the time she refused to move to the back of the bus in Montomery on December 1, 1955, the twenty-three-dollar-a-week seamstress at a big department store had been working in the NAACP for many years. She was taken into police custody that day and eventually fined ten dollars. Black leaders called a boycott. Rather than ride, people walked miles, and white women who drove black people around were stopped by the police. After 381 days, the U.S. Supreme Court struck down segregation on buses.

◄ **Fannie Lou Hamer,** daughter of sharecroppers in the Mississippi Delta, was harassed, shot at, and jailed and beaten bloody for working on voter registration in the South. In 1964, she walked into the national spotlight as one of the leaders of the Mississippi Freedom Democrats, who attempted to unseat the "regular" (all white) delegation to the national convention because they had not been fairly elected. In 1968, Hamer succeeded. Her work helped force political parties to rewrite their own rules and to push passage of the Voting Rights Act, both of which increased political participation by those who had been excluded. In 1971, she became one of the founders of the National Women's Political Caucus.

◄ **Ella Baker,** a field organizer for the NAACP and mentor to the Student Nonviolent Coordinating Committee, was a longtime activist who shaped the group's political vision. She believed in—and demonstrated—true grassroots organizing, empowering local people to act on their own behalf after the organizers had moved on. With little interest in celebrity or the grandstanding speeches of some male leaders, she was not famous outside activist circles.

Hundreds of black and white college students went South for what came to be called

The Roots of Women's Liberation

I am glad the American nation did not wait for the hearts of individual slave owners to change to abolish the slave system—for I suspect that I should still be running around on a plantation as a slave. And that really would not do.

Lorraine Hansberry

Our women played a major part at Wounded Knee [1973]. We had two or three pistol-packing mamas swaggering around with six-shooters dangling at their hips, taking their turns on the firing line, swapping lead with the feds. The Indian nurses bringing in the wounded under a hail of fire were braver than many warriors.

Mary Crow Dog, Lakota Woman, 1990

Angela Davis giving the Black Power salute upon her release from jail, Palo Alto, California, 1972.

Student sit-in at segregated lunch counter, Charlotte, North Carolina, February 9, 1960

Mrs. Gladys Bissonette
protesting the shooting of her
nephew by Bureau of Indian
Affairs officers during an
American Indian Movement
action on the Pine Ridge
Reservation in Wounded
Knee, South Dakota,
February 27, 1972

Partners Del Martin and Phyllis Lyon,
founders of the Daughters of Bilitis
and the journal, The Ladder, 1988

Women Strike for Peace
protesting the Vietnam
War, New York City,
August 26, 1970

Freedom Summer, 1964. They registered voters and taught in Freedom Schools, many staying beyond the summer. For some white women, this experience was an activist baptism; the analysis and vision of the movement carried over into working for women's liberation.

➤ *Viola Liuzzo,* a white part-time student, housewife, and mother of five, watched television news coverage of troopers attacking civil rights marchers in Selma, Alabama, and decided to act. Driving south from Detroit, she pitched in, organizing a second Selma-to-Montgomery march for March 25, 1965. At the end of the day, her car would ferry marchers back to Selma. On the highway, with a black male civil rights worker riding beside her, Viola Liuzzo was splattered with gunfire coming through her car window. She died at the scene.

The Equal Rights Amendment

"

Maybe [women] weren't at the Last Supper, but we're certainly going to be at the next one.

"

Congresswoman Bella Abzug to Congressman Emanuel Celler, who argued against the ERA because women are different from men, and "besides, they weren't even at the Last Supper."

In view of the intensity of discussion concerning sex equality as a basic human right, staleness plainly is not a reason for allowing the clock to run out on the proposed Equal Rights Amendment. Rather, the equal dignity of women and men before the law is among the most vibrant issues contemporary society faces.

Attorney Ruth Bader Ginsburg, arguing for extension of time to ratify the Equal Rights Amendment, 1978

Drafted by Alice Paul, suffragist and founder of the National Woman's Party, the Equal Rights Amendment was first introduced into Congress in 1923. It languished for nearly fifty years. Finally, prompted by the women's movement, it was debated and passed in 1972 and sent to the states for ratification. It looked like a shoo-in: twenty states passed it in the first six months. But the conservative opposition began raising money and organizing, bringing the process to a standstill in 1977, a year short of the congressional deadline. That summer, 100,000 supporters, dressed in white to echo the suffrage parades, marched in the capital. It was the largest demonstration for women's rights in American history. The deadline for ratification, virtually unique for a constitutional amendment, was extended to 1982. The amendment has yet to become law.

How the Women's Movement Changed the World

Before 1965, in the United States of America:

 ➣ Married women could not establish credit in their own names, which meant no credit cards or mortgages or other financial transactions were possible without a husband's agreement.

 ➣ Rape charges required a corroborating witness to be convincing in court—a woman's word alone was not good enough. A woman's past sexual history was allowed as testimony, usually to prove that she was "promiscuous" and had been "asking for it." A husband who raped his wife was not a rapist.

 ➣ Newspapers carried sex-segregated help-wanted ads. Employers routinely assigned certain jobs to women, others to men, with the women's jobs paying far less.

 ➣ There were few women in law or medical school and few visibly prominent in those professions.

*Equal Rights Amendment rally,
the White House, July 7, 1978*

≫ Women's ambitions as politicians, professionals, artists, or in any sphere outside the domestic were considered neurotic at best, crazy at worst.

≪ Women were addressed as "Miss" or "Mrs." even in irrelevant situations like booking airline seats, where there were obviously not special sections for married or unmarried women.

≫ Abortion was illegal. Sterilization without a woman's consent was common. Severe infections and deaths from illegal abortions were frequent. Birth control was not much discussed in public discourse and dispensing contraceptive information, even to married couples, was against the law in some states.

≪ *He* and *man* were considered universal words, applying to all humankind. There were chairmen, policemen, postmen, etc.

≫ Under most state laws, women were routinely not allowed to be administrators of estates.

≪ Most schools and colleges had few, if any, organized competitive sports for women. Male teams always had priority in terms of athletic scholarships, budgets, equipment, and playing time. Marathon running was considered too strenuous, and women were barred from such competitions, including the Olympics.

≫ Working women who became pregnant could be fired.

≪ The marriage contract was understood to be that men supported women financially and women provided domestic and sexual service to their husbands.

≫ An employer who insisted that in order to keep her job, a female employee have sex with him or submit to fondling was not breaking the law.

≪ Police called to scenes of domestic violence considered it a private matter and, at best, tried to calm the parties down.

≫ In schools and colleges, embarrassing, ridiculing, and generally denigrating female students was usual. There was little intellectual prestige for scholarship about women, and few women with advanced standing were on faculties.

≪ No woman anchored the news on television. Most women reporters wrote for the women's pages of newspapers. All women in media were paid less than men, except for those who owned the company.

≫ There was a 2 percent cap on enlisted women in the military and no women at the rank of general or admiral.

> ## " We've hardly cleared our throats. "
>
> *NOW president Wilma Scott Heide in 1974, to those who suggested that the women's movement had run its course*

We must guard what we have with vigilance and give up nothing. We have not come far enough to give up anything.
Patricia Bailey, Federal Trade Commissioner, 1983

In every generation women have to be taught their place one more time. The subordination of women is never accomplished for once and for all.

Theologian Rosemary Radford Reuther, 1986

Last Words

She risked everything that is dear to man—friends, fortune, comfort, health, life itself—for the one absorbing desire of her heart, that slavery be abolished and the union preserved.

Monument to Elizabeth Van Lew, spy, died 1900, Richmond, Virginia

There is a word sweeter than Mother, Home or Heaven—that word is Liberty.

Gravestone of Matilda Joslyn Gage, radical friend of Susan B. Anthony and historian of the first wave of the women's movement (died 1898, Fayetteville, New York)

She was a friend of John Brown.

Gravestone of Mary Ellen Pleasant, hotel owner and gold rush speculator, provider of funds in support of the raid on Harper's Ferry (died 1904, Napa, California)

" Failure is impossible. "

Susan B. Anthony's last public words, February 1906.

"
My definition
of courage is
making an
appointment
with the
gynecologist
and actually
showing up.
"

Joan Rivers

Pro-choice rally, New York City, 1992

CHAPTER 2

The Female Body

*T*he heavy skirts, bustles, long waists and longer points, filled with whalebones and other splints fit only to be used on the human frame in case of broken bones—this style of dress has induced more suffering than tightlacing, though that was a more speedy cause of death.
> The Water-Cure Journal, *1851*

I have an inalienable, constitutional and natural right to love whom I may, to love as long or as short a period as I can, to change that love every day if I please.
> *Victoria Woodhull, presidential candidate, 1872*

Be his. Be home. Be hard to forget. But be sure. Sure as Kotex napkins.
> *1970 ad*

Comedian Kate Clinton says that when she can't decide (politically) whether or not to shave her legs, she compromises and shaves just one.

We have been raised to fear the yes within ourselves, our deepest cravings. For the demands of our released expectations lead us inevitably into actions which will help bring our lives into accordance with our needs, our knowledge, our desires.
> *Audre Lorde*

I suppose it's too hard for men to admit the simple truth: for lesbians, sex with them is like peanut butter compared to caviar, like "The Donna Reed Show" competing with *Gone with the Wind*.
> *Jeanne Cordova*

Emma Amos, Take One, *stencil print, 1985–87*

Suzanne Opton, **Four Women, Vermont,** *1980*

Battleground and playground. Temple and sewer. A source of joy, grief, pleasure, pain, and political battles. An object of derision and mystification, shame and exploitation, covered up, publicly displayed, and constantly tinkered with. American history is a story about conflict over what the purpose of the female body is, how it is meant to work, and what should be done when it doesn't work properly.

At times, the struggle for women's bodies seems an effort to recapture what has been lost. In Colonial America, women were the experts in reproductive matters. Abortion was acceptable and legal until the point of "quickening," about midway through pregnancy, when the woman perceived fetal movement. Birthing and "lying in" were female rituals, attended by midwives, sisters, and friends: social rituals as well as natural events. In 1646, Francis Rayus was fined fifty shillings by a Maine court "for presuming to act the part of midwife."

Seal of New York Board of Lady Managers for the Columbian Exposition, 1893

After the American Revolution, male doctors began to interest themselves in childbirth. In 1847, when the American Medical Association was formed, the struggle for control of women's reproductive lives intensified. By 1900, birth control and abortion were outlawed, and births were doctor-attended and happened more often in hospitals.

The players in the political story of women's bodies are both men and women. Female slaves were shown naked at auctions, pinched and probed for their physical value. The slave system rested on abuse of black female bodies—for labor in the field or the household and as a legitimate object for rape and forced breeding. The modesty of the white lady did not apply.

The white female body—so frail, so subject to breaking down—was blamed for women's inferiority and need of protection. Being protected, more often than not, meant being excluded from life. In the struggle for women's rights—to vote, to study, to work, to compete in athletics, to have or not to have children, to be passionate or not and with whom—every step has involved encountering female flesh.

Unknown artist, Stop Forced Sterilization, 1980s

"It is very little to me to have the right to vote, to own property, etcetera, if I may not keep my body and its uses in my absolute right," said Lucy Stone in 1855. Exercising such a right has meant wresting control from people like Dr. Edward H. Clarke and Dr. S. Weir Mitchell, late-nineteenth-century so-called defenders of women's "health," interested mostly in preserving female reproductive capacity, proponents of an infamous "rest cure" designed to keep women away from higher education and assure, they said, the "safety" of female wombs. Wombs mattered more than women did.

Suffragist Harriot K. Hunt practiced medicine when the profession was still unlicensed and unregulated. She saw women's diseases as a result of submissiveness and promoted independence as a cure. In 1852, Dr. Hunt publicly protested paying taxes since she had no representation in the government. She told her patients to throw away the medicines male doctors had given them, drink a lot of water, and keep a diary.

"Our bodies, ourselves," long before it was articulated as a modern slogan, was an unarticulated rallying cry of Colonial women who used sponges as birth control, of dress reformers like Amelia Bloomer, who put first-wave feminists in loose Turkish trousers and long tunics, and of free love advocates like Victoria Woodhull. The women who won the vote were, on the whole, also fighters for birth control—for married women—because excessive childbearing endangered women's survival.

Information was a weapon against prejudice and superstition. The pioneers stood on soapboxes, wrote what they knew, opened clinics, and probed for real information on a subject shrouded in mythology. Many were ridiculed. Some were arrested. Progressive doctors and healers in the nineteenth century blamed female complaints on poor diets, restrictive clothing, and lack of exercise, not women's moral frailty. Midwives trained their daughters. Women passed information along informal networks—Jazz Age flappers whispered that acidic soda pop was useful as a douche. Emma Goldman and Margaret Sanger dispensed more scientific birth control information. Feminist health activists in the 1970s taught women to examine themselves and become acquainted with the sight of a cervix.

For women of color, the tyranny has been opposite. Forced sterilizations, often done without the woman's knowledge, sometimes when she was still a teenager in the hospital for, perhaps, an appendectomy, were the racist practice among doctors who treated young women at Indian schools in the nineteenth century, Mexican-American women throughout the Southwest, and black women everywhere.

The twentieth-century women's movement brought into the public arena previously shadowed, shame-drenched issues of female bodies. The personal has become most intensely political, that is, out of the closet and meant to be acted on. We speak openly now of periods and rape, orgasms and breast cancer. Abortion rights and the availability of birth control allow more control of our bodies by ourselves, but, equally important, firmly separate female sexuality from reproduction for the first time.

Sexuality, relatively smothered in the past, dominates the discourse of our time. In the nineteenth century, feminists considered exploitation of women's bodies the central issue and said little about female desire. We have come some distance from the vilification of lesbian sexuality in medical culture, the shunning of lesbians in political culture, and the silence of lesbians themselves. From lesbian feminists and theorists like Adrienne Rich, JoAnn Loulan, and Susie Bright, "the Dr. Ruth of lesbian sex," have come correctives to centuries of belief that women who loved women were frustrated men, deviants, and criminals. The cutting edge of the politics of desire may well be understanding the social construction of heterosexuality.

For all that it has been in our history, perhaps the most double-edged concept of the female body relates to consumerism. It is both a commodity to be peddled—from the slave system to beauty pageants—but also a market for the peddler's wares. There was always something to buy to fix women's bodies: pills for female disorders, some harmful, some not; menstrual technology from diapers to napkins to tampons to mini pads; preparations to cause abortion, from natural substances like quinine or juniper berries to the synthesized morning after pill, birth control pills, pessaries, diaphragms, ointments, and concoctions. Synthetic hormones to treat menopause have been on the market since the 1930s.

It is probably no accident that products aimed at improving health were nearly replaced by products promising improvements in physical appearance right after women got the vote. Arguments against female suffrage—as well as those against education and athletics—insisted that women moving out of their place would become masculinized. Assuaging such manipulated gender anxiety, a beauty culture thrived. A slew of self-made female millionaires emerged from the cosmetics industry in the 1920s: Harriet Hubbard Ayer, Helena Ruben-stein, Elizabeth Arden, and Sarah Breedlove Walker. Walker, the uneducated daughter of former slaves, built an empire on hair products for black women, particularly a hot comb for hair straightening and hair restoring formulas. Plastic surgeons went to work. The nose recon-struction done on Jewish comedian Fanny Brice, complete with pictures, was front-page news in the tabloids. Sound familiar?

The outsides of female bodies and how they are wrapped intersects politics, from the dress reformers of the 1850s to the inventors of brassieres, the originators of fashion maga-zines, and tycoons of department stores. The freedom to move is related to other freedoms, for Amelia Bloomer in her loose trousers through the dance costumes of Isadora Duncan and Martha Graham to the 1960s women's liberationists' rejection of girdles, garter belts, and bras.

The nineteenth-century revolution in dressing had quite a target to aim at. One reformer, describing the "semisuicidal" effects of the usual costume, pointed to the damage done by the excessive heat of inordinate amounts of clothing as well as the "dragging, bearing down sensations" of long, heavy skirts and the grim side effects of attempts to hold the body up under all that weight: "woman is harnessed into an abdominal supporter, wearing at the same time a much more efficient abdominal depressor in the shape of a bodice waist."

The new costume, the bloomer, consisted of trousers (straight or gathered around the ankles) worn under a full, below-the-knee skirt. Critics claimed the costume allowed women to make a display of themselves, but many women leapt at the chance. Dress reform picnics before the Civil War drew hundreds of participants.

Being able to move has been the motivating force of women who simply wanted to nav-igate their daily lives and of those with more strenuous aspirations, like mountaineer Annie Smith Peck, the first woman to reach the peak of the Matterhorn. The custom, toward the end of the nineteenth century, was for climbers to wear detachable floor-length skirts over their pants. One climber had been forced to scale the same peak twice in one day to retrieve the skirt she left on the summit, afraid to be seen entering an inn wearing only her climbing pants. In 1895, Peck climbed clad only in a pair of knickerbockers and received waves of deri-sive press coverage, which deterred her not at all. She continued to make major climbs well into her sixties.

Like all the rules about women, rigid ideas about clothing loosened when a different kind of dressing was necessary. During World War II, as women went to work for the defense industry, they had to dress for the work, which meant suspending conventional femininity. Movie star Veronica Lake, famed for her long blonde tresses, worn peek-a-boo style across her eyes, was persuaded to cut her hair and campaign for other women to do the same. Officials worried about long hair caught in machines. As more women wore trousers to work, major department stores began opening pants departments for women. Filene's in Boston had three slack bars in 1942. Skirts returned in the 1950s, shaped in a way that compensated for the trouser years: very wide, buttressed by layers of crinolines.

Some women, like Katharine Hepburn, kept their trousers. Historically, "renegade" women claimed freedom by adopting male clothing altogether. Since cross-dressing is an assumption of male privilege, the resistance and venom it causes reveals a passion to keep women in their place and in their skirts.

During the Civil War, women who dressed as men on the battlefields or during slave escapes were acceptable as long as they shed the disguise when the emergency was over. But Dr. Mary Walker, battlefield surgeon, lived in male attire and was buried in it. Some said the Medal of Honor awarded to her by President Andrew Johnson was rescinded in 1917 because of this habit. Supporters got the medal reinstated in 1977.

Even more transgressive, Charley Parkhurst, a California stagecoach driver, voted in a presidential election, but on "his" death in 1879, was discovered to be a Charlotte. There have been many Charlottes hiding their female bodies completely. A century later, the corpse of Billy Tipton, jazz musician, provided a shock to the funeral director when "he" turned out to be a "she."

American history, then, reads not only as a struggle for control of the female body, but as a series of oscillations between its safety and its danger and as the tension between exposure and concealment.

The Reproductive Body

Menstrual Technology: A Short History

Generally, the subject is "unmentionable." Researchers trying to learn how women on the wagon trains westward managed menstrual periods—or pregnancies and childbirths, for that matter—were stymied. The letters and diaries that have survived do not mention these intimate details.

Women in early America managed menstruation with no help from men. Sponges and fibers were the most usual materials.

In the nineteenth century, man-made products came on the market, often advertising in the growing numbers of women's magazines. The Comstock Laws of 1873, which outlawed sending contraceptive information or material through the mail, were often turned on menstrual products. Some were probably sold door-to-door. The belief that a great deal of blood was lost during menstruation led to enormous contraptions to contain it. For middle-class ladies, a deep sack or whole garment covered the lower torso. Vulcanized rubber, once it was invented, seemed a good material to use. So did oil silk, a silk fabric soaked in oil to make it waterproof, often used for rainwear.

> " It is as if the Almighty, in creating the female sex, had taken the uterus and built up a woman around it. "
>
> *Nineteenth-century male doctor*

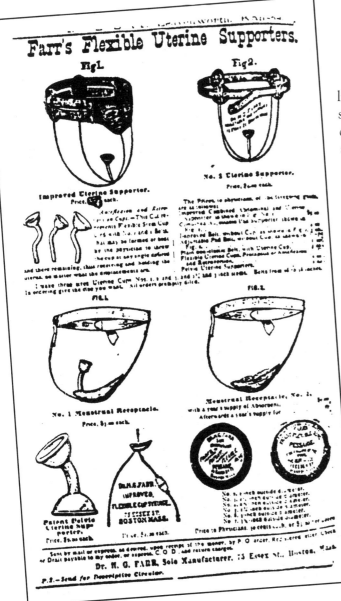

Menstrual receptacles

In 1905, napkins were made of linen and cheesecloth and attached to suspenders that went over the shoulders and joined together in both front and back.

Disposable sanitary napkins were invented in 1896, but the subject of menstruation was considered too indecent to allow advertising or marketing. Freer attitudes about women's bodies more than twenty years later allowed Kotex to be successful with its disposable sanitary napkins, using wood fiber wadding, launched in 1920.

Tampax, the first menstrual product to be used internally, was invented by Dr. Earle Cleveland Haas and developed by Denver businesswoman Gertrude S. Tenderich, who had a successful business in weight reduction products. Confronting cultural prudery in 1936, when the product was launched, Tenderich hired nurses to give public lectures on menstruation (and tampons) and crews of women to go door-to-door selling to housewives. Some religious leaders called the product immoral, claiming that it destroyed the physical evidence of virginity and provided a stimulus to masturbation.

Menstrual cups made of rubber or plastic and inserted into the vagina were developed in the 1950s.

Natural sponges, useful to women since colonial times, had renewed popularity in the 1960s and were used either externally or internally.

The discovery of toxic shock syndrome in the 1980s made many women wary of tampons. The women's health movement is currently crusading against the use of chlorine in tampons.

I am the mother of seven children. My girlhood was spent mostly in the open air. I early imbibed the idea that a girl is just as good as a boy, and I carried it out. I would walk five miles before breakfast, or ride ten on horseback. . . . I never compressed my body. . . . When my first four children were born, I suffered very little. I then made up my mind that it was totally unnecessary for me to suffer at all; so I dressed lightly, walked every day and took proper care of myself. The night before the birth I walked three miles. The child was born without a particle of pain. I bathed it and dressed it myself.

Elizabeth Cady Stanton on childbirth

The Midwife Trade: Onnie Lee Logan

In fifty-three years as an Alabama midwife, Onnie Lee Logan never lost a mother or a baby. In 1989, she told her story in *Motherwit*:

I was watchin' and takin' in what they [other midwives] was sayin' but I always see'd it a lil different that you could do or you could add to it. And that's the way I pro-gressed. Mo' and mo' like that. That's how come I say God give it to me. The bo'd a health didn't give it to me. Readin' books didn't give it to me. I progressed that outa my own mind. My own mind. Thinkin' and listenin' and knowledge that God give me.

Birth Control: Agitate, Educate, Organize, and Legislate

All the original methods of birth control, successful to different degrees, were invented by women. Before there was a medical technology to prevent conception, women in the colonies and on the frontier used cut lemons, lard, oil, or sponges, whose nontoxic properties have, prompted by the green movement, made them an option again for women in the 1990s.

Margaret Sanger worked in Lillian Wald's Visiting Nurse Service on New York's Lower East Side in the first decade of the twentieth century. She was inspired to fight for legalized birth control by hearing Emma Goldman speak on soapboxes about sexual freedom and by watching poor women try to abort themselves or sicken and die from continual pregnancies. Sanger's own mother had died at fifty after giving birth to eleven children and suffering seven miscarriages.

The struggle for legal birth control coincided with the last, most militant phase of the struggle for the vote

> **"**
> To look the whole world in the face with a go-to-hell look in the eyes; to have an ideal; to speak and act in defiance of convention.
> **"**
>
> *Margaret Sanger's urging to women, inaugural issue of her magazine,* The Woman Rebel, *in 1915*

and involved many of the same people, issues, and combination of conservative and radical factions. Socialist feminists were in the forefront. Both Goldman and Sanger went to jail. Sanger's staunch ally, Katherine McCormick, one of the first women to earn a biology degree at the Massachusetts Institute of Technology, wrote checks.

On October 16, 1916, Sanger opened the first birth control clinic in America, behind the curtained windows of a storefront tenement in Brooklyn. Advertising in English, Italian, and Yiddish, it served more than four hundred women in the nine days it operated. The police closed the clinic and dragged Sanger off to a patrol wagon.

This was a very long battle. In 1957, Enovid was approved by the FDA for treatment of menstrual disorders, but the secret soon leaked that the pill could be used for birth control. Thousands of women developed menstrual disorders and were handed prescriptions by their doctors. By 1960, despite intense opposition from religious groups, it was licensed as a contraceptive. A social revolution was in progress. By 1965, there were 700 tax-supported birth control clinics in America.

Barbara Seaman: Troublemaker

She had always believed women knew more about their bodies than male doctors did. As a young mother in the 1950s, she made the revolutionary decision to breast-feed her child at a time when medical belief favored infant formula as nutritionally superior. By the 1960s, Barbara Seaman had become a science writer for several major magazines and there had been limited evidence that the highly touted birth control pills on the market were dangerous to women's health. On the trail of a cover-up of potentially fatal side effects, Seaman published *The Doctor's Case against the Pill* in 1969, a year in which eight million U.S. women were taking oral contraceptives.

Exposing the potential for strokes and heart attacks as side effects, the limited testing and uninformed consent associated with distributing the Pill, Seaman was compared to Harriet Beecher Stowe, another woman who publicized a national evil. There were at least three important results of the enormous publicity she generated: the dangerously high doses of hormones in the pills were lowered; package inserts, describing potential side effects, were required; and large-scale political action by feminists around women's health issues began.

The Sterilization of Auntie C.

A member of the Blackfoot tribe tells the story of her Great-Auntie C.'s experience in the early twentieth century at an Indian boarding school:

At thirteen, in eighth grade, Auntie C. fell and broke her hip. At the Indian health clinic, she was given a hysterectomy. The school would not send her home because "they knew her other aunties would really come down and raise hell."

For a long time, Auntie C. was afraid to date men, ashamed to tell what happened to her. No man, she said, would want a woman who was "all used up." She did eventually marry and take in many foster children.

Auntie C. still doesn't trust doctors. She goes to her adopted child, a nurse, for medical attention. She refused to send her children to boarding school. Her grandniece, however, did go to such a school, but never went to the clinic. "I told all my friends not to go there," she says, "'cause they might not ever have kids."

Ruth Barnett, Abortionist

From 1918 until 1968, a year before her death at seventy-four, Ruth Barnett practiced as an abortionist in Portland, Oregon, unimpeded by the law. In approximately 40,000 operations, she never lost a patient. Rickie Solinger's book about Barnett (*The Abortionist: A Woman against the Law*) uses Barnett's colorful life story to point out the alternating waves of repression and tolerance about abortion in American history, whatever its legal status. In the 1940s, "abortion was not really considered a crime at all." In the family-oriented 1950s, "the old deal with the cops was off." Abortion prosecutions were about "enforcing norms of femininity." Large numbers of abortions among working women after World War II was "proof that women were resisting going back home."

"The danger for women before Roe v. Wade," Solinger says, "was not back alley abortionists, but the law."

Victorian Menopause

In the late nineteenth century, menopause was seen as a crisis needing medical intervention and was treated with bloodletting, leeches, arsenic, morphine, and acid injections to the cervix.

Menopause could lead to moral insanity or to erotomania. Moral insanity was often accepted as a legal defense in shoplifting cases, which were numerous.

The Sexual Body

In 1649 in Plymouth, Massachusetts, Goodwife Norman, the wife of Hugh Norman, and Mary Hammond were brought before the court "for leude behavior, each

COLONIAL MENOPAUSE

More than half the women accused as witches in seventeenth-century America were of menopausal age. A large number were charged with "sexual excess," as well as assertive and aggressive behavior.

It was considered unhealthy for men to have sex with women over fifty because the "impurities" that had had been released by menstrual flow were thought to be still lurking inside a woman when the flow stopped.

This time in a woman's life was referred to as "the cessation of the flower."

During childbearing years, a husband's impotence was grounds for divorce. Afterward, it was not.

with the other upon a bed." Mary got no punishment, but Goodwife Norman had "to make public acknowledgment of her unchaste behavior."

> Fully one-half of all women seldom or never experience any pleasure whatever in the sexual act. Now this is an impeachment of nature, a disgrace to our civilization.
> *Victoria Woodhull, 1873*

In 1906, when the *Ladies' Home Journal* published a series of articles on venereal disease, it lost over seventy-five thousand subscribers.

> To understand the lesbian as a sexual being, one must understand woman as a sexual being.
> *Phyllis Lyon and Del Martin,* Lesbian/Woman, *1972*

> If sex and creativity are often seen by dictators as subversive activities, it's because they lead to the knowledge that you own your own body (and with it your own voice) and that's the most revolutionary insight of all.
> *Erica Jong, 1972*

> So much ink has been spilled on the subject of the female orgasm since the sixties, it's no wonder guys sometimes feel that their orgasms are supporting actors in the sexual drama.
> *Wendy Dennis,* Hot and Bothered: Sex and Love in the '90s, *1992*

Abortion Landmarks

<u>1900:</u> Through the combined efforts of the American Medical Association and the antiobscenity movement, abortion is outlawed by every state in the nation. Under the Comstock Law, passed in 1873, sending obscene material through the mails is a criminal offense. Margaret Sanger is tried under the obscenity laws.

<u>1950s:</u> Therapeutic abortions are allowed in cases where it can be proven that the woman's life is in danger. In practice, this allows women with money to pay for psychiatrists' stipulations that they would kill themselves if they had to carry a child to term.

<u>1962:</u> Sherri Finkbine, mother of four, pregnant with her fifth child, learns that a sleeping pill she had been taking contains Thalidomide, a drug linked to grotesque fetal deformities. Her obstetrician schedules an abortion at a public hospital. To warn other women about the dangers of the drug, Finkbine talks to the newspapers. As a result, the abortion is canceled. The storm of controversy that erupts is the first modern public discussion of abortion. For many religious leaders, it challenges the purpose of marriage, which is to procreate.

<u>1960s:</u> The long public and legislative debate includes not just the opposition, but two wings of the proabortion movement: those favoring reform of the laws, others supporting repeal. California liberalizes its abortion laws in 1967. The

Some women know they're horny. Others don't, but they throw up instead. I see a lot of bingeing instead of masturbating.

Anonymous woman psychotherapist, 1995

Sex Radical: Angela Heywood

An early advocate of the joy of sex, Kansas magazine editor and sex reformer Heywood believed the liberation of men was integral to women's liberation and that society needed a basic readjustment of sexual expression. One of her favorite targets of attack was Anthony Comstock, the man who would eventually put Margaret Sanger in jail. His 1873 obscenity law, she said, made him the policeman of the American woman's genitals. Her idea of gender justice was to have Comstock's penis tied up by a length of wire and be inspected by a female Comstock. Offending males who removed the wire would be tried before a court of twelve women with the power to imprison them for ten years.

An equally fierce opponent of censorship, she campaigned for free use of the word *fuck*.

Shirley Chisholm at a pro-choice rally, New York City, May 6, 1972

We are related sexually; let us face the glad fact with all its ineffable joys. A woman might pretend that she wanted nothing of man, but her lady-nature knows it is the very great everything she wants to do with men. Lady Nature can put Madame Intellect behind the door, further than you can think while she revels with a man to her heart's content. . . . I used to think Passion was something bad, and was taught, by those who did not know, that Lust is the opposite of Love; I was mistaken, for the antithesis of Love is hate; while Lust means full, glowing, healthy animal heat.

The Ethics of Sexuality, *1881*

Is it "proper," "polite," for men to go to Washington to say, by penal law, fines and imprisonment, whether woman may continue her natural right to wash, rinse or wipe her own vaginal body opening—as well legislate when she may blow her nose, dry her eyes, or nurse her babe. . . . Whatever she may have been pleased to receive, from man's own, is his gift and her property. Women do not like rape and have a right to resist its results.

1893

Sex Research: Clelia Mosher

In work that did not become public until eighty years after she started it, Clelia Mosher asked married women to fill out questionnaires about their sexual lives. Among the things she discovered, beginning in 1892, was that most women knew almost nothing about sex before they married; most, including the postmenopausal women, experienced orgasms and sexual pleasure; and most used contraceptives: withdrawal, douching, condoms and cervical caps. Dr. Mosher, who had a medical practice in Stanford, California, after 1900, had also cru-

National Association for the Repeal of Abortion Laws is formed in 1969 at the end of the First National Conference on Abortion.

1967: Reverend Howard Moody of the progressive Judson Memorial Church in Greenwich Village forms the Clergy Consultation Service, which becomes a national network of referral services for abortions.

1969: The radical group Redstockings organizes a "speak-out" on abortion in New York City, where women describe their experiences with illegal abortions. Feminists in other cities follow suit.

1970: The New York legislature eliminates most restrictions on early abortions. Clinics spring up everywhere. Networks around the country organize to send women to New York, find them places to stay, and investigate the safety and efficiency of the clinics.

Early 1970s: Activists disrupt legislative hearings. A petitition circulates containing names of prominent women who admit to having abortions. In Chicago, The Janes, a collective originally made up of women from Chicago Women's Liberation, safely performs thousands of illegal abortions.

January 22, 1973: Supreme Court decision in *Roe v. Wade* essentially makes abortion legal. The National Association for Repeal of Abortion Laws does not close up shop, but, understanding that the struggle has only begun, becomes the National Abortion Rights Action League (NARAL). The decision's biggest impact is on poor women. Abortion is now defined as a normal medical procedure. Before 1973, a loose coalition of feminists and family planning advocates active in the population control movement had been vocal, visible, and effective, with weakly organized opposition, but the court's

saded against prevailing myths about menstruation, insisting that most menstrual difficulties were caused by constricted clothing and lack of exercise.

Crusading against Sex Censorship: The 1930s
Women struck two of the important blows against treating sex education materials as obscene. Mary Ware Dennett, birth control activist, was convicted of sending a pamphlet called *Sex Side of Life* through the mail, but the conviction was overturned in 1930. The next year, *Married Love* by British activist Marie Stopes was seized by U.S. customs officials, but the courts refused to declare it obscene and released it to the public.

The Great Cherry Myth
In 1981, sex researcher Mary Calderone confronted centuries of belief that the hymen forms a wall across the vaginal opening and that on first intercourse, it breaks and bleeds, causing pain. Every country in the world has rituals built around the breaking of "the cherry" as proof of a woman's innocence. Yet Calderone said the hymen stretched, not tore, that the stretching was hardly felt and caused little or no blood. Pain came from muscular tension, not rupture. The rest was pure sentimentality about female virginity. Masters and Johnson confirmed Calderone's finding in 1982 and Shere Hite's 1994 *Report on the Family: Growing Up Under Patriarchy* said that less than a fifth of the thousands of women she surveyed felt adequately taught about their own bodies.

Shere Hite: Troublemaker
It is not women who have a problem reaching orgasm, but the society that has a problem accepting how women do orgasm.

decision provokes opponents into action.

1976: The Hyde Amendment passes, banning Medicaid funding for abortions. Huge feminist demonstrations follow and the pro-choice movement is galvanized.

1978: Alice Faye Wattleton becomes the national president of the Planned Parenthood Association of America, the nation's oldest family planning agency. She is the only African-American and the first woman since Margaret Sanger to head the organization. During her fourteen-year tenure, she changes the conservative image of the organization to a militant defender of abortion rights.

1989: The Hyde Amendment has been challenged and upheld. Now, in *Wester vs. Reproductive Health Services*, the Supreme Court allows states to restrict abortion rights, which, over the following years, they do, imposing waiting periods and requiring parental consent.

1992: The biggest pro-choice demonstration in history marches on the nation's capital.

1995: The struggle for reproductive freedom is located in state legislatures.

"The facts show that people who are raped, who are truly raped, the juices don't flow, the body functions don't work and they don't get pregnant," says North Carolina legislator Henry Aldridge, using this nonsense to argue against funds for abortions for women who have been raped.

Violence against clinics and doctors' offices where abortions are performed escalates to murder. Clinic workers are killed in Boston.

The Hite Report, in 1976, upset a lot of applecarts. Hite's report on female sexuality was disturbing because, perhaps for the first time, she allowed women—3,000 had answered questionnaires for her book—to talk about how they defined sex. Although many feminists were attacking Sigmund Freud's idea that only vaginal orgasms represented mature female sexuality, Hite's work popularized the idea that many women preferred clitoral stimulation. She was roundly attacked, her methods called unscientific, her sample not representative. A *Washington Post* reviewer said the book was "about as intellectually provocative as the plumbing in my basement."

What's a Clitoris For?

The question came up on page 25 of the rather extraordinary catalogue of mail-order items sold by Eve's Garden, whose motto is, "We make pleasurable things for women." In the early 1970s, when a woman named Dell Williams first joined the National Organization for Women, the right to work and the right to equal pay were the marching themes. Williams made the right to enjoy one's own body an equally important aspect of being female.

She organized a conference on "Women's Sexuality" in 1973, attended by 1,400 women, probably the first gathering in history that created a safe space for women to share feelings and experiences about sexuality. To speak, Williams invited Betty Dodson, who was giving workshops teaching women to masturbate with vibrators and distributing a mimeographed flier called "Liberating Masturbation." My orgasm, myself.

Eve's Garden opened as a mail-order business the following year and, later, a New York shop. Vibrators—they never snore, let you down, or leave town—are still the best-selling items. In the biblical Garden of Eden, Eve's insistence on knowing for herself brought guilt and shame into paradise. Eve's Garden is devoted to the principle that knowledge will banish guilt and shame.

The answer to the question on page 25 is not given, but here, in full, is the question:

> Can a dildo, all by itself, bring you to orgasm? There's still a lot of controversy about the physical effects of penetration as the primary cause of orgasm. Orgasms can be felt in the vagina, but do they begin there? If so, what's a clitoris for?

The Joy of Lesbian Sex

> We slipped off the cotton shifts we had worn and moved against each other's damp breasts in the shadow of the roof's chimney, making moon, honor, love . . .
> *Audre Lorde,* Tar Beach, *1982*

Until the late 1960s, sex between women was illegal in many states and although upper-class women had managed to live in women's communities or women's political cultures without much trouble, working-class lesbian life thrived in bars, often owned by dubious characters and always in danger of being raided by police. Mental health professionals saw lesbianism as a developmental disorder for which heterosexuality was the cure. By 1973, when the American Psychiatric Association officially declassified "homosexuality per se" as a psychiatric disorder, the combined political efforts of lesbian feminists and the gay rights movement had done much to create a sex-positive lesbian culture.

Lesbian culture in the 1980s, often theatrical and outrageous, had a celebratory eroticism reflected in videos and workshops, sex shops, strip shows, books like JoAnn Loulan's *Lesbian Sex* (1984) and the magazine *On Our Backs*, edited by "sexpert" Susie Bright.

The Sexual Politics of Sex Research

Mainstream sex research and therapy deal mainly with how often and how successfully young (but not too young), white, middle-class, able-bodied, heterosexual couples complete the act of intercourse. It consistently isolates sex as something separate, self-enclosed, physical, focused closely on a few magic inches of mucous membrane. It engenders those terms we all know well, like "foreplay," "dysfunction" and "achieving" orgasm, as if orgasm were an assault on Mount Everest, complete with ropes and pickaxes.

Dr. Gina Ogden, Women Who Love Sex, *1994*

Clothing the Body

Dress/Redress

Let men be compelled to wear our dress for awhile and we should soon hear them advocating a change.

Amelia Bloomer, The Lily, *March 1851*

Some say the Turkish costume is not graceful. Grant it. For parlor dolls, who loll on crimson velvet couches and study attitudes before tall mirrors—for those who have no part to perform in the great drama of life, for whose heads, hearts and hands there is no work to do the drapery is all well. . . . But for us common place, every day, working characters, who wash and iron, bake and brew, carry water and fat babies up stairs and down, bring potatoes, apples and pans of milk from the cellar, run our own errands through mud or snow, shovel paths and work in the garden, why "the drapery" is quite too much—one might as well work with a ball and chain.

Elizabeth Cady Stanton, The Lily, *April 1851*

In the 1890s, the average skirt, worn over several layers of petticoats, was thirteen and

Susan Mogul photo collage, 1976

a half feet around the hem and the average waist measurement was twenty inches. This meant fifteen pounds of clothing hanging from a constricted waist. By the beginning of World War I, skirts were higher and narrower and waist size had increased by 40 percent. Women's health improved immeasurably.

> The man did not have to please the woman by the small size of his feet, but by the large size of his bank account. His feet were organs of locomotion, hers of sex attraction.
>
> This corset is as idiotic as a snug rubber band around a pair of shears."
>
> *Charlotte Perkins Gilman*, The Forerunner, *1915*

Mrs. Custer's Clothes

During the long summers, when we women were left alone and had nothing to fill up our time except work that we purposely made to occupy the lonely hours, there came to be great improvement in our stitchery.

Harper's Bazaar was as thoroughly read out there as at any point in its wide wanderings. The question of clothes was not a serious one, for we dared, when so far beyond the railroad, to wear things out of date. Sometimes boots or shoes were ordered by mail and sent separately, on account of bulk or postage. . . . Fortunately, we had no city toilets to compete with, and it took a good deal to disfigure fresh, healthful happy women. . . .

A charge of our brave men was made through the town hunting for black hair to re-model the antique coiffures of their better halves. It was no easy task, for the sun fades and streaks the glossiest locks out there, and the wind breaks and dries the silkiest mane.

From Following the Guidon, *Elizabeth Bacon Custer's account of garrison life during the period of the most extensive military activity against the Plains Indians, from 1867 to 1869*

Amelia Bloomer in dress reform costume, 1850s

Breasts

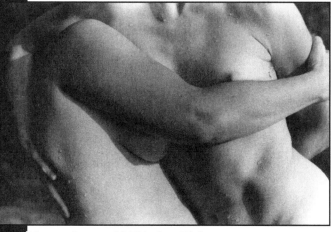

Morgan Gwenwald, This One Night, 1985

When female slaves were portrayed in art sympathetically, they were shown as having the classic spherical breasts. When they were portrayed unsympathetically, they were shown with long, hanging, animal-like breasts.

Londa Schiebinger, professor of history, Pennsylvania State University

While male clothing styles evolved to bring the male body more clearly into focus, female clothing was a form of selective exposure. A woman's arms and head might be fairly intelligible; her pelvis and legs were always a mystery, her feet a sometime thing, and her bosom a constantly changing theatrical presentation.

Anne Hollander

In 1858, while Sojourner Truth was giving a series of lectures in Silver Lake, Indiana, on the abolition of slavery, a rumor circulated in the audience that she was a man posing as a woman. At her final talk, a man rose and challenged her to prove the rumor false by having her breasts examined by some of the women present. His challenge was voted on: a resounding "aye." Truth appeared undaunted. She said that her breasts had suckled many a white babe, to the exclusion of her own offspring, and that many of these had grown to be better men than those in the audience. She revealed her breasts, saying it was not to her shame that she did so, but to theirs.

American women's actual breast size has not been increasing. The average is 36B and has been for half a century or more.

And what's this pooching out over the top half of my suit? Two delinquent orbs that remind me, not surprisingly, of Baskin-Robbins double-scoop vanilla.
Tracy Young, A Few (More) Words about Breasts, 1992

After my diagnosis, I cherished my breasts, like two puppies rescued from the ASPCA, and touched them often, amazed at their softness and weight. . . . I wondered how I'd ever done without them.
Karen De Balbian Verster, "Tabula Rasa," in The Breast: An Anthology, 1995

In 1994, manufacturers of silicon breast implants settled a class action suit brought by women who had been harmed by the implants. The manufacturers paid $4.2 billion.
Janet Van Winkle of Kirkwood, Missouri, founder of American Silicone Implant Survivors group, has 75,000 women on her mailing list.

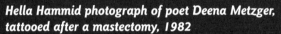

Duane Michals photograph of artist Louise Bourgeois in latex costume she designed and made, 1970

Hella Hammid photograph of poet Deena Metzger, tattooed after a mastectomy, 1982

The Bra Story

The First Bra

Caresse Crosby was the essence of the Roaring Twenties and the "new woman." Born into the Social Register as Polly Jacob, married first to Dick Peabody of Boston's Peabody Museum family, mother of two, she ran off to Paris in 1921 with the younger banker/poet Harry Crosby to live *la vie boheme* with a lot of money. She rode down the Champs Elysées naked on a baby elephant, dabbled in opium and orgies and, with Harry, started Black Sun Press, publishing James Joyce, D. H. Lawrence, and Ezra Pound.

She was also the inventor of the brassiere. Brought up in undergarments that encased her "in a sort of boxlike armor of whalebone and pink cordage [that] ran upwards from the knee to under the armpit," when she was still Polly Jacob, dressing for dinner, she asked her maid for two silk handkerchiefs, some pink ribbon, a needle, and thread. She called it a backless brassiere, made it for eager friends, and patented the design in 1914.

Defying the mores of her class, which scorned trade, Crosby had several hundred garments made and took them to New York stores herself. Nobody was interested. A family friend eventually sold the patent to the Warner Brothers Corset Company for $1,500. She estimated that Warner's made $15 million over the years.

The Second Bra

A Jewish refugee from Russia, who stood less than five feet tall and was said to ask male business associates to sit down so they wouldn't tower over her, took the next step. In the early 1920s, Ida Cohen Rosenthal, dressmaker, added tucks to make cups and snaps for firmer support. She gave the garment away as a sales device, but it was so popular that, in 1923, she and her husband started the Maiden Form brassiere company. William Rosenthal suggested making different sizes. By the 1960s, the company's gross annual income was $40 million. When Ida Rosenthal died in 1973, the company passed to her daughter.

The Wonderbra

Since push-up bras had been available for at least a decade, the Wonderbra's American debut in the spring of 1994 was a triumph of marketing over merchandise. Promoted as "a safe alternative to breast implants, the look without the surgery," Wonderbras are being sold as examples of "freedom" and as "confidence-boosters."

The Future of Underwear

Shape-changers on manufacturers' drawing boards for the 1990s:

- Pantyhose that "lift and separate the buttocks"
- Tummy Terminator and Waist Eliminator, promising "liposuction without the surgery"

Roberta Elins of the Fashion Institute of Technology thinks women who remember girdles will resist these products in 1995: "Whether a woman will buy something that is not comfortable has a lot to do with her age and her politics—her feminist politics."

Nylon Day: May 15, 1940

In 1938, the DuPont Chemical Company announced the development of a new synthetic called nylon, which promised to be indestructible. The "miracle yarn" was shown at the 1939 World's Fair and as hosiery manufacturers went into production, stores agreed to withhold sales until May 15, 1940. Women lined up hours before stores opened. No consumer item in history ever caused such nationwide pandemonium.

Although the clamor—manipulated by marketers and the stores themselves—was treated as an example of female lunacy in matters of fashion, the truth is that nylons were much less expensive than the traditional silk stockings and, while not indestructible, certainly lasted longer. Women's urgency to get them was most likely economic.

Chicago activists Barbara Stratton, Oretha Smith, and Lauren Bogle in women's liberation demonstration, September 5, 1969. For tossing bras into the river, they received citations for river pollution.

The Healthy Body and the Sick Body

I am very tired of the battle with giant wrongs, and would like to have some one younger and stronger arise to say what ought to be said, still more to do what ought to be done. Enough! If I felt these things in privileged America, the cries of mothers and wives beaten at night by sons and husbands for their diversion after drinking . . ."
Margaret Fuller, reporting from Italy, 1848

Lydia Pinkham: Charlatan or Savior?

Lydia Pinkham, who saw herself as "the savior of her sex," one of the many nineteenth-century women who believed women suffered needlessly at the hands of doctors, came from Lynn, Massachusetts, a working-class town where abolitionist leader Frederick Douglass lived. Her Quaker family was deeply involved in antislavery, temperance, and spiritualism. Married to a man with a lot of get-rich-quick schemes, she had a baby a year for three years.

Her folk remedy to cure "female complaints," which encompassed everything from painful menstruation to a prolapsed uterus, was made of unicorn root, life root, black cohosh, pleurisy root, and fengugreek seed macerated and suspended in alcohol. The alcohol was stronger than table wine or sherry, although Pinkham's family, temperance supporters, had all "taken the pledge."

In the spring of 1875, Lydia, her three sons, and her daughter, launched the concoction, brewed on a stove in the cellar, as a patent medicine. A four-page "guide for women" to accompany it became advertising copy. The medicine sold, mostly to druggists in Boston, then New York. It was not a runaway success until son Dan suggested putting Lydia's picture on the wrapper.

Smith Brothers Cough Drops and Buffalo Bill Cody's Wild West Show used images of the bearded brothers and the swaggering Cody, but nobody had used a woman in advertising. Lydia Pinkham, at sixty, in black dress and white lace collar, an idealized grandmother, became a national figure. When women wrote for advice, she responded with sane talk of diet and exercise. By 1881, sales of Mrs. Pinkham's pills were almost $200,000 a year.

Edward Bok, editor of the *Ladies' Home Journal*, attacked patent medicines for their lack of medical authority. A temperance advocate who once deleted a drinking scene from a story by Rudyard Kipling, he singled out Lydia Pinkham and the alcohol content of her remedy. In 1905, the *Journal* published a photograph of Mrs. Pinkham's grave. This was somewhat disturbing to customers who had still been receiving letters of advice from Pinkham's company, over her signature, in the twenty-two years since her death.

It was not, however, catastrophic. The company survived in the family until the 1960s.

Fat Is a (White?) Feminist Issue

In 1984, *Glamour* magazine found that 75 percent of the women they asked, aged 18 to 35, believed they were fat. Forty-five percent of the underweight women thought they were too fat. Respondents chose losing 10–15 pounds above success in work or in love as their most desired goal.

> She is called Twiggy because she looks as though a strong gale would snap her in two and dash her to the ground. . . . Her legs look as though she had not enough milk as a baby and her face has that expression one feels Londoners wore in the blitz.
> Vogue *magazine's description of the model Twiggy in 1965*

> I want to weigh myself now; I lean toward the scale in the next room, imagine standing there, lining up the balance. But I don't do it. Going this long, starting to break the scale's spell—it's like waking up suddenly sober.
> *Sallie Tisdale,* The Weight That Women Carry, *1994*

> Guys will say "oh, she looks so good" when some girl walks by and you look up and she's a rail.
> *Anonymous New York high school girl, 1995*

> The Barbie doll used to come with her own scale, set at 110 and her own diet guide: "How to Lose Weight: Don't Eat."

In 1995, the journal *Human Organization* published a study reporting that:

≪ While 90 percent of the white junior high and high school girls studied voiced dissatisfaction with their weight, 70 percent of African-American teens were satisfied with their bodies.

≫ Almost two-thirds of the black teens defined beauty as "the right attitude." They also said that "women get more beautiful as they age" and that being "fat" is defined as taking up two seats on the bus.

≪ In white, middle-class America, part of the great American Dream is to be able to make yourself over. In the black community, as one girl put it, "if you think negatively about yourself, you won't get anywhere."

> There is simply no such thing as anorexia among native peoples in North America. . . . The grave concern with slenderness is itself seen as absurd. Native people would be very concerned about a person who was willfully wasting away, but you just don't find it, except perhaps among highly acculturated Indians.
> *Dr. Spero Manson, medical anthropologist, 1995*

Today, the average model weighs 23 percent less than the average American. A generation ago, it was 8 percent less.

Eighty percent of ten-year-old girls have dieted. Two-thirds of girls thirteen to eighteen are trying to lose weight.

Great Cross-Dressers in American History

"I FEEL TWO NATURES STRUGGLING WITHIN ME"

T. Westerman cartoon, 1915

Women in the garb of the opposite sex gives rein to the idea that women's sexual fantasy is much broader, and includes a predatory side.
Anne Hollander, Sex and Suits

Women in the garb of the opposite sex also points to choices women make about what to do with their female bodies.

Their reasons are many and not always sexual, although the implications often are. Women have worn men's clothes and passed as men to get and perform jobs they would otherwise have been barred from. Both the Revolutionary War and the Civil War produced verifiable legends of women in disguise on the battlefield. In the nineteenth century West, stagecoach driver was a popular cross-dressed occupation. Calamity Jane, like many working women, rejected female attire, as she did female company and a traditionally female life. It's hard to rope a steer in corset and crinolines.

Sometimes, a woman in men's clothes is showing her internal gender identity and sometimes she isn't. Sometimes she is a lesbian and sometimes she isn't.

At various times, wearing pants has been a simple act of rebellion or protest:

In 1915, when painter and gallery owner Betty Parsons was fifteen, she locked herself in her room and refused to eat, telling her parents through the closed door that she was born to be an artist and wanted to leave Miss Chapin's Finishing School. She emerged from her room wearing trousers with her hair slicked across one side, like a boy, a cigarette hanging from her lip. Her father promised art classes if Parsons would go back to Miss Chapin's, which she did. Without the trousers.

Or something more metaphysical:

I just want us to be boys together. I want to dress like you and go out and make the world look at us differently, make them wonder about us, make them stare and ask those silly questions. . . . Don't worry when we come home I will be a girl for you again but for now I want us to be boys together.
bell hooks, Black Looks: Race and Representation, *1992*

When playwright Noel Coward ran into novelist Edna Ferber and both were wearing nearly identical suits, he said, "Edna, you look almost like a man." "So do you," she replied.

The beast [of fashion] relies on a kind of uncertainty principle of its own. It makes money by trying to make us feel unsure about how we look, disassembling us part by part, feature by feature, outfit by outfit, and then selling us what it says are the pieces we need to be whole again.
Connie Porter, 1995

Dr. Mary E. Walker,
c. 1910

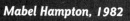

Mabel Hampton, 1982

Calamity Jane, also
known as Martha
Jane Canary Burke,
1895

Contesting Beauty

1968: Demonstrators, mostly members of Redstockings in New York City, appear at the Miss America pageant in Atlantic City, New Jersey, carrying signs protesting the exploitation of women. They crown a pig "Miss America" and throw objects of torture, including girdles, bras, and high-heeled shoes, into a "Freedom Trash Can" on the boardwalk. Contrary to all subsequent mythology, nobody ever burns a bra.

1971: A judge sentences a woman to lose three pounds a week or go to prison.

Oprah Winfrey is the first black winner of the Miss Fire Prevention beauty pageant in Nashville, Tennessee.

1972: As Miss Black Nashville, Oprah Winfrey wins a four-year scholarship to Tennessee State University.

A woman is fired by the Playboy Club of New York for "losing her bunny image." She sues. Beauty, the court rules, is something that can legally gain or lose some women their jobs. "All women are bunnies," Gloria Steinem says.

1975: Catherine McDermott sues the Xerox Corporation for withdrawing a job offer on the grounds of her weight.

1979: Sculptor and antirape organiz-

er Nikki Craft and activist Ann Simonton begin annual protests against the Miss California pageant in Santa Cruz. Simonton appears in a bathing suit, dragging bathroom scales from a chain around her ankle. Craft stages a public vomiting of Nestle's Crunch bars and Kellogg's Cornflakes, sponsors of the pageant.

1980s: California counter-pageants, called Myth America, become larger than the Miss California pageant itself.

1985: More than 1,000 feminists demonstrate against the Miss California pageant in Santa Cruz, California. Ann Simonton parodies the swimsuit contest by wearing a suit made of meat. "Judge meat, not women," the protesters chant. Simonton and Chris Adams, another protester, spill their blood on the steps of the pageant building, because, Adams explains: "As a survivor of sexual abuse, symbolically that's my blood that is being walked on here." As a result, the pageant is moved south to San Diego.

> I want people to understand the connection between violence against women and objectifying women in pageants.
> *Ann Simonton, 1985*

> They are not the example of womanhood I would like to follow. Many of them are fat. They don't take care of themselves. They're not even clean.
> *Lisa Davenport, Miss California, on the protesters, 1985*

1987: In San Diego, Simonton shaves her head in protest at the sixty-fourth annual Miss California pageant.

1988: Undercover feminist Michelle Anderson, a student at the University of California at Santa Cruz, spends eighteen months and $5,000 training to win the Miss Santa Cruz beauty contest. She goes on to San Diego where, as Miss California is being crowned, Anderson pulls from her bra a banner reading, "Pageants Hurt All Women."

> Prizes given out hardly cover the winner's gown and performance coaching expenses. The sponsors benefit the most financially. Pageants don't encourage education, they reinforce the message that women's predominant career is still to please men.
> *Ann Simonton, 1989*

1995: Staci Baldwin, five feet, two inches tall, size two dress, enters the state of Washington's pageant on the way to the Miss Universe competition. She pays a $600 entrance fee and buys a white beaded evening gown and bathing suit. One of her role models is Michelle Pfeiffer, whose Miss California contest win helped launch her career. Baldwin is named Miss Washington. But when her twenty-seventh birthday comes in June, the pageant says she is too old to compete for the bigger crown. She sues. She says: "I know that I'm not old. Look how beautiful Elizabeth Taylor is. Do people call her old?"

Ann Simonton in a 30-pound bologna dress, protesting the Miss California Beauty Contest, 1982

We live in a society where there is a very narrow conception of what is beautiful. It is usually pale, blonde and a size seven, which leaves out 95 percent of the women in this country. And black women are usually the farthest from that ideal.

Susan Taylor, editor-in-chief, Essence *magazine, 1995*

Lucky Strike ad, 1920s

My mother persistently affirmed my Blackness by offering her descriptive personal narrative of learning to love herself as a Black woman. She told me stories of wearing clothespins on her nose to make it look thinner and of special bleaching creams used by her friends to look lighter. Later, when she had gained a stronger sense of self-identity, she, like many Black women in the late sixties and early seventies, wore a large Afro. Then, in the late seventies, she cut her hair very close to her scalp.

Jocelyn Maria Taylor, "Testimony of a Naked Woman," in Afrekete: An Anthology of Black Lesbian Writing, *1995*

Smoking Is a Feminist Issue

The marketing of addiction to girls and young women should be viewed with the same sense of urgency as violence against women and reproductive choice.

Heidi Holland, Massachusetts Prevention Center

∽ In 1989, Gabriela Sabatini's trophy in the Virginia Slims tennis tournament showed a woman with a racket in one hand and a cigarette in the other.

∽ Smoking-related illness is the leading cause of death among women in the United States. By the year 2000, women's lung cancer rates may surpass men's.

∽ There is evidence that nicotine addiction is more powerful physiologically and psychologically for women.

∽ Twenty percent of pregnant women still smoke.

∽ Smoking rates among teenage girls are climbing. Among twelve- to thirteen-year-olds who smoke, virtually all are also dieting.

∽ Groups fighting the tobacco companies' targeting of young women are STAT (Stop Teenage Addiction to Tobacco) and Women and Girls Against Tobacco.

The Story of *Our Bodies, Ourselves*

In the spring of 1969, a women's liberation conference in Boston included a workshop about women and their bodies. Some workshop participants started teaching Know Your Bodies courses at women's centers and conferences in New England. They also collected names of doctors who treated women knowledgeably and well; they added information about women's health and published a newsprint pamphlet the next year. It sold for seventy-five cents. Two years and 200,000 copies later, the pamphlet became a book, *Our Bodies, Ourselves*. Revised in 1976 and 1979, it has sold over 3 million copies and has been translated into fourteen foreign editions.

The collective that created the book was activist and has remained so. Currently on their agenda: opposing hormone replacement therapy and critiquing images of women in advertising (high-heeled shoes and obsessive thinness are health issues); supporting midwifery care and urging more breast cancer research.

The most important issue, according to Judy Norsigian, an original member of the collective, is access to health care. "There is much more about women's health research in the media," she says, "than about access. One-fifth of women under thirty have no health insurance; 18 percent of single mothers have none."

Defending Black Women's Lives: The Black Women's Health Project

∽ Infant mortality among African-Americans is double that in the white population.

∽ Forty percent of black women are obese, defined as health-endangering overweight.

The Body as Art/The Art of the Body

Judy Chicago broke the menstrual taboo in modern art. Her 1971 lithograph *Red Flag* shows a hand removing a reddened tampon by pulling on a string. In an elaborate shrine to female culture called *Womanhouse*, constructed in California the same year, Chicago's "Menstruation Bathroom" is a gauze-covered room, white, clean, and deodorized, with Modess and Tampax boxes on shelves, a wastebasket overflowing with used napkins.

When women artists in New York protested the sexism of the Whitney Museum in 1970, they hung tampons throughout the building.

The conceptual artist Nicolino was planning to assemble 10,000 donated bras in the spring of 1996 and fly them over the Grand Canyon. "We'll have a chain of these iconic objects and we'll span the greatest cleavage on the planet," she says.

Lorna Simpson,
Portrait.

"They tried to wisper
sweet nothings."

Ana Mendieta, from
"Tree of Life" series of
photographs, 1977

Anita Steckel, Giant Woman on
New York, montage, 1977

≈ Fifty-two percent of all women with AIDS are African-American.

≈ Eighty percent of all pediatric AIDS cases occur among blacks and Latinos.

≈ African-American women have the poorest survival rate for breast cancer of any racial group.

These are the issues addressed by the National Black Women's Health Project, the self-help and advocacy organization started by Byllye Avery, of the Harvard School of Public Health, in 1981. Since most activists in the women's health movement of the 1970s were white, Avery's intention was to draw women of color into the arena.

Defining health as "not merely the absence of illness, but the active promotion of physical, spiritual, mental and emotional wellness of this and future generations," the organization is the model for the National Latina Health Project and Native American Women's Health Research Center.

Is Pornography Violence against Women?

Seventeen magazine reported in 1995 that 89 percent of girls surveyed had experienced unwanted sexual comments, gestures, or looks.

Pornography is a systematic practice of exploitation and subordination based on sex that differently harms and disadvantages women. The harm of pornography includes dehumanization, psychic assault, sexual exploitation, forced sex, forced prostitution, physical injury, and social and sexual terrorism and inferiority presented as entertainment.

Model civil rights ordinance, written by Andrea Dworkin and Catherine MacKinnon, 1983

The range of feminist imagination and expression in the realm of sexuality has barely begun to find voice. Women need the freedom and the socially recognized space to appropriate for themselves the robustness of what traditionally has been male language . . . [We] fear that as more women's writing and art on sexual themes emerges which is unladylike, unfeminine, aggressive, power-charged, pushy, vulgar, urgent, confident and intense, the traditional foes of women's attempts to step out of their "proper place" will find an effective tool of repression in the ordinance.

Feminists against Censorship Task Force, 1985

I, too, recoil in pain and incomprehension whenever I hear about the latest psychopath who has shot his mother, machine-gunned his co-workers, raped his daughter or slashed a prostitute. I notice that such men are more likely to have read the Bible than pornography, but I do not hold either script responsible for their actions.

Susie Bright, 1995

Last Words

Why A Woman Can't Be Pope

Everyone knows that under her robes,
there would be breasts . . .

Sandra Kohler, "The Country of Women," 1995

> **"** I stand here before you feeling like I own the earth because of twenty years in a sport. That's what we're fighting for—to make sure that everybody out there, every little girl and every high school girl and every 55-year-old woman ashamed of her fat, could feel like I feel—like she owns the earth. **"**
>
> *Swimmer Diana Nyad, 1983*

CHAPTER 3
The Female Body in Motion

*I*f I am asked to explain why I learned the bicycle I should say I did it as an act of grace, if not of actual religion.

Frances Willard, Women's Christian Temperance Union leader who coined the group's motto: "Do Everything," 1895

I preach freedom of the mind through freedom of the body: women, for example —out of the prison of corsets.

Isadora Duncan, 1922

I always knew what I wanted to be when I grew up. My goal was to be the greatest athlete who ever lived.

Babe Didrikson Zaharias

Dance is the fist with which I fight the sickening ignorance of prejudice. Instead of growing twisted like a gnarled tree inside myself, I am able to dance out my anger and frustration.

Dancer/choreographer Pearl Primus, 1968

You can't ride winners if the trainers don't put you on any horses. . . . All I ever ride are long shots. The male jockeys get the Cadillacs and I get the Volkswagens— if I'm lucky.

Jockey Robyn Smith, 1978

Yolanda M. Lopez: "Portrait of the Artist as Virgin of Guadalupe" from Guadalupe Triptych, 1978.

Seth Eastman, Squaws Playing Ball on the Prairie, *1849*

*I*n no area of American life has the scorn of being "unwomanly" been more easily or more consistently hurled than in athletics. Annie Peck climbs the world's highest mountain in 1895. Helen Wills in 1925 serves a tennis ball so hard that a man can't return it. A female person named Babe Didrikson Zaharias throws a baseball 296 feet in 1934. Others leap hurdles, participate in shot puts, and race horses. Are they unwomanly? The answer depends on what year it is, where it is, and what the woman's race and class are.

Except for the battlefield, no turf has been defended as male more ferociously than the baseball diamond, the basketball court, the wrestling ring, and the racecourse. For most of our history, sports culture—the contests, the teams, the locker rooms, the sportswriters—was masculine. An exertion-contorted face and a sweat-drenched body have threatened the status quo of gender ideas more directly than a female hand dropping a ballot into a box or cashing a paycheck. The struggle for women's sports, then, has been vigorous.

During America's early years, nobody worried much about fragile ovaries in need of rest and protection or frail constitutions ready to expire at any expenditure of physical energy when female labor was necessary. Nobody thought the back-breaking exertion of slave women threatened their constitutions. On the frontier, where social customs were less restricted than they were in cities, many women farmed and homesteaded from sunup to sundown, drove wagons, herded cattle, shot rifles, and rode horseback. For amusement, they might race, on horseback or on foot.

By the middle of the nineteenth century, restrictions on female movement had set in and reformers made exercise part of their progressive agenda. Catharine Beecher published *A Course of Calisthenics for Young Ladies* in 1832; a school run by the abolitionist Grimké sisters before the Civil War had girls' exercises in the gymnasium and competitions in rowing, swimming, and high diving.

By the end of the century, sport had become a refined way for white women and men to spend time together. Winslow Homer's paintings show Victorian ladies in mixed company hitting croquet balls, easily done in Victorian clothing. Charles Dana Gibson's 1890s creation, the Gibson Girl, decidedly white and aristocratic, bicycled, golfed, and played tennis.

The Becker sisters branding cattle on their Rio Grande ranch, 1894

Other sports—and women of other classes—were curiosities, in the same category as a talking dog. People came to gape when Nell Saunders stepped into a boxing ring and raised her gloves against Rose Harland in 1876. Saunders won. Her prize was a silver butter dish. In 1891, Alice Williams and Sadie Morgan wrestled. Both wore their hair short, a violation of convention all by itself. The short hair was not an act of defiance, as it would be for Jazz Age flappers, but a safety measure, to prevent hair pulling.

Dance did not have to be defended as male turf, but the pioneers in moving the female body around in space and in public did have to contend with questions of class. For most of American history, the Puritan heritage prevailed. While dance was an integral part of religious and social life among Native Americans and Latins, and had a place in black entertainment, it remained a "folk" concept. There was a meager tradition of social dancing and almost none of theatrical dancing in white culture. When European ballet companies toured the country in the 1840s, they belonged to the realm of the disreputable. The women, after all, showed their legs.

The change began, along with many other changes, in the 1890s. Those who promoted the change were "tainted" women from the ballet corps and vaudeville—Loie Fuller, Isadora Duncan, and Ruth St. Denis—women who embodied and acted out the decades-long

Frances Benjamin Johnston photograph, **Girls' Gym Class at Western High School,** *Washington, D.C., 1899*

attempts to free women's minds and bodies. Their work paralleled the efforts to open athletics to women, provoked perhaps more controversy, and was equally fascinating to advanced thinkers of the day, particularly photographers, who rushed to capture the daring new female body in motion.

That the pioneers of dance were businesswomen also escaped public notice. Female athletes, like Western sharpshooters and bronc riders, were breadwinners, although that was harder to accomplish than being an oddity. Until the 1970s, it was difficult for the American public to understand that women did anything at all for serious financial reasons, not merely for "pin money." In immigrant and African-American neighborhoods, sports, especially baseball, basketball, and track and field, were tickets out of poverty and ghettos for men, but the fact that they might be the same for women took some time to sink in.

Yet nineteenth-century America was no athletic paradise. Consider the clothes. Vassar's baseball players took to the field in thirty pounds of attire, including wide, floor-length skirts and high-button shoes. Imagine stealing third. In the next century, the All American Girls Baseball League was also wardrobe-challenged: they were forced to wear short skirts. Imagine their skin after stealing third.

Reformer Amelia Bloomer's loose pants and tunic were worn by suffragists and athletes alike, underscoring the link between women's political and physical freedom. While jeering crowds followed Elizabeth Cady Stanton, Susan B.

Pitcher, all-female Giants baseball team, c. 1910

Althea Gibson, Wimbledon, England, 1956

Anthony, and their allies until they couldn't take it anymore, athletes kept the costume. From 1890 to 1920, hundreds of women played professional baseball in what was called the Bloomer League.

On campuses, the idea of female prowess and glory suffered a severe setback. By the 1920s, those worried about how "mannish" American women were becoming—casting votes, entering professions, and all that—somehow convinced everyone that wanting to win might be all right for immigrants and working-class girls, but was unfeminine for nice, white, middle-class girls at elite schools. One by one, throughout the decade, schools and colleges ended competitive sports for women. The rules changed: physical education became a way of keeping a woman healthy and improving her looks.

Even so, a woman who rejected everything about middle-class white femininity became the greatest female athlete of all time. Babe Didrikson Zaharias was so record-breaking good that the usual questions about the femininity of female athletes and Zaharias's sexuality in particular, were confined to muttering out of earshot. In the mid-1940s, a journalist commenting on the fact that she not only set records in track and field, but excelled at basketball, baseball, and football—she would later add the title of America's greatest woman golfer to her achievements—asked: "Is there anything at all you don't play?"

"Yeah," Zaharias said, "dolls."

The spotlight that shone on female athletes only saw the white ones. Off the sports pages of mainstream newspapers, black women were performing athletic feats without the ensuing fame. Ora Washington won seven consecutive singles titles in the American Tennis Association and challenged reigning champion Helen Wills, who refused to play her. No tennis player spoke up about the sport's segregation until Alice Marble threw her weight behind Althea Gibson in 1950, challenging the United States Lawn Tennis Association's ruling against Gibson's participation in the championships. Gibson not only broke the color line in American tennis but won the championship that year. In 1957 and 1958, she became the first black American to win the Wimbledon singles title.

The dancers did better. While French audiences celebrated the "savagery" of African dancing in the hypersexed persona of Josephine Baker, it was left to other Americans in the 1920s and 1930s to bring wider aspects of African movements to white audiences. Helen Tamiris was the first white choreographer to use black music and to show black life in her dances—in *Negro Spirituals* (1928) and *How Long Brethren?* (1937). Katherine Dunham, an anthropologist as well as choreographer and dancer, integrated the physical vocabulary of Africa and the Caribbean into ballet and modern dance in the 1930s.

World War II provided an excuse for female sports, as it did for female welders and shipyard workers. Chewing gum magnate Philip K. Wrigley filled the empty ballparks of the Midwest with teenagers batting and running bases. The All American Girls Baseball League, which began as a softball league, eventually allowed nearly 600 women to earn a living on the diamond. To counter the stereotypes and make women's baseball nonthreatening to the public, Wrigley not only insisted on short-skirted outfits, but put his players under Helena Ruben-

Katherine Dunham, c. 1955

stein's tutelage to learn "charm." This was sometimes welcome, sometimes tough. "It was hard to walk in high heels with a book on your head when you had a charley horse," said catcher Lavonne "Pepper" Paire.

Pearl Primus, born in Trinidad and raised in New York, an athlete who set college records as a sprinter, an anthropologist also, embodied a fiercer esthetic. "My body is built for heavy stomping, powerful dignity," she said. The indigenous movements, particularly Haitian, that went into her dancing were kept close to their original form, less adapted to mainstream taste.

One way a female body can move is to put itself on the line. Josephine Baker returned to America to march on Washington with Dr. Martin Luther King, Jr., in 1963. Katherine Dunham, once dance director for the New York Labor Stage, spent the 1940s and 1950s filing lawsuits and publicly condemning segregation. In 1992, when the U.S. government began deporting Haitian boat refugees, she went on a hunger strike in protest. Only the persuasion of exiled President Aristide could convince her to stop.

The dancers did nothing less than take the female body seriously and, as women were doing in every other part of American life, from the 1890s onward, expand its options. A woman's body could have something to "say" about war and motherhood, as it did for Isadora Duncan, who not only made those bold themes the subject of her dances, but performed while visibly pregnant. It could speak of violence and rage, as it did for Martha Graham. It could, under its own steam, without male arms to lift it or lead it, stomp or fly, be dignified or silly. A woman's body could/can be or do anything.

An athletic female born after the 1970s is in luck. The old questions still arise and barricades are set in her path, but the ammunition with which to fight back is in place because of the extraordinary seventies alliance of feminists and athletes, who were sometimes the same person. Because of Billie Jean King and many others, female athletes today have pictures of female gold medalists on their girlhood bedroom walls. Most of all, they have an attitude that didn't exist before: not "Why would a woman want to be an athlete?" but "Why not?"

> Skating, driving hoop and other boyishy sports may be practised to great advantage by little girls provided they can be pursued within the enclosure of a garden or court; in the street, of course, they would be highly improper. It is true, such games are rather violent, and sometimes noisy, but they tend to form a vigorous constitution and girls who are habitually lady-like, will never allow themselves to be rude and vulgar, even in play.
>
> *Lydia Marie Child,* The Little Girls' Own Book, *1847*

For Suffrage, for Mountains

Anna Dickinson may have been the only suffrage leader who loved climbing mountains. The "Queen of the Lyceum," a gifted speaker, she boasted that she had been on top of more of America's great mountains than any woman alive. On trips to Colorado in the 1870s, she alternated giving speeches with going up some fourteen-thousand-foot mountains on a mule or a horse. In 1873, the *Boulder County News* made much of the fact that she wore trousers on her way to the summit.

The Amazon of the Nineteenth Century

Etta Hattan, known as "Jaguarina" and "Ideal Amazon of the Age," embodied the theatricality of athletic contests. Wearing exotic costumes, creating an aura of paganism that took the event out of the realm of ordinary sports, she challenged and defeated men in a series of mounted broadsword contests, from 1884 to the end of the century. In San Francisco in 1887, her opponent was so chagrined at being beaten by a woman that he harangued the referee.

SWEATING COLLEGE WOMEN: VASSAR LEADS THE WAY

Vassar College opened in 1865 with a separate building called the Calisthenium and a catalogue that explicitly said, "A suitable portion of each day is set aside for physical exercise and every young lady is required to observe it as one of her college duties." Although some of the exercise promoted for women in these years was aimed at making them fit for childbirth and was at a level of strenuousness equivalent to an hour of house cleaning, there was also sport, whose function was defensible largely on the grounds of fun.

In its second year, Vassar had two baseball clubs and games were held every weekend. Smith, Mount Holyoke, and Wellesley followed. Although male sport was endorsed not only as mere fun, but as preparation for winning in the world—learning the rules of combat, acquiring team skills—the same could not be said of the huffing and puffing going on in women's schools.

The Bloomer League

> I got in shape beating rugs and chopping wood.
> *Lizzie Murphy, Bloomer League first baseman*

Most women who played hardball in the Bloomer League at the end of the nineteenth century came from farms or the urban working class. Men in drag and fright wigs also played on the teams.

Many of the best players were pitchers, including the first woman signed to a minor league contract, Lizzie Arlington, who played in a regulation minor league game in 1898. Six-foot-tall Amanda Clement, whose mother had been one of the original settlers of the Dakota Territory, was the first woman paid to umpire a game. In 1904, in Iowa, the scheduled umpire didn't show up for an amateur game and she took over. A semipro team, impressed, asked her to umpire. She did, for six years, using her pay to put herself through college.

Pitcher Alta Weiss, who used her pay to go to medical school, wore the Bloomer costume, but Lizzie Murphy, first baseman, wore a standard man's outfit. For twenty years, she earned her living playing ball.

The Bloomers introduced night baseball, which the major leagues didn't adopt until 1935. Wrigley Field was not permanently lighted until the 1980s.

THE GIRL WHO STRUCK OUT BABE RUTH

In 1904, seventeen-year-old Virne Beatrice "Jackie" Mitchell of Chattanooga, Tennessee, struck out both Babe Ruth and Lou Gehrig. Playing in an exhibition game between the Chattanooga Lookouts, who hoped to cash in on the publicity surrounding their girl pitcher, this was her public debut. The papers said it was all a combination of a joke, a publicity stunt, and male chivalry, but Mitchell insisted the strikeouts were entirely serious.

Why Women Should Be Umpires

All the official baseball umpires of the country should be women.

The only objection that is found in this day to baseball is rowdyism. Now, if women were umpiring none of this would happen. Do you suppose any ball player in the country would step up to a good-looking girl and say to her, "you color-blind, pickle-brained, cross-eyed idiot." Of course he wouldn't. Then there's the crowd. There's a good deal of cowardliness about the roasting of umpires by crowds, because hardly any of the fans that shout all sorts of insults from the bleacher would have the nerve to say anything of the kind to the umpire's face. . . .

Amanda Clement, 1906

Annie Oakley

Her real name was Phoebe Ann Mosey, she was five feet tall, weighed a little over one hundred pounds, and was the first female Western superstar. As a child in Ohio, fatherless since she was eight, Mosey hunted to help the family income. By the time she was fifteen, her reputation as a crack shot led her community to pit her against a visiting star sharpshooter. She not only beat Frank Butler in their contest, she married him. Together, Butler and impresario William F. ("Buffalo Bill") Cody packaged "Annie Oakley." She joined Buffalo Bill's show in 1885, three years after he started.

She saw herself as an athlete, a wage earner, and a performer. Opposed to suffrage and the emerging "new woman" of the late nineteenth and early twentieth century, she nonetheless was an early fan of the bicycle and an increasingly strong advocate for women's participation in both sports and the national economy. "I don't like bloomers or bloomer women," she said in 1897, "but I think that sport and healthful exercise make women better, healthier and happier." In 1901, she was more emphatic: "God intended woman to be outside as well as men, and they do not know what they are missing when they stay cooped up in the house with a novel."

Believing that women should "know how to handle guns as well as they handle babies," Oakley taught many how to use firearms to protect themselves. That she inspired a female following is evident from her offer to President William McKinley, on the eve of the Spanish-American War in 1898, to provide a "Company of fifty lady sharpshooters." She was brushed off.

Rodeos and Wild West Shows

It was easier in the Western states and territories, where women's hard physical labor was essential to daily life, for women to become athletes. The skills girls learned on ranches translated easily to exhibitions and competitions in the public arena. Beginning in 1882, when Buffalo Bill Cody first packaged rodeo contests, women earned money and prizes by competing as sharpshooters, riders, and ropers. Some tried to do so in heavy skirts; others adopted the controversial culottes or men's clothing. Those who rode astride, as most rodeo and wild West show riders did, were criticized for unladylike behavior and for allegedly impairing their reproductive organs.

The early rodeo queens were sportswomen and showpeople—like champion Lucille Mulhall, who once, at the request of Teddy Roosevelt, roped a wolf, and sharpshooter May Lillie from Philadelphia, who had attended Smith College and whose husband, "Pawnee Bill," put the first bronc-riding women into his wild West show in 1906. In the 1920s, the heyday, the most famous celebrities, combining athleticism with showmanship, were bronc riders, trick riders, and relay racers. Enjoying a camaraderie with male peers unmatched by women in other sports, they traveled all over the country and competed at the prestigious annual rodeo in New York's Madison Square Garden.

Rodeo performer Jessie Roberts on bucking horse Grey Ghost, 1930s

During World War II, the sport's popularity waned. Trick riding had been dropped as a contest, then bronc riding. Barrel racing, less showy and daring, became the standard female event on the circuit. Female rodeo participants were more often chosen for their looks than their skill.

In 1948, the Girls Rodeo Association began resurrecting the sport; in 1981, *Women* replaced *Girls* in the group's name. The new generation is more focused on the professional athleticism of the competitions, less on the glitter, and has over one million dollars in prize money up for grabs every year.

Bernarr MacFadden: Good Guy or Bad Guy?

Part of the opposition to women's sports was horror at the "nakedness" of some of the participants.

In 1899, health faddist Bernarr MacFadden took over *Physical Culture* magazine and started promoting physical culture for women. In 1905, he staged "Physical Culture Show" in New York's Madison Square Garden, billed as a search for the world's most perfectly developed female. Shapely young women in union suits paraded before an audience of 20,000. Anthony Comstock, enforcer of Victorian morality, the man who would prosecute Margaret Sanger for obscenity, threatened to arrest MacFadden and close him down, but the show went on.

Girl Scouts Move; Camp Fire Girls Sit

Juliette Low, a great supporter of women's athletics, founded the Girl Scouts of America in 1912. Along with vaguely military uniforms, the scout program emphasized calisthenics, hiking, and basketball. Physical education specialist Luther Gulick objected and organized the Camp Fire Girls in opposition. Dressed like what a white man thought of as demure Indian maidens, their major activity was singing songs around a suitably domestic campfire.

That Sears Girl

> You offered to pace me, not chase me.
> *Eleanora Randolph Sears to two lagging male companions, on an eleven-hour, five-minute walk from Providence, Rhode Island, to Boston*

In 1910, Eleanora Randolph Sears created a scandal by wearing jodphurs and riding astride while playing against men in a polo game. Sears, a descendant of Thomas Jefferson, also won five tennis championships playing doubles, where her style was described as "hard." She raced cars, rode in equestrian events, and was one of the first prominent women to wear pants and short hair in public.

Sportsclothes

☞ In 1867, the Dolly Vardens of Philadelphia, a women's baseball team, wore shocking red calico dresses that stopped above their ankles.

☞ Defying convention in order to be able to move was the motivating force of women who simply wanted to navigate their daily lives and of those with more strenuous aspirations, like mountaineer Annie Smith Peck, the first woman to reach the peak of the Matterhorn. Custom said climbers wore skirts, as Fay Fuller did when she climbed Mount Rainier in 1890. One climber was forced to scale the same peak twice in one day

Bathers being arrested for violating ordinance against wearing revealing swimwear, Chicago, 1922

to retrieve the skirt she left on the summit, afraid to be seen entering an inn wearing only her climbing pants.

☞ Annie Peck, whose motivation was to set foot where no man had stepped before, went up the Matterhorn in 1895 in knickerbockers, tunic, and a felt hat tied by a veil. The waves of derisive press coverage provoked by her costume deterred her not at all. She continued to make major climbs well into her sixties.

☞ Tennis, the sport that revolutionized the clothing worn by upper-class women, was brought to the United States from Bermuda in 1874 by Mary Ewing Outerbridge, charter member of the exclusive Ladies Club for Outdoor Sports. One of the earliest tournaments was at the Staten Island Cricket Club. Women's colleges quickly adopted the sport and the first college tournament was played in 1887. In 1893, Ava Willing Astor scandalously defied her mother-in-law, Caroline Astor, by wearing bloomers on the courts in Newport, Rhode Island. In 1902, the rules of the game changed, and women's tournaments became the less strenuous two out of three sets, instead of the original three out of five. They still are.

☞ By the 1920s, the female body had become a marketable commodity on a larger scale than ever before. Show-biz impresario Flo Ziegfeld and Hollywood agents scouted swimming and tennis meets for great-looking women. Among the actresses who had their starts as swimmers were Esther Williams and Eleanor Holm. Williams, 1939 freestyle champion, was discovered at the San Francisco World's Fair Aquacade.

☞ Pictures of night club girls in skimpy clothes could be censored in the mail, but not swimmers in one-piece garments. The Florida real estate boom was built on girl swimmers in ads.

Climbers on
Mount Hood,
Washington, 1913

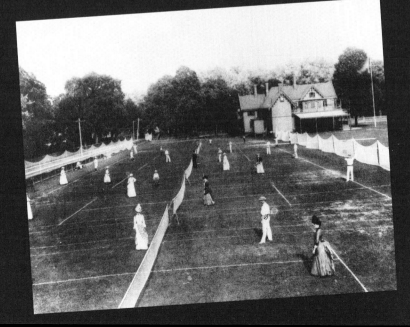

Alice Austen photograph,
First U.S. Tennis Courts,
Staten Island, New York,
1874

Ruth St. Denis as Radha, 1906

The Politics of Olympic Gold

In August 1920, the Nineteenth Amendment was passed, and a team of American women competed in the Olympic Games. Neither had been easily accomplished. Baron Pierre de Coubertin, the modern Olympic Games' founder, was adamant that women violated the "purity" of Olympic competition and that "female applause as reward for men's prowess was the proper female sphere."

The Roaring Twenties: Sports Celebrities

The sphere of female prowess became the spotlight of celebrity in the 1920s, an era of sports heroes, the decade of Babe Ruth and Jack Dempsey. In 1926, on her second try, the eighteen-year-old daughter of a New York delicatessen owner became the first woman to swim the English Channel. Gertrude Ederle beat the record time of the five previous male swimmers across the Channel by almost two hours and returned to a tumultuous ticker tape parade. Ederle's record stood until 1950, when it was broken by Florence Chadwick, a California stenographer, who also became the first swimmer to cross the Channel in both directions. Helen Wills dominated tennis and the newspapers, winning every singles match she played from 1926 to 1933. Her record of eight Wimbledon crowns lasted until Martina Navratilova broke it with her ninth win in 1990.

"New" Women

Like the women who came after them, Loie Fuller, Isadora Duncan, and Ruth St. Denis made the business of allowing the female body to move into a business, supporting themselves and others by creating dances and establishing schools. They were rebels. St. Denis, who came from a family of women reformers and doctors, was a great believer in physical education for girls, setting her against prevailing conceptions of the sickly, dependent female body.

All three found more receptive audiences and greater support in Europe than they did in America, but their work paved the way for the next generation.

Isadora Duncan: Emancipation from Puritanism

If my art is symbolic of one thing, it is symbolic of the freedom of woman and her emancipation from the hide-bound conventions that are the warp and woof of New England Puritanism.

I would rather dance completely nude than strut in half-clothed suggestiveness, as many women do today on the streets of America.

Lori Bellilove and Company performing work by Isadora Duncan, 1995

In 1901, Isadora Duncan threw off her corsets and modeled herself on Botticelli's *Primavera*, a copy of which her mother always hung in every boardinghouse they lived in. Once her waist and ribs were free to move, once she had put sandals on her feet and Grecian-style draperies on her body, Duncan became the whole show—her body was the scenery and, although she was likely the first to use concert music, Chopin especially, for her dances—her body was also the music.

Duncan rejected the conventional lives of women in society, denounced marriage and, later in her life, sided with the Russian Revolution and became an outspoken critic of capitalism.

She performed all over the world, founding schools in many of the countries she visited. Her life was a series of ups and downs, great successes and dismal failures, many lovers and three children, and a constant struggle for money. She was the toast of the radicals, especially during the years before and after World War I, not only for her dancing but because she embodied everything about "the new woman" that the world found shocking.

In a Category of Her Own: Josephine Baker

> Sex was a pleasurable form of exercise, like dancing.
> *Phyllis Rose,* Jazz Cleopatra: Josephine Baker in Her Time, *1989*

In the 1920s, the female body that was given center stage in the culture was not the S shape of the Victorians—protruding bust, narrow waist, extended derriere—but something looser and wilder. As a dancer, Baker not only embodied the new, but the African-American. She brought with her to the Paris stage in 1925 the moves of black musical comedy: the Charleston, the Black Bottom, jazz dancing, and tap. To these she added her own personal stamp—dancing with her eyes crossed, among other gestures—and the shocking, stimulating nakedness that branded her the ultimate "primitive" to white audiences.

Baker had worked since she was eight years old, first as a domestic in St. Louis, Missouri, then as a show biz runaway. Still a teenager, she made it to the stage in the most important black musical comedies of the early 1920s: *Shuffle Along* and *Chocolate Dandies*, where she was discovered and hired for *La Revue Negre*, which would play Paris. She debuted dancing the Charleston to "Yes, Sir, That's My Baby" and became one of the biggest celebrities of all time. In the Folies-Bergère, she danced in a costume of rhinestone-studded bananas around her hips.

One of the earliest self-created female legends, she went about Paris with a leopard wearing a diamond choker, had clothes made for her extraordinary body by the newest designers, and was praised by artists, including Picasso, who called her "the Nefertiti of now." Although she became a singer and then a national heroine for her Resistance work during World War II, it was for moving her body the modern, African-American way she did that she first became an international sensation.

Martha Graham

Modern dance isn't anything except one thing in my mind: the freedom of women in America. . . . It comes in as a moment of emancipation, the moment when an emergence took place from behind the bustle.

All things I do are in every woman. Every woman is Medea. Every woman is Jocasta. There comes a time when a woman is a mother to her husband. Clytemnestra is every woman when she kills.

Martha Graham, 1946

Women in the 1970s, freed by a movement that has validated the expression of female experience, may be able to bring to the theatre of words the depths of female feeling that Graham has brought to the dance.

Honor Moore, The New Women's Theatre, *1977*

As a child, Graham saw Ruth St. Denis dance and knew what she would make of her own life. Although her psychiatrist father wanted to send her to Vassar, she studied with St. Denis and then joined her company. In 1923, she came to New York to work as an exotic solo dancer in *The Greenwich Village Follies* and to encounter the world of modern theater. Her spare, psychological, dramatic style and its theatrical influences were present from her 1926 debut.

Her work became part of the way American women were able to see themselves. In *Frontier,* she paid tribute to the vision, independence, and strength of the pioneer woman. *American Provincials* has as its background the world of Nathaniel Hawthorne's *Scarlet Letter.* Poet Emily Dickinson's imagination is the landscape of *Letter to the World.*

She created Amazonian women on her stages, societies of women and matriarchies, violent, sexual women who disrupted families. She broke all the rules, including the one that said powerful women should hide their power. As choreographer and director of her own school, Graham was notoriously what some called assertive and others abrasive.

Although her career was the most important one of its time of any woman in any of the arts, her daring work initially terrified many critics, who called it "bitter," "intellectual," and "cold." She outlived the critics, leaving behind when she died in 1992, a seventy-year contribution to art, politics, and bodily imaginations.

Dance, Drama, Modernism, and the Female Body

Martha Graham and Doris Humphrey were modernists. In 1929, Graham said that she aimed in her dances for the tempo of modern life: "nervous, sharp and zigzag." Each brought to the stage a new and thoroughly American art form. Graham was passionate about the "psyche of the land" being found in its movement, believing that great art, which was her intention, "must belong to the country in which it flourishes, not be a pale copy of some art form perfected by another culture and another people."

The indigenous, female-centered drama created by American women choreographers had never existed before, nor had their new way of seeing the female body. As dancers and makers of dances, they emphasized the power and expressiveness of the female body. And that changed everything.

Sports

"The Babe"

In Beaumont, Texas, Babe Didrikson practiced hurdles by jumping over neighbors' hedges. A girl who wanted to be an athlete had to play with boys, and so she did.

Competitive sports for women in the 1920s and 1930s were in industrial leagues. The Employers Casualty Insurance Company of Dallas sponsored a basketball team called the Golden Cyclones, who played (shockingly) in shorts and jerseys. A young woman who stood about five feet, four inches, weighed 105 to 110 pounds, lean and wiry, with short hair, no makeup and a penchant for sweatsuits instead of dresses, led her team to a national championship. Five thousand people a night came to watch Babe Didrikson—"The Texas Tornado"—and the Cyclones.

She persuaded the company to sponsor a track team and broke three world records herself in 1930. In 1932, she was the whole team herself at the women's national amateur track championships, scoring points in seven events, winning five, and establishing three world records. Olympic rules limited her to three events: javelin (won the gold), high jump (silver), and eighty-meter hurdles (gold).

Agreeing to appear in a Dodge automobile ad, Didrikson incurred the anger of those who believed amateur sportswomen should not earn money.

The small newspaper coverage allotted women's sports commented obsessively on the athletes' looks. Didrikson was ridiculed, but it didn't stop her. She toured with an all-male baseball team, establishing a woman's record that still stands for throwing a baseball 296 feet. In 1934, she pitched exhibition games for three major league teams.

After a stab at boxing, she became a golfer, and by 1946, she had won seventeen tournaments in a row. The Ladies Professional Golf Association, the oldest professional sports organization for women in the country, had started in 1944, but didn't take off until 1949, when Babe Didrikson, then married to boxer George Zaharias, started playing on the tour. Driving a golf ball more than 300 yards, she turned a polite ladies' dance into an aggressive game. The LPGA, which brought more money and prestige to the sport, is her lasting legacy.

Babe Didrikson, Los Angeles, July 31, 1932

After a cancer operation, she won her third U.S. Open in 1954, two years before her death at age forty-three.

A League of Their Own

By the mid-1930s, women's baseball had given way in popularity to softball, a game that relied almost entirely on the pitcher, was less expensive to run and promote, and less difficult to play. Many organizations supported it—Eastman Kodak had a team—although none had supported baseball.

In 1943, Chicago Cubs baseball team owner Philip K. Wrigley, whose chewing gum was advertised to workers in offices and factories as an antidote to thirst and nervous tension, started a girls' softball league. Although Wrigley didn't believe women could play baseball, the game quickly evolved from underhand pitching to overhand and became . . . baseball!

Players were required to wear makeup on the field and have long hair. No "masculinized" women in the All American Girls Baseball League.

Its first year, the league had four teams, 108 games, and 176,000 fans. Admission was a dollar, the same as men's games. In its second year, two more teams were added and attendance rose 50 percent. It all took place in medium-sized Midwestern cities, where factories were fueling the war effort.

The most outstanding player was Dorothy Kamenshek of the Rockford Peaches in Rockford, Illinois. A great first baseman, she had the highest lifetime batting average in the league. Bill Allington, tough manager and ex-player, was hired in 1944.

Kamenshek retired in 1952, went to college, and became a physical therapist. "One thing about our league," she said, years later, "it gave a lot of us the courage to go on to professional careers at a time when women didn't do things like that."

The All-American Girls' Baseball Squad being lectured by their coach, 1951

At the end of the 1944 season, Wrigley changed his mind about supporting the women and the sport. The threat to men's baseball was passing; the war would end sooner than he thought. He sold the All American Girls Baseball League for $10,000 and it survived another decade.

Baseball's women had little recognition until an exhibit at the National Baseball Hall of Fame opened in 1988.

Running

After much controversy five women's track and field events were added to the 1928 Olympics. Unlike swimming or tennis, track was considered a masculinizing sport. When some female runners collapsed after the 800-meter race, the critics rushed in again. Protesters, male and female, objected to the strenuousness of the events, urging officials to suspend the newly added competitions. Some wanted to eliminate female athletes altogether. The women stayed, but their medium- and long-distance races were withdrawn. Until 1960, there were no Olympic women's races longer than 200 meters.

Both track and basketball were popular women's sports in the 1920s and 1930s, but media coverage was consistently negative. Organized attempts to remove them from school and international competition resulted in white women abandoning track and field in particular; black women took it over.

At the 1948 Olympics, Alice Coachman became the first African-American woman to win an Olympic medal, a gold in the high jump. A track and basketball star at Tuskegee Institute, which became a training ground for female runners, Coachman had been raised in Georgia with nine siblings and a father who whipped her when she left the house to practice with the high school basketball team or to run. He wanted his daughters to be "dainty, sitting on the front porch."

Her victory set the stage for track and field dominance by American black women:

Wilma Rudolph, who had been unable to walk without a brace as a child because of illness, won Olympic medals in relays and the 200-meter race.

Sprinter Wyomia Tyus, whose family thought athletics unfeminine, broke records at the Mexico City Olympics in 1968.

Willye B. White, five-time Olympian, started competing in 1956. At sixteen, she won a silver medal in the long jump. "I just wanted to get out of the house," she said. "That was why I turned to sports. It was the only way I could stay out past 5 o'clock. And I was good at it, too. . . . As far as what was traditional and nontraditional, I had no idea. All I knew was it was just an escape for me not to have to go to the cotton fields during the summer."

Joan Benoit won the first women's marathon at the Olympics in 1984 in just under two and a half hours.

Wilma Rudolph winning the quarter final heat, Summer Olympics, Rome, 1960

The Future

In 1963, the first female marathon runners were almost an hour and a half slower than the best male runners. Twenty years later, the fastest women were within fifteen minutes of the winning male speed. Female sprinters are now within a fraction of a second of the top male speeds and some experts predict that early in the next century, women will match male runners.

Althea Gibson's Inspiration

My smash was considered revolutionary in women's tennis, but Althea Gibson elevated the stroke to a new level with her combination of power and ease.
Champion Alice Marble

> Mom is a strong woman . . . the first one to say that she was no delicate flower in those days. She used to love to ride, and because there wasn't much chance of her going to a riding stable, she used to ride not only horses, but cows, hogs and everything.
>
> *From Althea Gibson's autobiography,* I Always Wanted to Be Somebody, *1958*

The Fight for Women's Basketball

In the 1890s, when it was invented, basketball was seen as a perfect recreation for women because it was an indoor game, played in a small, confined space. It became extremely popular in settlement houses, where peach buckets were often used as baskets. On college campuses, it became an undergraduate passion.

The reaction came from female physical education specialists, often at the women's colleges, who were worried about the frenzy of the sport, its roughness, and what was coming to be thought of as its masculinity. Many an undergraduate in the 1920s was steered toward more ladylike, noncontact sports, tennis and golf especially. For decades, they struggled to minimize intercollegiate competitions and to impose rules for girls' basketball that limited the players' exertion, had six women on a side, confined to certain areas of the court, which was shorter than the men's court to begin with. One of the opponents' primary concerns was the "tussling" that went on. Girls' rules minimized physical contact.

Two segments of the population paid little attention. At black schools, women's basketball went on with all the fervor it always had. Among working-class young women, industrial leagues sponsored full-court basketball; the "protectors" of femininity objected to the short-shorts worn in those leagues.

The resistance faded in the late 1960s. American women dominated Olympic basketball competition in the 1980s, and the on-and-off push for a professional women's league picked up steam in the 1990s. While major stars have been playing in other countries, the National Basketball Association has started talking about endorsing women. In 1995, Sheryl Swoopes became the first female player to have a Nike shoe named after her.

Battle of the Sexes

1925

Helen Wills, who came from the University of California, was considered the essence of girlness, and was often contrasted to the mannish, boyish, drinking, smoking, shocking flappers of her time. The all-American girl, a Chris Evert prototype, she was cool on the court and often called "Little Miss Poker Face."

Her success was so huge that schools that had dropped women's tennis took it up again and Charlie Chaplin said that watching her play tennis was the most beautiful thing he'd ever seen.

Basketball player Lisa Leslie (far right) presents T-shirts to Supreme Court Justices Sandra Day O'Connor (left) and Ruth Bader Ginsburg (center) as part of publicity campaign for a national team for women's basketball, February 7, 1995

Cheerleading in the 1950s

The trick is to be up in the air with a big Ipana smile on your face, touching the heels of your saddle shoes to the back of your head, bending your elbows as close as you can get them behind you. This makes your short red dress rise, revealing a quick glimpse of thigh and underpants. It also makes your 16-year-old tits, aided and abetted by stuffings of cotton or the professional padding of Maidenform, stick far out.

I am doing this of my own free will on a spring afternoon in Madison Square Garden. The year is 1957, halfway between my sixteenth and seventeenth birthdays. I have aimed at, plotted and waited for this moment. It is living up to my expectations. The Garden is crowded. This is the play-off game for the New York City championships: Forest Hills against Boys High.

The old Madison Square Garden smells like a locker room, which is what makes it such a triumph that I find myself at the center of attention in it. I am a star at last on male turf. There are ten of us at halftime in the middle of the wooden floor with all the lights out except for the spotlight shining on us. I turn my face upward into the smell of sweat, into the applause and whistles dropping like confetti from the tiers of spectator seats above me.

We played some humid swimming meets in Far Rockaway and Flushing, tottering at the edge of the pool and getting our hair all fuzzy, but basketball was the main attraction. (There was no football. Rumor said a boy had once been killed on the field and the sport discontinued.) Cheerleaders as a group were married to the basketball team as a group. We played wife.

Our job was to support the team. We were the decorative touches in the gyms they played. We had some "prestige" in the city because the team was so good that year. They had a little prestige rub off on them, too, for Forest Hills was known for the good-looking stuck-up bitches there. We learned to cater to the boys' moods, not to talk to Gary after he had a bad game (he would glower and shake us off), and yes to *be* there when he or Stanley or Steve came out of the locker room all showered and handsome. We were there for them always, peppy and smiling. Boys had acceptable temper tantrums on the court, but cheerleaders never did. We were expected to be consistently "happy," like the Rockettes at Radio City Music Hall.

We were the best athletic supporters that ever lived.

We paired off, cheerleader and basketball player, like a socialite wife and corporation executive, leading lady and leading man. My social life was defined by my "status." I only went out with jocks. "Who's *he*?" or "What a creep!" applied to boys who wore desert boots or girls who were "brains." We knew kids "like us" in other middle-class ghettos in the city, and we stayed away from the Greek and Italian kids in our school, from "rocks" like Howie and Dominic who played cards and drank and "laid girls," and from girls like Carole and Anita whom we called "hitter chicks" and who, we whispered, went all the way.

Cheerleaders had a reputation for chastity. No one ever said it, but we all understood it. On top of the general fifties hang-ups about sex, cheerleaders had a special role to play. Vestal virgins in the rites of puberty. Jewish madonnas.

Half the time, in real "civilian" life, I had to keep pulling those gray flannel skirts down, making sure "nothing showed," keeping my legs crossed. I would have been incarcerated on the spot by my mother if, one morning, I refused to layer the top of my body with a bra and all its padding followed by a slip followed by a blouse. Even if I were to evade Mother, my peers would have condemned me as a "slut" if I appeared less than dressed.

The other half the time, as a cheerleader, I dropped a skimpy red costume over only my bra and panties and got out there in the middle of a gym full of screaming spectators to wiggle my hips all over the place.

What does it do to the mind of a 16-year-old girl to be Marilyn Monroe one moment and Goody Two-Shoes the next? I don't know, but it sure wasn't sane.

Every time I say "sure" when I mean "no," every time I smile brightly when I'm exploding with rage, every time I imagine my man's achievement is my own, I know the cheerleader never really died. I feel her shaking her ass inside me and I hear a breathless, girlish voice mutter "T-E-A-M, Yea, Team."

—Louise Bernikow, Ms. *magazine*, 1973.

In 1925, Helen Wills played seven different men in exhibitions and beat them all. Her managers said this was being done to show how good she really was. In September, she played the top-ranked male college player, and her blistering serve gave her a single-set victory, 6-4. The press kept saying the men who lost had been behaving like gentlemen, but Phil Neer, the collegiate champion who lost to her, would say decades later that he had really tried to win.

1951

Leonard Crawley, British golf journalist, was skeptical of the abilities of women golfers and the chances of their tour surviving. Babe Didrikson Zaharias took a women's team to Wentworth, one of England's finest courses, to challenge the six best male amateurs. Crawley offered to let Zaharias shave off his mustache if the men lost. The women won, 6½-2½, sweeping every singles match. All mustaches, however, remained firmly in place.

1973: The Drop Shot Heard Around the World

Bobby Riggs, fifty-five-year-old former champion, a vocal opponent of women getting equal prize money, challenged Margaret Court, former champion, and beat the nervous, choked Court on Mother's Day, 1973. Billie Jean King, twenty-six years younger than Riggs, the leading women's player since the late sixties, the activist who had done more than anyone else to bring equality to women's tennis, fought back. On September 20 of that year, Houston's Astrodome held 30,000 spectators, and an estimated 40 million people were watching on television. The purse was $100,000. New York Congresswoman Bella Abzug made book on the floor of the House of Representatives. King came in on a Cleopatra-like litter borne by bare-chested musclemen. Riggs arrived in a rickshaw pulled by buxom young women.

King defeated Riggs 6-4, 6-3, and 6-3.

> It is small wonder that the American male has a strong affinity for sports. He has learned that this is one area where there is no doubt about sexual differences and where his biology is not obsolete. Athletics help assure his difference from women in a world where his functions have come to resemble theirs.
>
> *Psychiatrist Arnold R. Beisser, 1967*

Athletes and Feminists: The 1970s

The 1970s women's movement revived sports as a feminist issue, but it had a legal orientation, unlike the past. Also, for the first time, women athletes were political. Among the feminist agitators were skier Suzy Chaffee, swimmer Donna de Varona, and tennis champion Billie Jean King.

The Pressure Pays Off: A Time Line of Women's Sports in the Second Wave

1967–1972: Bernice Gera fights through the courts for the right to work as a minor league umpire.

1969: Owner and trainer Mary Keim puts Diane Crump on Merre Indian at Hialeah, making her the first

Katherine Switzer evading Boston Athletic Association official, Boston Marathon, April 19, 1967

female jockey to compete against men on a major U.S. flat track.

1970: Crump is the first woman to ride in the Kentucky Derby. Male

jockeys complain that her presence interferes with their concentration because they worry about her safety.

1972: Officials of the Boston marathon relent and officially allow women to enter the race. Many ran unofficially before, including Roberta Bengay, who leaped from behind the bushes near the starting line in 1966, finishing ahead of two-thirds of the male runners, and Katherine Switzer, who entered the 1967 marathon under her brother's name and ran with a

cap covering her hair until she was discovered. Officials trying to chase Switzer off the course resembled nothing so much as the Keystone Cops. She outran them all and finished the race.

Bernice Gera is the first woman to umpire a professional baseball

game. Eventually, threats and criticism will drive her away from umpiring, but not from baseball. She will take a job in the New York Mets front office.

Billie Jean King is named *Sports Illustrated* magazine's first Sportswoman of the Year.

1974: The Women's Professional Football League is founded, with seven teams and ten games a year.

Teams from Queens College in New York and Immaculata College in Philadelphia engage in the first women's basketball game to be played in Madison Square Garden. Scheduled as an opener to a men's collegiate game, the contest draws 12,000 spectators, most of whom leave after the heated contest, which Queens wins by four points.

1975: Eleven-year-old Karren Stead of Pennsylvania is the first female to win the soapbox derby, driving a fiberglass racer she designed and built herself.

The Amateur Athletic Union sponsors power-lifting for women.

Distance swimmer Diana Nyad sets a record of seven hours and fifty-seven minutes swimming around Manhattan Island.

1976: The first women's Olympic basketball event is part of the summer games in Montreal, Canada. The United States team wins a silver medal. Team member Nancy Lieberman goes on to become a fitness coach for tennis player Martina Navratilova.

1977: The Women's Basketball Association, the first professional league, is formed. Eight thousand spectators watch the first game.

Janet Guthrie, physicist and aerospace engineer, is the first woman to drive in the Indianapolis 500, the world's toughest auto race. She has to quit because of mechanical trouble.

Shirley Muldowney, who started by racing the family car at a local drag strip in Schenectady, New York—even though in *Rebel without a Cause,* Natalie Wood's only role was to drop the flag that started the boys' drag race—wins the National Hot Rod Association race. She will win again in 1980 and 1982.

1978: Driving with a broken right wrist, reaching across her body to shift gears with her left hand, Janet Guthrie finishes ninth against thirty-

three of the world's most famous drivers in the Indianapolis 500.

Rugby, a direct-contact sport played with no protective gear, has been outlawed for women, but now there are over eighty clubs on college campuses. A player at Brown University says, "Women are not taught to be physically aggressive and are usually not the instigators of physical contact—in sports and in social activities. Women are not initiated into contact sports at an early age. With rugby, you have to break that cultural barrier. You have to push and shove with abandon and aggressiveness."

Linda Williams of Houston, Texas, becomes the first female player on a high school varsity baseball team, playing right field for the

Wheatley High School Wildcats after a judge orders the school to let her play.

Melissa Ladtke, a writer for *Sports Illustrated,* wins a court decision forcing the New York Yankees to let her interview players in the locker room.

1981: Julie Krone starts racing horses. She will ride to the winner's circle close to 3,000 times. In 1993, she becomes the only woman to win a Triple Crown race. On her wedding day in 1995, she rides a full schedule of races.

1985: Libby Riddles is the first woman to win the Iditarod Trail Sled Dog Race, crossing 1,100 miles of Alaskan wilderness in just over seventeen days.

Hoboken Little League players, 1974

Gender equality in sports was unheard of before the feminist seventies, when the idea that playing fields were exclusively male turf began to be exposed in all its maddening nuances and slowly dismantled. Billie Jean King, whose first experience in competitive tennis was being barred from a tournament for wearing white shorts instead of a white skirt, led eight other players out of the United States Lawn Tennis Association. In 1971, King and the others established the first professional tour, the Virginia Slims circuit. The first woman to earn over $100,000 in one sport in a single year, King went on to start *Womansports* magazine, forcing other media outlets to pay attention to female athletes, and the activist Women's Sports Foundation.

Title IX: The Tidal Wave:

"

No person in the United States shall, on the basis of sex, be excluded from participation in, be denied the benefits of, or be subject to discrimination under any education program or activity receiving Federal financial assistance.

"

The revolution was not only about money, recognition, and respect, but about changing consciousness with respect to women's bodies and what they could do. The imagery of seventies feminism was Amazonian: women did amazing things in all fields. As women gained political clout, they were also insistent on gaining physical strength, forming self-defense schools, and investigating their own socialization into physical passivity.

The more the concept of sex roles underwent serious research, the less sure anyone was about what, if any, women's real physical limitations might be. Studies of Olympic athletes showed absolutely no correlation between stages of the menstrual cycle and athletic performance. The only immutable ascertainable differences between female and male bodies that affected sports performance and had nothing to do with culture and training were found to be women's greater percentage of body fat and lower center of gravity.

When feminists first started pushing, 7 percent of college athletic scholarships went to women; today, more than a third do. When female athletes were oddities, their coaches were always male and the people who made the money were fathers and male managers or captains of industry who used their likenesses to sell products. The story now is somewhat different, but far from over. Serious training of female athletes is so new that the limits of female possibility are still unknown.

The umbrella was education, but the impact of Title IX, written and maneuvered through Congress by Congresswomen Edith Green of Oregon and Patsy Mink of Hawaii, was most visible in school athletics. When hearings on sex discrimination in education were held in June 1970, no representative from the federal educational establishment testified—and the general attitude was that there was no problem. Green, Mink, and their allies in the women's movement seemed to be mad Cassandras. In 1972, when Title IX passed, few understood its implications.

In most schools and universities, women's physical education received a pittance of the total athletic expenditure. This meant paltry equipment, little access to playing fields and gymnasiums, virtually no scholarships, and puny salaries for female coaches. Under Title IX, all these practices were illegal. The male athletic lobby fought long and hard to undo the legislation and is still fighting today.

The problem for women was enforcement, which was dismal. Once women got wind of the tool Title IX could become in the battle for sports equality, complaints were filed and then forgotten. In 1975, Senator John Tower tried to exempt "revenue-producing sports," all of which were men's sports, from government reprisals. Four years after the passage of Title IX only five complaints had been resolved, and no school had lost any federal funding.

But activists didn't go away. Nearly a quarter century after Title IX, numbers and amounts of athletic scholarships have risen dramatically, participation by girls and college women has skyrocketed, and competitions have increased. The outstanding performance of American women at the 1996 Olympics was a direct result of changes brought by this legislation. On the other hand, the rise of athletic programs for women created new coaching jobs, many of which were filled by men. In 1972, 90 percent of the coaches of intercollegiate female sports were female; by 1987, only 50 percent were.

The Burning Tree Country Club in Bethesda, Maryland, is still male-only. Women are allowed in the clubhouse one day only—during the Christmas holiday season, to do their shopping in the pro shop.

Little League

Founded in 1939, the Little League grew rapidly after World War II and excluded girls for its first thirty-five years. By the 1960s, girls were trying to play and being turned away and communities erupted in bitter disputes over the matter. The old bugaboo about injuring private parts came up again. By 1974, parents had filed suit against the organization in fifteen states. In Delaware, Yankees manager Dallas Green filed on behalf of his nine-year-old daughter. The policy was officially changed on June 12, 1974.

The game has produced many heroines in its short life, including nine-year-old Brianne Stepherson, who pitched thirty-six innings in her team's 1989 season without allowing a single run to score and who batted .685.

Going coed has also had unwelcome repercussions, including considerable sexual harassment. In 1975, a suburban Little League in Michigan insisted that a female player comply with regulations by wearing an athletic supporter.

Some journalists were recently playing Yale University's golf course right after an NCAA women's tournament. One of them whistled, calling to a woman driving by in a golf cart, "Are you the beer lady?"

"No," she said, "I'm the Yale coach," and drove away.

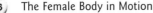

Crashing the Boxing Ring

Dallas Malloy took her name from ex-fighter Terry Molloy, the character Marlon Brando played in *On the Waterfront*. The teenager wanted to box, and she wanted the sport's governing body, U.S.A. Boxing, to sanction it. Canada, Finland, and Sweden have women's programs in international amateur competition. When the Americans refused, she sued, with the help of the American Civil Liberties Union. In November 1993, Malloy won a unanimous decision over her opponent in the first women's match under official auspices. Malloy's only regret: "I wanted to knock her out."

The Lavender Menace in Sports

Questions about Babe Zaharias's love life were one reason she said she didn't like to talk to women reporters, who always wanted to know when she was going to get married. Although she married, the tomboy image did not disappear. Although it is known today that she was a lesbian, her contemporaries in the press and public decided to treat her as an athlete, a female person in a class by herself, with virtually no gender identity.

Talk about lesbians in the girls' baseball leagues during World War II was always denied. The most unanswered question is not who is a lesbian or does athletics "make" women lesbian, but: When does homophobia become an important factor in women's sports? Part of the answer involves money. When male sponsors get nervous, when there is more financial gain in the sport, the "lavender menace" of lesbians in sports crops up strongly.

> The tour was a subculture of gay culture. Every dyke with two nickels to rub together got to Palm Springs for the Dinah Shore. It was the event.
> *Lynn Greer, former golfer on the Ladies Professional Golf Association tour*

> Everybody misses the boat. There are certainly lesbians, as there are gay male golfers, but nobody talks about them. But that doesn't matter. As if lesbianism was a negative. That bothers me. We watch golfers because they're good golfers, not because of their lipstick. We don't watch male golfers because they're good looking. If companies have not signed on the women's tour because there are lesbians, we should examine that.
> *Martina Navratilova replying to comments by Ben Wright of CBS about lesbians in the Ladies Professional Golf Association, May 23, 1995*

Social Dancing: Who Leads?

One of the most difficult aspects of ballroom dance for many women is not strictly technical, but seems to be gender related. In learning to follow the lead unhesitatingly, women typically encounter a stubborn problem—to move forward with uninterrupted vigor. . . . His body blocks the path and the female, reluctant to push him out of the way . . . must learn to dance aggressively, even as she follows the male's lead, fulfilling her prescribed, apparently passive/feminine role. That is, ironically, she must be aggressive precisely in order to appear non-aggressive and pliable. Men do not have this problem.

Sally Peters, From Eroticism to Transcendence: Ballroom Dance and the Female Body, *1991*

Last Words

In 1994, a dance class at the University of California was thrown into an uproar. The instructor, Sunni Bloland, reminded her pupils that dancing was a form of courtship and asked any couples that got engaged to let her know. But one couple was already engaged: Ruti Kadish and Nicole Berner. Bloland told the lesbian lovers that they could only stay in her class if they each danced with men, as followers. The couple filed a gender-discrimination complaint, which led the department to decree that gender would no longer determine whether a student led or followed. It added, however, that each student had to pick a role at the beginning of the semester and stick to it.

Ballroom dance lesson, Fred Astaire Dance Studio, New York City, 1996

Students going to chapel, twenty-fifth anniversary celebration, Tuskegee Institute, Tuskegee, Alabama, 1906

CHAPTER 4

The Female Mind

*A*s for training young ladies through a long intellectual course, as we do young men, it can never be done. They will die in the process.
Reverend John Todd, early nineteenth century

Educate a woman and you educate a family.
Slogan of La Liga Femenil Mexicanista, *founded by Jovita Idar in 1911 to educate Mexican children in America*

In intellect, there is no sex.
M. Carey Thomas, first president of Bryn Mawr College

It is hard to apply oneself to study when there is no money to pay for food and lodging. I almost never explain these things when folks are asking me why don't I do this and that.
Zora Neale Hurston

An academy that was a Forest of Arden and a Fifth Avenue department store combined.
Mary McCarthy on Vassar College

The male professor looks at the woman student knitting in the first row and reminds her that Freud says knitting is a form of masturbation. "Professor," the woman answers, "when I knit, I knit and when I masturbate, I masturbate."
Apocryphal story told on campuses of women's colleges in the 1950s

When we got around to books, I was finally set, as our minister would say, on solid ground. I gorged on books. I sneaked them at night. I rubbed their spines and sniffed in the musty smell of them in the library.
Lorene Cary, Black Ice, *1991*

Protest against admitting male students, Texas Women's University, Denton, Texas, 1995

Sod schoolhouse, Custer County, Nebraska, 1886

woman's mind was a useless appendage, frail, like her body, and as much in need of protection. Her real purpose, motherhood, was not thought to require mental skills. A female scholar was as anomalous as a female weight lifter. As late as the 1930s, Mary McCarthy could say that Vassar College was "an introduction into mental life for its own sake, even into mental athletics, hitherto banned to the sex, like field sports and throwing the javelin."

Homelife and dame schools taught colonial daughters of the elite the skills necessary for their place in society: reading (a Christian education implied reading the Bible), sewing (stitching initials on clothing and household linens), and the more ornamental needlework of samplers, which became one of white women's most accomplished folk arts.

The history of growing female minds has a strong streak of larceny running through it. It was illegal to teach slaves to read until after the Civil War, but the rebellious white abolitionists Angelina and Sarah Grimké shared the forbidden world of reading with their slaves. Women of all races

Post–Civil War Freedman's Spelling Book

pounded at the gates of education, but they also took it where they could: surreptitious forays into a brother's schoolbooks late at night, raids on a father's library, picking the brains of anyone possessing the secrets of knowledge.

Seeing what was possible, often enough, provoked action. Emma Willard, an early crusader for women's education, realized how inadequate her own learning was when she picked up the textbooks in mathematics and philosophy used by her nephew, a student at Vermont's

Astronomer Maria Mitchell with her class in front of observatory, Vassar College, 1870

Middlebury College. After running a school at home, a typical undertaking, Willard raised public money for a Female Seminary in Troy, New York, in 1821, which taught trigonometry, physiology, chemistry, and natural philosophy, all previously thought too difficult for women.

The Moravian Female Academy, the most advanced in the South, had opened in Salem, North Carolina, in 1802. Oberlin College, coeducational and open to any woman, white or black, began in 1833. Woman's rights activist Lucy Stone, who had been a teacher since the age of sixteen in order to put herself through college, was one of the first women admitted to Oberlin's regular course of study. When she graduated at the top of her class in 1847, she was forced to sit in the audience while a male student read her valedictory speech.

Faced with such insults and with the stubborn refusal of most men's colleges to admit women—or, if they did admit them, to provide an equally rigorous education—an epidemic of women's colleges swept the Northeast: Vassar (1865), Radcliffe (1874), Smith (1875). The purpose was compensatory, to provide what male institutions denied. Women's schools were seen as distinctly second rate by Elizabeth Cady Stanton, student at Emma Willard's Troy seminary, who yearned for Clark University with her brothers and male friends.

The pioneers—Willard; Mary Lyon of Mount Holyoke Seminary; and M. Carey Thomas, the crusading first president of Bryn Mawr College—went against the grain. So, too, did their students, most of whom defied their families and culture to attend. They all dissembled: schools were needed, advanced women said, to create better wives and mothers. "Stupid mothers never did and stupid mothers never will, furnish this world with brilliant sons," wrote educator Helen Gardener in 1891.

The first college-educated generation furnished the world with few sons. More than half the graduates of women's colleges at the end of the nineteenth century did not marry. In a time of general agreement that three children per couple was needed for the republic to survive, this was tantamount to treason.

Faculty who married had to resign, leaving all-female communities where students and teachers received educations in matters not covered by lectures and textbooks. They learned

Bryn Mawr students marching for suffrage down Fifth Avenue, New York City, 1909

about female possibility by seeing the intelligence, scholarship, and determination of those around them, not visible in the larger culture. They found mentors and role models. Many grew ambitious and independent. They formed friendships and support networks. Some fell in love with each other.

Naturally, there was a reaction, much muttering about woman's sphere and carping about delicate women wearing themselves out. Critics insisted that women were being "masculinized" by higher learning. Athletics and studies, they said, "muscularized" a woman's mind "beyond the harmonious vigor to make her man's companion." Even worse, female graduates went into "lifelong homosexuality."

Schools exposed women to life outside the home, to lessons in class distinctions, and to ideas that might never have entered their family circles. They moved into that forbidden sphere, politics and public life. Mary Harriman, daughter of a railroad titan and financier, was so taken by a talk on her college campus by settlement worker Jane Addams that she determined to organize her debutante friends to "do more than come out." The organization she started in 1901 was called the Junior League.

Less than two decades later, undergraduates were marching under school banners in suffrage parades and being arrested at demonstrations. In 1919, the president of Mount Holyoke College declared women's education "a feministic movement, the natural expression of a fun-

Lesbian Herstory Archives contingent, Lesbian and Gay rights parade, New York City, June 29, 1978

damental principle that women . . . have a share in the inalienable right of human beings to self-development." No more mothers-of-brilliant-sons arguments.

Women were edged out of higher education by the GI Bill, which brought veterans of World War II and the Korean War flocking to campuses. By the mid-1950s, although women returned to campuses in significant numbers, the seriousness of the early struggle for women's education had been obliterated in an emphatic return of the ideology of motherhood. College became a place to get an "M.R.S. degree." Child study became the most popular major at Vassar. In high schools, "home economics" was required, while boys studied "shop," and the lack of athletic opportunities drove active young women into cheerleading.

A decade later, the situation was very different. Civil rights legislation made it officially illegal to discriminate on the basis of gender in student admissions, faculty hiring and promotion, and appointments to administrative positions and trusteeships. The battles fought by women, especially in class action suits brought by female professors, to enforce these standards, were arduous and largely victorious, resulting in cash settlements and changes in the country's most respected institutions.

Debates about coeducation versus single-sex schools resurfaced. When anthropologist Margaret Mead, herself a product of a Barnard College education, spoke at Radcliffe in 1969, she was firmly opposed to sharing classrooms with male students. "Twenty-four hours a day with boys can be appalling," she said. "It's bad enough to have to eat breakfast every day with your husband." Enrollments at women's schools rose.

Feminist pressure for structural change in courses of study and institutional structures has evolved into intense scrutiny of something less tangible: attitudes. Scholars and activists are exposing the glass ceiling that may settle on girls as early as kindergarten. Women's Studies programs and campus feminism groups in the late 1980s and 1990s have nurtured feminist thinking and action about the social conditions under which women learn, especially the problems of sexual harassment and date rape. Controversial codes of sexual behavior and yearly Take Back the Night marches have replaced older generations' rituals of pep rallies and panty raids.

Beyond the shaping and exercising of female minds through education lies the question of exactly how those minds function. Now we enter a desert. There is virtually no serious thinking about female psychology before the twentieth century.

There is, however, a lot of so-called female insanity. Although female mental diseases, in their time, were thought to be related to physiology, modern eyes see the considerable influence of sexual politics. Women disobedient or aggressive toward husbands, sons, and brothers could be labeled insane. Married women were especially vulnerable, since they had no legal rights at all.

Twentieth-century women brought to the field of psychology new answers to old questions and raised a whole new set of questions. The relationship of the female mind to the female body was always up for interpretation. In 1916, Leta Stetter Hollingworth attacked the idea that women's thinking abilities declined during their menstrual periods. She named "the motherhood mandate," pointing out that women who did not choose motherhood were not, as common opinion had it, abnormal or nuts. She spent—or was railroaded into spending—most of her professional life teaching and studying child psychology.

> **Did You Know?**
>
> After the Nineteenth Amendment passed, American women, giddy with possibility, went to school in large numbers. In 1920, nearly half the country's undergraduate students were female. Over the next five decades, the number steadily declined.

As women broke new ground in every area of American life during the 1920s, new insights into the female mind were inevitable. Karen Horney, one of the first to insist on a girl's relationship with her mother as critical to her development, and the first to describe "womb envy" in men, said, in 1926, that the psychology of women up to that time "actually represents a deposit of the desires and disappointments of men."

*Sampler embroidered by Sarah Chandler at
Mrs. Dohl's Seminary, Boston, 1808*

In the psychoanalytic mainstream, women formed professional associations, achieved institutional power, and contributed to theory. Dr. Annie Reich advocated treating female submissiveness as a pathology; Dr. Phyllis Greenacre wrote *The Child Wife As Ideal*.

Post–World War II America was not a hospitable place for female psychologists. While male mental health professionals had contributed "usefully" to the work of the war, women had been shunted aside. The powerful drug Thorazine appeared in 1954 and shifted attention from the tantalizing work of pioneers theorizing the female psyche to the efficacy of the pharmacy in controlling it.

By the late 1960s and 1970s, a new generation of feminists in the field, literary critics, and ordinary women were analyzing the sexual politics of understanding and treating women's minds. Traditional research on sex differences was faulted for everything from underlying ideology to methodological design. A radical troublemaking psychologist named Phyllis Chesler, author of *Women and Madness* in 1972, asked the mental health profession for a million dollars in reparations for the abuse inflicted on women over the years.

The psychology of women became a recognized part of the American Psychological Association in 1973. A large-scale feminist attack on Freud was mitigated later in the decade, when psychoanalytic methods and language reentered feminist theory and literary criticism. In the 1980s, the new feminist attitudes in psychology influenced theories, treatment, and activism in relation to eating disorders, childhood abuse, battered women's syndrome, and the construction of gender.

What the Samplers Say

Recently, samplers have become clues to the history of female education. In 1991, Mary Jane Edmonds published her findings that the samplers were probably done in schools for girls, designed by teachers, long before women's education officially began. Working from what she found to be recognizable motifs and regional patterns, Edmonds, among others, situates samplers firmly as folk art and specifically in private boarding or day schools. (Married women did not make samplers, but were more utilitarian with their needlework.) Many of the designer/teachers and sites of the schools are identifiable. Most surviving forms of this art, which disappeared after 1840, come from New England and the Eastern seaboard.

Prudence Crandall's School Goes Up in Flames

Prudence Crandall, a Quaker woman in Canterbury, Connecticut, admitted black girls to her elegant school, which angered the white girls' parents. Crandall closed down in 1831 and defiantly reopened two years later as a teacher-training boarding school exclusively for "Negro girls." Antiabolitionists and opponents of education for girls attacked. Town residents persuaded the state legislature to pass an act prohibiting "private schools for nonresident colored persons." Its passage was marked in the town of Canterbury by the ringing of church bells. Crandall was twice arrested and convicted, but let off by the Supreme Court on what was called a technicality.

She persevered, keeping her school open although all shops and meetinghouses in the town were closed to her and her pupils; doctors wouldn't treat them; her well was filled with manure; rotten eggs and stones were hurled at her house, in which she taught. In 1834, the school was set on fire and burned to the ground.

Should Women Be Educated?

No, I will not give a dollar; all a woman needs to know is how to read the New Testament, and to spin and weave clothing.
Man refusing to contribute to the founding of Wesleyan College in Macon, Georgia, which, in 1836, became the first in the world chartered to grant degrees to women

Let the young ladies of this republic continue another half century to receive what has, during the last twenty years, been considered a genteel education, and there will not be energy enough in the country, mental or physical, to guide the helm of state or to defend its priceless institutions.
A lady, 1836

Mount Holyoke Female Seminary, South Hadley, Massachusetts, 1840

Woman, having received from her Creator the same intellectual constitution as man, has the same right as man to intellectual culture and development.

Matthew Vassar, self-taught brewer, founder of Vassar College, at his first speech to the board of trustees, 1861

Mount Holyoke Seminary

Opened in 1837, Mary Lyon's school was the first to aim at including women who were not from the upper class. Fees at Mount Holyoke were lower than elsewhere partly because students did some of the housework. The school's aim was to turn out good Christian women and badly needed teachers, especially missionary teachers for some of the first Indian schools.

Emily Dickinson was an early pupil, but her reports home indicate only that she liked the food a lot.

The Nineteenth-Century Girls' Schools

The Diet

Certain foods, it was believed, especially highly flavored dishes and meats, aroused the sexual appetites. Therefore, girls' diets were regulated to protect them from unhealthy desires. Since protein deprivation was considered a cure for female masturbation, female boarding schools were likely vegetarian.

Curriculum

At Mount Holyoke Seminary, two or three major subjects were taken intensively for six to ten weeks. Extras—composition, calisthenics, and vocal music—were available throughout the year. Latin became a requirement in 1846. There were lectures on character, manners, and the amenities of group living. Visiting lecturers talked about architecture or the philosophy of history. Students attended two services at the village church on Sundays, did Bible lessons over the weekend, spent a half hour morning and evening alone in private devotion, and took scriptural instruction.

The Discipline

Every day, students reported on their own conduct. Among the items that required reporting at Mount Holyoke Seminary were:

- Absence from school exercise
- Absence from domestic work
- Failure in walking
- Spending time with others when it is not time for entering rooms
- Loud speaking after the retiring bell
- Throwing things from the window
- Taking tea out without permission
- Speaking above a whisper in the washroom
- Speaking above a whisper in the ironing room

> *Let woman be educated to the highest practicable point; not only because it is her right, but because it is essential to the world's progress.*
>
> *Horace Mann, Massachusetts congressman and first president of Antioch College, 1853*

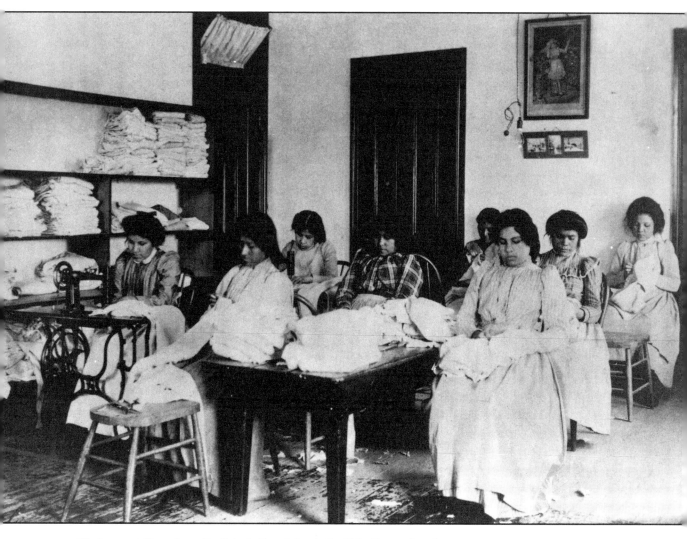

Clothes-mending class, Carlisle Indian School, Carlisle, Pennsylvania, 1900

"Educating" Native Americans

A nation is not conquered until the hearts of its women are on the ground.
Blackfeet saying

Throughout the late nineteenth and early twentieth centuries, the U.S. government tried to assimilate the native population by removing Native American children from their homes and families and sending them to white schools.

Graduates of the Cherokee Young Ladies Seminary, Oklahoma, 1875

The Indian School system was developed to aid the military and "legal" establishment in processing the resigned, defeated young Natives who fell into its hands. Schools were erected all over the West, mid-west, and, eventually in the East, where the star colonial establishment, Carlisle Indian School, was located. My great-grandmother got her education there. She learned how to be a literate, modest, excruciatingly exacting maid for well-to-do white farmers' and ranchers' wives. She didn't follow exactly the course laid out for her and became the farmer-rancher's wife instead. The bitter fruits of her efforts are still being eaten by her grandchildren, great-grandchildren and her great-great-grandchildren. I wonder if we will recover from the poisonous effects of the Indian-saving.

Paula Gunn Allen, writer, 1993

The Cherokee Female Seminary was established in 1850 by the Cherokee Chief and Council and missionaries to the Cherokee Nation. The Cherokee had long believed in equal education for men and women, and the school represented not only accession to white life, but the nation's will to survive.

The seminary, in Oklahoma, was modeled after Mount Holyoke Seminary in the East, where a number of Cherokee women had already been students. Mount Holyoke sent its graduates as administrators and teachers of Latin and English.

Full-blooded and half-blooded women were separated and the schools supervised the girls' behavior far more than the boys'. Many Indian women used the "civilization" and knowledge of white ways acquired in these schools in reform and resistance movements on behalf of their people.

Educating Black Women

I had a white playmate about this time [1860], named Katie O'Connor . . . [who] told me, if I would promise not to tell her father, she would give me some lessons. On my promise not to do so, and getting her mother's consent, she gave me lessons about four months, every evening. At the end of this time she was put into the convent permanently and I have never seen her since.

Susie King Taylor, who would escape from slavery in Sea Islands, Georgia, during the Civil War

Everything is new and strange and inspiring. There is a quickening of the pulse, and a glowing of its self-consciousness. Aha, I can rival that! I can aspire to that! I can honor my name and vindicate my race! Something like this is the enthusiasm which stirs the genius of young Africa in America and the memory of past oppression and the fact of present attempted repression only serve to gather momentum for its irrepressible powers.

Anna Julia Cooper, 1892, graduate of Oberlin College, describing the post-Emancipation generation

Taken together, these girls seemed more certain than I that they deserved our good fortune. They were sorry for people who were poorer than they, but they did not feel guilty to think of the resources we were sucking up—forest, meadows and ponds, the erudition of well-educated teachers, water for roaring showers, heat that blew out of

In [my] magnificent education . . . I encountered some crazy Frenchmen, namely Sartre, Anhouil and Breton, who knew Eurocentrism was irrational, which left me to surmise that I, too, could address the world, act as my own agent and define and design the symbols from Akan sculpture to Chuck Berry that I hold dear.

Ntozake Shange, writer, looking back on her 1970s education, 1996

opened windows everywhere, food not eaten but mixed together for disgusting fun after lunch. They took it as their due. It was boot-camp preparation for America's leaders, which we were told we would one day be. They gave no indication that they worried that others, smarter or more worthy, might, at that very moment, be giving up hope of getting what we had.

Lorene Cary, the first female black student at the traditionally white and historically male Saint Paul's preparatory school, 1991

Zora Neale Hurston at College

It was only when I was off in college, away from my native surroundings, that I could see myself like somebody else and stand off and look . . . then I had to have the spyglass of Anthropology to look through at that.

Of Mules and Men

Dormitory, Barnard College, 1900

Ellen Swallow Richards, first female member, with the chemistry faculty, Massachusetts Institute of Technology, 1900

In 1925, Annie Nathan Meyer, founder of Barnard College, arranged a scholarship for twenty-four-year-old Zora Neale Hurston. Hurston, Florida-born, with two years at Howard University behind her, a fledgling writer who had been a manicurist in Washington, D.C., was drawn to New York by the Harlem Renaissance. She worked as a secretary to novelist Fannie Hurst.

The only black student at Barnard, Hurston became a serious social scientist as a result of studying anthropology under Gladys Reichard, Ruth Benedict, and the famous Franz Boas. Her subject would be cultural anthropology and folklore, African-American culture, and especially its literature.

With Boas, she worked on research refuting racist ideas about race and intelligence, work he had already accomplished in relation to Native American culture. She stood on a Harlem street corner measuring heads to prove that there was plenty of room in African-American skulls for the brain. Through Boas and Barnard anthropologist Elsie Clews Parsons, Hurston won a six-month grant to go off on her own and collect African-American folklore.

Educating White Women

It would be ridiculous to talk of male and female atmospheres, male and female springs or rains, male and female sunshine . . . how much more ridiculous is it in relation to mind, to soul, to thought, where there is as undeniably no such thing as sex, to talk of male and female education and of male and female schools.

Susan B. Anthony and Elizabeth Cady Stanton, 1857

I'm glad Brown isn't co-ed because if I met on the campus and in recitation and in society the right kind of girls—the womanly, tender, emotional kind—I am afraid I might get interested in something besides study, but if we had a lot of those coldly intellectual females—those prospective old maid doctors and lawyers who are all very useful members of society no doubt—the glorious "co-ed" influence in polishing my manners, etc. would amount to just about nothing at all, for I don't admire a manly woman or a womanly man.

Brown undergraduate, 1895

Before I myself went to college I had never seen but one college woman. I had heard that such a woman was staying at the house of an acquaintance. I went to see her with fear. Even if she had appeared in hoofs and horns I was determined to go to college all the same. But it was a relief to find this Vassar graduate tall and handsome and dressed like other women.

M. Carey Thomas, president of Bryn Mawr College

Bad Guy: Dr. Edward H. Clarke

Prestigious Harvard Medical School Professor Edward H. Clarke fulminated in *Sex in Education* (1873) that higher education harmed not only women, creating awful menstrual difficulties, but—obviously more important—their future offspring. Among the horrors he predicted for educated women were "monstrous brains and puny bodies; abnormally active cerebation and abnormally weak digestion; flowing thought and constipated bowels."

Among those who responded, poet Julia Ward Howe insisted that "boys as well as girls break down under severe study; men as well as women and at least as often." She recommended "a milder and more human regime" for the good of all students.

Still, many doctors adopted Dr. Clarke's ideas, including a Philadelphia physician who prevented many young women from attending Bryn Mawr College, prescribing instead a rest cure that kept them in bed for weeks or months without books or visitors. Writer Charlotte

Peace demonstration on the Vassar College campus, April 22, 1937

Perkins Gilman was driven to the brink of insanity by such a cure and wrote about it in her short story, "The Yellow Wallpaper."

This same physician insisted to M. Carey Thomas, future Bryn Mawr president, that no woman could study and remain healthy. Although Thomas looked fine, he said, "he was convinced that she had some secret disease that must show itself sooner or later."

Gilman eventually recovered, and Thomas never manifested any secret diseases.

Ellen Swallow Richards: Great Dropout

Ellen Swallow Richards graduated from Vassar College in 1870 and got both B.S. and M.A. degrees from MIT, where she was a special student in chemistry. Two years later, claiming her professors did not want a woman to get the first doctorate in chemistry, she dropped out of the program. The laboratory she set up to study "sanity chemistry"—the purity of air, water, and food—was the world's first, and her work there led to passage of the first Food and Drug Act in Massachusetts. Although considered a founder of home economics, she is actually one of the first ecologists.

Educating Activists

➤ Florence Kelley, one of the first women admitted to Cornell University, graduated in 1882 with an undergraduate thesis on the history of the legal status of children. Kelley put her studies to good use as a leading twentieth-century reformer, working mostly with the Trade Union League.

➤ In 1885, eighteen-year-old Annie Nathan Meyer had enrolled in the Collegiate Course for Women at Columbia College. Denied the right to attend lectures, she still was required to take the same examinations as the men. Her father insisted that "men hate intelligent wives," but Meyer believed that votes for women, without equal education, was self-defeating. She raised money and persuaded the Columbia trustees to approve the establishment of Barnard.

➤ When settlement workers began moving into the industrial neighborhoods of America's cities—to Jane Addams's Hull House in Chicago and Lillian Wald's Henry Street Settlement in New York—making themselves useful to the waves of immigrants at the end of the nineteenth and first decades of the twentieth centuries, more than 90 percent of them were college graduates whose awareness of social problems and passion to help solve them came from teachers and classmates at school.

Backlash

At the end of the nineteenth century, after ninety-eight graduating women collected more awards and honors than male students, California's Stanford University created a quota for female enrollment—one female to three males—that remained until 1933.

Campus Politics: The 1930s

Student political activity in the first years of the Depression was a prelude to the mass student movement that would develop as fascism brought the world closer to war. In 1933, mass peace meetings were held on U.S. campuses and a peace magazine was edited cooperatively by Bryn Mawr, Wellesley, and Vassar.

Vassar in particular was a hotbed of activism in the largest, most effective, most radical student movement in American history until the New Left of the 1960s. In 1935, a contingent lobbied the New York State legislature against a bill that would have imposed a loyalty oath on college students. The bill was defeated. In 1937, the third student peace strike on campus was held in pouring rain with signs that said: "Careers Not Conscription," "Sanity Not Slaughter," and "Scholarships Not Battleships."

The First Big-League Novel of Female Academic Life

Mary McCarthy's novel, *The Group*, published in 1963, chronicles the lives of eight Vassar undergraduates in the class of 1933 and includes material that was considered shocking, such as lesbianism and what must be the first diaphragm-fitting scene in literature. The book was said at the time to have ruined a first-rate literary career. Male critics derided its "triviality." Norman Mailer called it "the best novel the editors of the women's magazines ever conceived of in their secret ambitions."

National Association for the Advancement of Colored People (NAACP) poster, 1946

Immediately after publication, the book shot to the top of the best-seller lists and stayed there for nearly two years. When the novel became a film starring Candice Bergen in 1966, the campus scenes were shot at Connecticut College because of Vassar's disapproval.

Between 1950 and 1960, the number of women age eighteen to twenty-four enrolled in college increased by 47 percent. From 1960 to 1970, the number increased by 168 percent.

Between 1950 and 1960, the number of women earning bachelor's degrees rose by 35 percent. From 1960 to 1970, the number rose by 146 percent.

> It was with some degree of pain, but mainly a feeling of resignation, that I accepted my guidance counselor's advice to take a commercial course in high school. This was standard advice for the majority of girls in my class. I know now that the programming or "channeling" of girls of the poor into subservient job training is no accident. It is the very core of our educational system.
>
> Madeline Belkin, "Drowning in the Stew Pool," Up from Under *(feminist newspaper)*, 1970

Campus Politics: The 1960s

In 1961, Charlayne Hunter was the first female black student to enter the University of Georgia in Athens, Georgia, with the whole world watching. Two thousand students armed with rocks stoned her dormitory window her first night in residence. After graduation, she became a reporter at the *New York Times* and then, as Charlayne Hunter-Gault, on public television.

> In most projects, in many "radical" marriages and in the National Office, women frequently get relegated to "female" types of work—dish washing, cooking, cleaning, clerical work, etc. . . . In an atmosphere where men are competing for prestige, women are easily dismissed and women, accustomed to being dismissed, come to believe their ideas aren't worth taking the time of the conferences.
>
> Students for a Democratic Society memo, 1965

> Girls Say Yes to Guys Who Say No
> *Antidraft slogan, late sixties*

In one of the buildings occupied by student activists on the campus of Columbia University in 1968, women cooked for 300 protesters, three times a day, in a kitchen the size of a telephone booth.

SENATE REJECTS CARSWELL, 51-45

Hunter College students blocking staircase during student lockout, New York City, April 9, 1970

The Radical Origins of Women's Studies

Mississippi's Freedom Summer in 1964 brought Northern college students, including female ones, into the civil rights movement. Women's participation in New Left politics and antiwar activism at college or graduate school—and their increasing frustration at being allowed to make coffee but not policy—fueled the movement for women's liberation. Out of women's liberation came women's studies.

The first unofficial courses given by women on campuses and at women's centers in the late 1960s, were meant to help radical women understand their place in society. Quickly, the vision that regular courses of study denied the existence of women in nearly every field ignited a joint push by a fringe of young teachers, with recent degrees based on traditional scholarship, eager to explore feminist issues in their work, and students afire with the mood of women's liberation.

The existence of women's studies in high schools, colleges, and universities is the result of decades of agitation and resistance. Becoming institutionalized and academically respectable, however, has somewhat dulled the activist edge of the first courses and programs, whose motto may well have been, in the words of Margaret Sanger: "Educate women to rebel."

> We women are doing pretty well. We're almost back to where we were in the twenties.
> *Margaret Mead, 1976*

The Other Side of the Coeducation Debate

In May 1990, facing declining enrollment and financial woes, the trustees of Mills College in Oakland, California, voted to accept undergraduate men for the first time in the school's 138-year history. Mills was not alone. Since the 1960s, the number of women's colleges had dropped from 298 to 94. More and more all-female schools were going coed.

Mills students rebelled. Wearing T-shirts that said, "Better Dead than Coed" and "Mills College: Not a girl's school without men, but a women's college without boys," they barricaded administration buildings and the president's house. Two hundred fifty students kept a twenty-four-hour protest vigil, sleeping on the ground outside school buildings as sympathetic alumnae dropped off food, coffee, and encouragement.

"Hell hath no fury like a woman scorned" read the banner outside Mills Hall. Black shrouds were draped over the bell tower and the library. Around the country, all-women's colleges rallied, picketing, marching, and writing letters. Some shaved their heads in protest.

After nearly two weeks, the board agreed to reconsider. Eventually, the decision was reversed.

Protesting racial discrimination, University of California, Berkeley, March 22, 1990

Campus Politics: The 1990s

Advance scouts for *Playboy* magazine, looking for models for its "Women of the Ivy League" issue, met pickets and demonstrators at Cornell, Columbia, Yale, Brown, and other universities. At Yale and Brown, women students offered to pay the magazine's modeling fees—$250 for partial nudes, $500 for full nudes—to those who would refuse to pose. Yale students organized a "Women of the Ivy League" magazine of their own, featuring writing and art from female students at eight Ivy League schools.

Rhodes Scholarships, which sent undergraduates with "capacities for scholarship and leadership"—President Bill Clinton was one—to Oxford University were not open to women until 1975. That year, Great Britain's Sex Discrimination Act was passed. In the first year that women were eligible, twenty-four of the seventy-two Rhodes scholars were female, including thirteen from the United States.

Perfect Score

On her first day of kindergarten, Brooke Cowley was visibly upset. Her mother thought it was separation anxiety, but the child looked up and said: "I thought this was going to be college."

In June 1995, Brooke, a junior at Wamogo High School in Litchfield, Connecticut, was one of the twenty-five students out of two million who got all the answers right on the national Scholastic Aptitude Tests. Cowley has also won honors in Latin, for student artwork, sings in a choir, and does community volunteering. Her divorced mother, a telephone operator, raised Brooke and her sister alone.

Now she is "seriously interested in cognitive neuroscience," but she also likes history.

Women Who Dared: The Teachers

> Behind the mists of ruin and rapine waved the calico dresses of women who dared.
>
> W. E. B. Du Bois, The Souls of Black Folk, *describing the women teachers, black and white, of the Freedman's Bureau who taught black people in the South after Emancipation*

The feminization of teaching started in the 1830s, as the public school system expanded and the need for teachers grew. It quickly became the profession for middle-class women, for whom bargaining for money was considered undignified. Female teachers normally got 30 to 50 percent of what men with comparable qualifications were paid. This is one of the things that enraged and humiliated Lucy Stone, Lucretia Mott, and Susan B. Anthony and turned them into feminists.

For black women, teaching was an enterprise of racial self-consciousness, since schooling black children had sinister connotations to white Southerners. The outspoken social and political activists were lifelong teachers.

Did You Know?

On October 24, 1901, Anna Edson Taylor, a Michigan schoolteacher, became the only woman to go over Niagara Falls in a barrel and the first person to survive the stunt.

Sara Porter

Sara Porter was the intellectually voracious oldest daughter of a pastor in Farmington, Connecticut. Her brother Noah was president of Yale. The first female student at Farmington Academy, she became, at sixteen, its first female instructor. In 1843, after teaching at young ladies' schools in Springfield, Buffalo, and Philadelphia, she began taking in boarding students. She taught all the academic subjects: Latin, French, German, chemistry, natural philosophy, and rhetoric. By breakfast time, she had read for hours and done her correspondence. Afternoons, she led country walks. At fifty, she learned Greek. At sixty-five, Hebrew. She was reported to require very little sleep.

Jacqueline Kennedy Onassis was a graduate of Miss Porter's School.

Margaret Fuller: Unofficial Education

Margaret Fuller, writer, teacher, and one of the first to make her mark as a female intellectual, was not invited to teach at nearby Harvard. Nor, perhaps, would she have cared to. Instead, once a week, over four springs and winters, from 1839 to 1842, Fuller "taught" in a bookstore owned by bluestocking Elizabeth Peabody. Educated Boston women paid a fee, and Fuller, in what she called "Conversations," provided what she hoped was training for a lifetime of thought and education that would change the status of women. The women who came were wives and daughters of important men. They discussed education, fine arts, Greek mythology, and other grandiose topics far from women's sphere. Fuller's method was Socratic, and her intention was to encourage women to be courageous, think for themselves, and speak their minds, risking "that others should think their saying crude, shallow, or tasteless." When Fuller decided to invite men, they dominated the talk and so she reverted to her original all-female group the following year.

Clara Barton: Great Dropout

In 1852, Clara Barton started one of the first free schools in New Jersey in a one-room cottage. Within a year, she had 600 pupils. Pleased town officials planned a three-story expansion, but when they assigned a male principal to supervise her, Barton resigned.

Rebecca Pennell: Female Professor

When Antioch College opened in Ohio, which was considered the West in 1852, Rebecca Pennell was "Professor of Physical Geography, Drawing, Natural History, Civil History and Didactics." The first female professor in America was thirty-one years old.

She had been raised in a progressive Massachusetts family and was one of three in the first class of the state's first grammar school. For a decade, she taught and then became a school principal, distinguishing herself by advocating the new teaching, seeing education not as a pouring-in process, but a drawing-out one. Her uncle, Horace Mann, educational reformer and Antioch's first president, invited her to help plan a school where men and women would be educated on equal footing.

In 1855, she married a younger man, the college's assistant treasurer. She remained at Antioch, a controversial figure, often accused of being power hungry, a Cleopatra, a snake. Yet when Horace Mann died, students begged her to stay.

She left, however, for St. Louis, where Mary Institute had opened to serve the growing frontier community. Its founders believed that a woman's education was no longer "finished when she had learned to work a fire-screen or dance a polka or drum a sentimental tune upon an unhappy piano."

After twenty-five years of teaching, she retired.

Good Guy/Bad Guy: Asa Mercer

The first president of the University of Washington wanted to bring women to the Pacific Northwest. He went East in 1864, stopping first at Lowell, Massachusetts, a mill town, recruiting "young ladies" to migrate to Washington Territory as teachers. Twenty-five signed on and paid him $225 passage money. On his next trip, he signed up 400 women, although the press accused him of "seeking to carry off young girls for the benefit of miserable old bachelors." When his ship sailed from the East Coast, south to Rio, then to San Francisco, a journey of four months, a *New York Times* reporter went along. Mercer married one of the women six weeks after their arrival. The others found work and all married, except Elizabeth Ordway, who insisted she really wanted to be a schoolteacher and "Nothing would induce me to relinquish the advantages of single blessedness."

Lucy Laney and Mary McLeod Bethune

In 1886, when the state had no public black high schools and the only education available was vocational training, Lucy Laney, daughter of former slaves who had bought their freedom, graduate of the first class at Atlanta University, established the Haines Normal and Industrial Institute in Augusta, Georgia. The school, which survived for half a century, offered liberal arts courses.

Mary McLeod Bethune, also the daughter of former slaves, the last-born child of seventeen and the first born in freedom, was encouraged by a mission school teacher in South Carolina to pursue further education. She wanted to become a missionary to Africa, but after studying at Moody Bible School in Chicago, she learned that only whites were sent to Africa. Returning to the South, she taught at Lucy Laney's school and, inspired by Laney, turned to education as a way to "uplift the race." Bethune's school for Negro girls opened in Daytona, Florida, in 1904, followed by a hospital to train black nurses. The school became a college, merging with a men's college in 1925 to become Bethune-Cookman College.

A lifetime's activism in the black club movement, fighting against school segregation and for prison reform, led to a government appointment in Franklin Roosevelt's New Deal. The first black person with a high federal position, Bethune became a close friend of Eleanor Roosevelt. She was the first woman to have a respected place in the black power structure.

In 1974, the first statue to honor any black woman leader in a public park was erected to her in Washington, D.C.

Firsts

➤ The first school to train young black women as teachers was opened by Myrtilla Minder in Washington, D.C., in 1851.

➤ Charlotte Forten became the first black teacher of white children in Salem, Massachusetts, in 1856.

➤ The first laws guaranteeing equal pay for teachers regardless of sex were passed in Wyoming Territory in 1869 and the State of California in 1873. They were not enforced.

➤ Effie Chew was the first Chinese-American public schoolteacher in 1918.

Academics/Activists

In 1915, with the First World War looming, the peace movement was less controversial than suffrage. An antimilitarism protest meeting, the International Congress of Women at The Hague, was attended by women from neutral and belligerent countries, including academic women. Among them was Professor Emily Greene Balch of the Department of Economics and Sociology at Wellesley College. The public's accepting mood changed in 1917, when war was declared. Pacifism became disloyalty at best, treason at worst. When Balch came up for reappointment at Wellesley in 1919, she was not rehired. A trade unionist and social reformer, Balch would win the Nobel Peace Prize for her work with the Women's International League for Peace and Freedom in 1946.

On January 20, 1932, Mary Woolley, the president of Mount Holyoke College, sailed to Europe as the only woman member of a delegation to international disarmament talks in Geneva. When her ship was near European shores, Ruth Nichols and Mabel Vernon, pioneer aviators, flew out in a hydroplane to meet her. They brought flowers from Eleanor Roosevelt, then First Lady of New York State and they brought Lillian D. Wald, settlement house founder and representative of the Women's International League for Peace and Freedom. Wald had with her sixteen trunks containing half a million signatures on petitions for peace that had been collected by eleven national women's groups.

On the morning of February 6, a truck pulled by a tractor rolled up to the meeting site. Into the great hall, fifteen women carried boxes filled with the American petitions and similar collections from around the world, the signatures numbering in the millions.

An unidentified male delegate said about Miss Woolley, "Perhaps we can use her to pacify the peace organizations."

Teachers Are Workers

In 1853, Susan B. Anthony attended the New York Teachers' Convention and rose to speak on the question of why teaching was not a respected profession. Although women formed a large portion of the membership, they did not speak at meetings. After a half-hour debate, Anthony was allowed to talk. She said, "So long as society says a woman is incompetent to be a lawyer, minister or doctor, but has ample ability to be a teacher, that every man

Carol Sun, Herstory, painting from the "China Mary" series, 1991

of you who chooses this profession tacitly acknowledges that he has no more brains than a woman?"

In the 1890s, Chicago teachers, led by Catherine Goggin, went on strike for better pay. Goggin suggested getting corporations to pay their taxes and using that for teachers' pay.

Navaho teacher, Navaho children, and the written Navaho language, July 21, 1948

Marriage Is Not Misconduct: Teachers, 1908

New York City teachers fought for equal pay for equal work and for an end to forcing teachers to resign when they married. Authorities were known to search the schools for pregnant teachers. High school English teacher Henrietta Rodman argued that teachers could be fired for misconduct, but that "marriage is not misconduct." She charged the Board of Education with "mother-baiting" in a letter to the *New York Tribune*, which got her suspended. In 1916, the Teacher's League that Rodman helped found became the American Federation of Teachers.

The Healthy Mind and the Sick Mind

I am angry nearly every day of my life, but I have learned not to show it; and I still try to hope not to feel it, though it may take me another forty years to do it.
Louisa May Alcott

What's your excuse?
Congresswoman Patsy Mink in response to a male politician's objection that "raging hormones" left women unfit for political life, 1960s

As women, we shouldn't emulate men, but should look to women's experience— what women actually do—and realize that a lot of so-called "deficiencies" can be reframed as the seeds of strength.
Jean Baker Miller, author of Toward a New Psychology of Women *(1976) and director of education at the Stone Center, Wellesley College.*

Was Elizabeth Packard Crazy?

In 1860, Elizabeth Packard was committed by her husband to the state hospital in Jacksonville, Illinois. A Presbyterian minister, he had collected neighbors' signatures on a petition claiming insanity and had two doctors examine her. The doctors took her pulse, did not question her, and pronounced her insane. Elizabeth Packard said her commitment was caused by her defiance of her domestic role. When she forgot to iron her husband's wristbands in time for his Sunday sermon, he said her mind was slipping. When she did not wish to hear him read from the Bible on female obedience, he said she was mad. She openly defended abolitionist John Brown. She refused to stay home all day.

After three years, Packard was released from the asylum into her husband's care. But she managed to turn the tables by having friends and supporters file a writ of habeas corpus against him. She won her case and set out on her own to crusade for married women's rights and protective legislation for the insane. She wrote books and worked with lawyer Myra Bradwell to get Illinois to pass a law allowing married women the right to control their own property. She brought inordinate amounts of publicity to conditions in insane asylums, earning her the perpetual enmity of the medical establishment, which preferred keeping such matters confidential.

Was Mary Todd Lincoln Crazy?

She shopped. In the ten years between the night her husband was murdered as he sat beside her at Ford's Theatre and the day an old family friend asked her to come to the courthouse to be judged insane, Mary Todd Lincoln had moved from place to place, seen two sons buried, and shopped. She bought curtains in multiples and gloves she would never wear. She spent a lot of time in stores, talking with salespeople more than they were accustomed to having a lady do.

Women's Education Time Line

1778: A Quaker grammar school opens to educate rural mothers, who are responsible for educating their children.

1793: Katy Ferguson's School for the Poor is established in New York City.

1814: Emma Hart Willard starts a school in her home in Middlebury, Vermont.

1821: Emma Hart Willard's Troy Seminary opens in New York State, the first to receive public funding.

1824: First public high school for girls opens in Worcester, Massachusetts.

1832: Catherine Beecher becomes head of the Western Female Institute in Cincinnati.

1834: Prudence Crandall's school in Connecticut burns and closes.

1836: Georgia Female College is chartered.

1837: Oberlin College admits women. Mary Lyon starts Mount Holyoke Seminary in Amherst, Massachusetts.

1847: Catharine Beecher takes seventy young women from New England westward to be teachers.

1849: Elizabeth Blackwell is the first female graduate of an American medical school.

1850: First federal census to measure basic literacy reports white men and women nearly equal. Only half the black women surveyed are literate.

1853: Antioch College opens in Ohio, admitting women.

1862: Charlotte Forten becomes the first Northern black woman to travel to South Carolina to help educate former slaves.

1865: Vassar College opens, with astonomer Maria Mitchell on its faculty. Mitchell stays at Vassar until 1889.

1869: Fannie J. Coffin, a freed slave, the first black person to graduate from Oberlin College (1865), becomes principal of the Institute for Colored Youth in Philadelphia, introducing a training program for teachers and an industrial curriculum.

1870: Swarthmore College opens, admits women. The University of Michigan opens to women.

1872: Cornell University admits women.

1873: Dr. Edward H. Clarke publishes Sex in Education.

1875: Smith and Wellesley colleges open.

1876: Dr. Mary Putnam Jacobi answers Dr. Edward Clarke with The Question of Rest for Women During Menstruation.

1879: The first formal arrangements to admit women to Harvard University are made and the Harvard Annex opens.

1881: Spelman College for black women established in Atlanta, Georgia.

1885: Bryn Mawr College opens, the first to offer graduate programs for women. Goucher College opens.

1886: Lucy Laney establishes a normal school in Augusta, Georgia.

1889: Barnard College opens at Columbia University, the only affiliated college in the world with full official sanction and recognition from its affiliated University.

1890: Total holders of baccalaureate degrees in the United States: 2,500 white women, 300 black men, 30 black women.

1894: Harvard Annex becomes Radcliffe College.

1904: Mary McLeod Bethune, after teaching in Lucy Laney's school for a year, opens the Daytona Normal and Industrial School for Negro Girls.
    Stanford University adopts quotas for female students.

1930: Women college presidents, professors, and instructors are 32.5 percent of the total.

1931: Lucy Sprague Mitchell (Radcliffe, 1900), first dean of women at the University of California, starts the Cooperative School for Teachers, which will become the Bank Street School.

1938: The appointment of a man to succeed Mary Woolley as president of Mount Holyoke College causes enormous controversy. Woolley feels so betrayed that she refuses to return to the school again.

1948: After twenty-five years in the Columbia University Anthropology Department, the renowned Ruth Benedict is finally named a full professor. She is sixty-one years old and among the students she has taught is Margaret Mead.

1961: Charlayne Hunter becomes the first black female student at the University of Georgia

1968: Strikes by Third World students at San Francisco State College—and in Berkeley in 1969—call attention to the need for ethnic studies. Courses on black history, Asian-American history, and Latino history begin around the country.

1969: Twenty women historians form the Coordinating Committee on Women in the Historical Profession to support the separate but related issues of women in the profession and the field of women's history.
    Vassar College admits men.

1970: First congressional hearings on sex discrimination in education.

San Diego State College adopts the first official, integrated women's studies program.

1972: Title IX, federal legislation penalizing educational institutions for gender discrimination, is passed.

1974: *Signs: Journal of Women in Culture and Society*, publishing new feminist scholarship, begins.

1975: Jill K. Conway becomes the first woman president of Smith College, on its hundredth anniversary.

1977: Founding convention of the National Women's Studies Association, San Francisco. Lesbian caucus formed, begins to formulate Lesbian Studies curriculum.

1981: Spelman College in Atlanta opens a Women's Center and starts women's studies programs.

1987: Goucher College in Maryland goes coed.

1990: Mills College students rebel against an administration decision to admit male students. Decision withdrawn.

Kate Millett, Domestic Scene, sculpture, 1987

In 1875, a jury in a Chicago courtroom found her guilty of insanity. Medical experts who had never examined her testified that she was insane. The star witness was her only surviving son, Robert Lincoln, whose descriptions to the experts of his mother's mad behavior formed the basis of their opinions. Robert Lincoln's motivation appears to be a combination of family dynamics and greed, for among other things, Mary Lincoln retained control of her money. She was, however, addicted to the drug chloral hydrate and had been for many years a practicing spiritualist.

After the three months and three weeks in a mental hospital, she was rescued by Myra Bradwell, the first woman lawyer in Illinois. The two women had known each other previously; Mary Todd Lincoln, who was against suffrage for women, disapproved of Bradwell's public life. Determined to free Mary Lincoln, Bradwell enlisted the help of her husband, a powerful judge, and together, threatening a mass publicity campaign, they convinced the authorities to let her go.

More Crazy Ladies

It is now 21 years since people found out that I was crazy and all because I could not fall in with every vulgar belief that was fashionable. I could never be led by everything and everybody.
Phoebe B. Davis, New York, 1856

It is a very fashionable and easy thing now to make a person out to be insane. If a man tires of his wife, and if he fooled after some other woman, it is not a very difficult matter to get her in an institution of this kind. Belladonna and chloroform will give her the appearance of being crazy enough, and after the asylum doors have closed upon her, adieu to the beautiful world and all home associations.
Ada Metcalf, Illinois, 1876

Charlotte Perkins Gilman Saves Her Own Life

In April 1887, Gilman, who had been working as a commercial artist and was beginning to write, put herself in treatment for nervous exhaustion and breakdown with the most famous neurologist of her time, Dr. S. Weir Mitchell, a staunch proponent of keeping women in their sphere. For a month, Gilman received the rest cure in the doctor's Philadelphia sanitarium. His instructions, on release, were, "Live as domestic a life as possible. . . . Have but two hours' intellectual life a day.

In 1857, unmarried, thirty-two-year-old Adriana Brinckle sold some furniture she no longer needed. Charges were brought against her for selling furniture that was her father's property. Her physician-father and a judge friend sentenced her to twenty-eight years in a psychiatric hospital for the crime of embarrassing family honor.

And never touch pen, brush or pencil as long as you live." Following his directions rigidly, she "came perilously near to losing my mind." By November, she "decided to cast off Dr. Mitchell bodily and do exactly what I pleased." In 1890, she wrote "The Yellow Wallpaper," a short story based on the enforced rest prescribed by Dr. Mitchell, but with an ending opposite to what happened in her own life. Gilman said she wrote the story "to save people from being driven crazy." The first person she saved was herself.

Karen Horney and Clara Thompson: Troublemakers

When one begins, as I did, to analyze men only after a fairly long experience of analyzing women, one receives a most surprising impression of the intensity of this envy of pregnancy, childbirth and motherhood, as well as of breasts and of the act of suckling. . . . Is not the tremendous strength in man of the impulse to creative work in every field precisely due to their feelings of playing a relatively small part in the creation of living beings, which constantly impels them to an overcompensation in achievement?

Karen Horney, "The Flight from Womanhood," 1926

. . . Freud's idea that women have envy because they have no penis is symbolically true in this culture. The woman envies the greater freedom of the man, his greater opportunities, and his relative lack of conflict about his fundamental drives. The penis as a symbol of aggression stands for the freedom to be, to force one's way, to get what one wants. These are the characteristics which a woman envies in a man.

Clara Thompson, Penis Envy in Woman, *1943*

Between 1922 and 1935, in fourteen different papers, Karen Horney, one of the first women to study medicine in Germany, a Berlin psychoanalyst who came to New York, countered Freud's theories about women. Her sister rebel, American Clara Thompson, got a medical degree in 1920 and worked along similar theoretical lines. In the 1940s, Horney and Thompson, with Frieda Fromm-Reichmann, seceded from orthodox psychoanalysis to create the William Alanson White Psychiatric Foundation. Their program for training psychoanalysts included aspects of anthropology, political science, and social psychology.

Psychology Constructs the Female: 1968

Psychologists have set about describing the true nature of women with a certainty and a sense of their own infallibility rarely found in the secular world. . . . A woman's true nature is that of a happy servant . . . [but] there is not the tiniest shred of evidence that these fantasies of servitude and childish dependence have anything to do with woman's true potential. Psychology has nothing to say about what women are really like, what they need and what they want, essentially because psychology does not know.

Naomi Weisstein, Associate Professor of Psychology and member of the Chicago Women's Liberation Rock Band

Phyllis Chesler: Troublemaker

For a woman to be healthy, she must "adjust" to and accept the behavioral norms for her sex—passivity, acquiescence, self-sacrifice, and lack of ambition—even though these kinds of "loser" behaviors are generally regarded as socially undesirable (i.e. nonmasculine).

Women and Madness, *1972*

Without a radical feminist movement moving in the world, you would never have heard of it, no one would have cared about it, other feminists couldn't have inspired it, blessed it, passed it round from hand to hand.

Phyllis Chesler on Women and Madness, *in 1995*

How White Is Women's Psychology?

It is actually misleading and dysfunctional to engage in a discussion of Black mothers and daughters patterned along the lines of white theoretical writing. . . .

Gloria Josephs, 1984

Since Black mothers have a distinctive relationship to White patriarchy, they may be less likely to socialize their daughters into their proscribed role as subordinates.

Patricia Hill Collins

Do Women Think Differently?

In 1982, Carol Gilligan's book *In a Different Voice: Psychological Theory and Women's Development*, claimed that Freud's idea that men have a better-developed sense of morality than women was nonsense. Women's concept of morality, she said, was just different. She named male morality "an ethics of justice" and female morality "an ethics of care."

As we have listened for centuries to the voices of men and the theories of development that their experience informs, so we have come more recently to notice not only the silence of women but the difficulty in hearing what they say when they speak. Yet in the different voice of women lies the truth of an ethic of care, the tie between relationship and responsibility and the origins of aggression in the failure of connection.

Carol Gilligan, In a Different Voice, *1982*

Rethinking Freud

Dora viewed the sexual attentions of her father's associate, Herr K, as unwanted and uninvited. She responded to them with revulsion. . . . Freud evidently viewed Herr K's lecherous advances as acceptable behavior, although Herr K was married and Dora was only fourteen and the daughter of a close family friend. We can surmise that the cultural belief in the primacy of men's sexual needs prevented Freud from seeing Dora's revulsion as genuine.

Rachel T. Hare-Mustin and Jeanne Marecek, Gender and the Meaning of Difference, *1990.*

Paternal child rape was being tied into a noose to hang those the new experts identi-fied as the real culprits: the mothers who "failed to protect" . . . in 1984, social work sen-timentality promised salvation for Amelia in the ABC TV movie, "Something About Amelia"—and the actor-daddy said he was ashamed of himself, and the actress-mother looked as though, after a suitable period of family "treatment" (during which she acknowl-edged she had made him do it), she might welcome poor-ashamed-of-himself daddy back into the marital bed.

Louise Armstrong, author of Rocking the Cradle of Sexual Politics: What Happened When Women Said Incest, *1994*

Nicole Hollander cartoon, 1991

Last Words

I am assuming that therapy ought to be about the work of healing those of us who have thought we were crazy, and of liberating, or empowering, all of us to realize ourselves as active moral agents in the work of justice, near and far. I am assuming that healthy moral agents want to help bring down the blasphemous canopies of heterosexism and homophobia; sexism and misogyny; capitalist exploitation, poverty, and class woundedness; racism and white supremacist attitudes and actions. I am assuming that therapy ought to fan those flames in our hearts and souls.

Carter Heyward, Episcopal priest and ethicist, 1993

Poet/writer Audre Lorde,
1934–1992

CHAPTER 5 Writers and Artists

*W*oman's strongest vindication for speaking [is] that the world needs to hear her voice.

Anna Julia Cooper, black writer and activist, 1892

Mary Cassatt's visit home, long after she had become famous in Europe, was reported in the Philadelphia newspaper as the arrival of "Mary Cassatt, sister of Mr. Cassatt, President of the Pennsylvania Railroad, who has been studying painting in France and owns the smallest Pekingese dog in the world."

Any fool can make a quilt; and, after we had made a couple of dozen over twenty years ago, we quit the business with a conviction that nobody but a fool would spend so much time in cutting bits of dry goods into yet smaller bits and sewing them together again, just for the sake of making believe that they were busy at practical work.

Abigail Scott Duniway, The New Northwest, *July 1880*

I would like you to think of my interests. That is your primary concern, because I am the one to steer the course, the pilot. . . . I want you to stop writing fiction.

F. Scott Fitzgerald to Zelda Fitzgerald

It says in the Torah, only through a man has a woman an existence. Only through a man can a woman enter heaven.

Father to daughter in The Bread Givers *by Anzia Yezierska, 1925*

I put on the page a third look at what I've seen in life—the reinvented experience of a cross-eyed working-class lesbian, addicted to violence, language and hope, who has made the decision to live, is determined to live, on the page and on the street, for me and mine.

Dorothy Allison, Trash, *1988*

Florine Stettheimer, **The Cathedrals of Art,** *1929*

*N*othing disappears from the historical record quite so fast as a woman artist. On college reading lists, poet Muriel Rukeyser used to say, women writers only came "after Easter." A few white writers—Emily Dickinson, British novelist Jane Austen, perhaps Virginia Woolf—were considered worth noticing. Yet women have been at the heart of all the arts in America.

In 1678, Anne Bradstreet, the country's first poet, showed what her gender was up against:

> *If what I do prove well, it won't advance,*
> *They'll say it's stolen, or else it was by chance*

From Bradstreet on, only (white) tokens survive the historical wipeout with any force: the writers Dickinson and Stein, the painters Cassatt and O'Keeffe, sometimes the photographer Bourke-White. Women's achievements continued to be called "stolen" or "by chance" long after Bradstreet lay down her pen. Escaped slave Harriet Jacobs and Margaret Mitchell, author of *Gone with the Wind*, were at first considered frauds whose writing must have been done by others. After young sculptor Vickie Ream persuaded Abraham Lincoln to sit for her, people spoke only of her feminine "wiles," not her art. Bourke-White was whispered to have "used" men to get her pictures, especially those on the World War II battlefield.

A rescue mission has been going full tilt for twenty-five years, retrieving artists and writers from archives and attics. Because the lives and work of women of color are even less represented than those of white women and the lives and work of lesbians less than heterosexual women, the biggest excavations have been in those areas.

Stubborn they all were, those setting pen to paper against the

> **In 1955, the Ford Motor Company sent the poet Marianne Moore two model Edsels, hoping she would come up with a clever name for the car. She didn't.**

> **"I think I am one of the few who gives our country any voice of its own."**
>
> *Georgia O'Keeffe*

odds and against the grain, all the way back to Anne Bradstreet and Phyllis Wheatley, white and black, seventeenth-century poets, early New Englanders, both transported from elsewhere—Bradstreet from England, Wheatley from Africa—but only one of her own free will.

Stubborn and ingenious. Somehow, Mrs. Harriet E. Wilson, a black woman, wrote a novel about interracial marriage and racism, *Our Nig*, in 1859. Julia Ward Howe became famous with "The Battle Hymn of the Republic" and the Jewish Emma Lazarus's words were inscribed on the base of the Statue of Liberty. When women insisted on speaking in public, as they did during the Abolition struggle, they also wrote.

By the 1920s, women were part—often the vanguard—of modern literature and the Harlem Renaissance. Their numbers were unmatched until the 1970s, when the women's movement found its second collective voice in the work of poets like Alice Walker, June Jordan, Adrienne Rich, and Audre Lorde, novelists like Marge Piercy, Erica Jong, and Rita Mae · Brown, as well as essayists, critics, columnists, and dramatists.

Writing since the 1970s has expanded on two fronts: excavation is the first, interpretation the second. Neither Emily Dickinson nor Gertrude Stein turn out to be incomprehensible, as rumored, only subversive. Alcott's dark side comes to light, as do the lesbian text in Djuna Barnes's work and the subtext in Willa Cather's writing.

The past two decades have seen the erosion of the exclusively white idea of a woman writer. Black critics and writers have elaborated on an unearthed female literary past and created new work in every genre. Chicanas and Latinas, Native Americans and Asian-Americans have made large niches in the literary and feminist worlds with a literature that puts on the page the dramas of ethnic identity and female selfhood. The canon of real American writing, in all its diversity and layers, is larger than ever.

For a long time, there were no female painters or sculptors at all in public consciousness. In schools, women writers came "after Easter," but visual artists never came. The catch-up has been slow. If the nineteenth-century women's movement inspired more writers than visual artists, the twentieth century has more than made up for it.

Feminism has redefined art to extend beyond oils or watercolors, what Gertrude Stein collected, or what museums bought for their walls. It has redeemed what was once disparagingly called crafts or the decorative arts, the traditional artistry of women not in the white mainstream. The blankets woven by Navajo women have influenced many painters, including Jasper Johns and Frank Stella. The work of Native American potter Maria Montoya, who perfected a technique for making black pottery, was once so admired that she was asked to lay the cornerstone when construction began on Rockefeller Center. Pioneer photographer Gertrude Stanton Kasebier always credited her Iowa grandmother, "an artist with her loom who made her own designs." Women investigating the origins of quilting found not only social echoes of their own concerns—early quilting bees were a "cover" for profound conversation—but principles of design and texture.

While nineteenth-century white "ladies" learned to draw, becoming a serious artist was

Native American women doing lace work and quilting, Minnesota, 1895

another matter. Two who made their mark—Sarah Peale and Lily Spencer—came from the only environments likely to produce them: progressive families, where art was not forbidden to women.

The first women's movement, spilling over into the early twentieth century, inspired and created possibilities for artists of all kinds. Modernism arrived with women in it, as did other rebellions, like Surrealism. The Depression years, so bleak for most of the country, and especially bleak for jobless women, brought gender-blind government support for the arts, a historical first. Many artists, including sculptor Louise Nevelson, were assistants to the great mural painters, Rivera and Orozco, shaping their art as well as paying the rent.

World War II opened doors for women that were slammed shut in the 1950s. "Little women" were enshrined again, and female artists went into hiding. Young abstract expressionist painter Miriam Schapiro came to New York and found many women, but, "With them I had only 'girl talk.' The men would get together in studios to talk about their work. The women really didn't respect each other deeply. . . . We talked about our love lives, shared each other's romances. . . we never came together over painting."

By the late sixties, women's liberation had spawned a feminist art movement. Radical white women joined antiwar, antiracism, radical organizations first, and they quickly organized women artists within them. Women of color gravitated toward art groups based on ethnicity first—the Black Emergency Cultural Coalition, the *Taller Boricua*, the Asian-American Basement Workshop—and struggled on both fronts, race and gender, as they did in the political arena.

The female-centered quality of the art, playing off a commonly understood male tradition, lent itself to wit, parody, and irony. As women's experience became the focus of poems, novels, stories, and polemics, the female body emerged in the visual arts differently than before, and the female gaze changed everything.

"Once the women's movement was under way," Miriam Shapiro said, the fifties women "came together again. Then most of us could connect on a new plane."

In the beginning, making art with a camera was like living on the frontier: there were no rules. As women do when the social structure is loose, when there are few male precedents to live up to or overcome, they took to photography early. Doing so did mean violating norms of acceptable female behavior: they left their homes; they were ambitious; they earned money.

Without women, the history of photography as an art form is incomplete. The camera work of Berenice Abbott and Imogen Cunningham was in the vanguard of modernism.

Women's work in photography is also remarkably rich in social and political content. In the 1920s and 1930s, Doris Ullman discovered Gullah life in South Carolina, Tina Modotti aimed her camera at workers and artists in Mexico, Consuelo Kanaga and Jesse Beale captured black street life in New York.

The camera as an agent of social change, as witness, and as a means of honoring what others ignore are themes running from that time to ours, connecting Dorothea Lange's images of country women, begun in the mid-1930s, and of Japanese-Americans being herded into internment camps in 1941 to Susan Meiselas's pictures of the Nicaraguan Sandanistas or Haitian uprising.

The photojournalists in particular were often as physically daring as any athlete. Margaret Bourke-White and other "girl photographers" during the Second World War were intrepid. Famous for crawling to the top of skyscrapers in peacetime for a picture, they trudged through battlefields under fire during the war. Bourke-White and Lee Miller brought the world unimaginable images of the Final Solution, their emotional courage as crucial to getting those pictures as physical bravery was. In the 1960s, the controversial Diane Arbus, inspired by the work of Lisette Model, who had photographed on the streets of New York two decades before, showed a different version of emotional courage as she investigated the margins of normal life.

Restored are not only specific artists, but their female mentors and friends, their circles of support and connections. Nineteenth-century feminist philanthropist Louisine Havemeyer encouraged and supported the painter Mary Cassatt and used her own impressive art collection to raise money for Alice Paul's militant suffrage work. Photographer Gertrude Kasebier helped the younger Laura Gilpin, America's first woman landscape photographer. Unlike other journals in the 1940s, Lillian Smith and Paula Snelling's magazine, *The New South*, gave space to black writers and to women. Georgia O'Keeffe's sisters helped her through despair: painter Dorothy Brett and patron Mabel Dodge introduced her to New Mexico, where she found a new visual vocabulary.

When the pieces are laid together, it becomes clear that women together, in movements, matter, just as individual artists do. The artists appear in clumps, at times of feminist activity across the board. Feminist movements help encourage women artists, assuring an audience for what they do: at the turn of the century, when education in particular opened new doors for women; during the 1920s, after the vote was won, a time of progressive feminist and antiracist politics and a sexual revolution; and in the 1970s, the most broad-based feminist upheaval in American history.

Influence works the other way, too. Writing and making art are dangerous activities. They inspire women to misbehave. They challenge orthodoxies of all kinds. "The artist," rocker-poet Patti Smith said in 1971, is "a saint, but with a cowboy mouth." Artists provide encouragement to girls trapped in cute pink bedrooms when the world says no.

The lives of female artists show the interaction between imagination and the conditions of real life. Money is always an issue, as are families, marriage, and sex. The strategies for survival differ: Dickinson lived at home, but Louisa May Alcott went into the world as the family breadwinner. Nella Larsen worked as a nurse. Berenice Abbott went to Paris. It is easier to name the women who married and had children—they stand out—than those who did not. Whatever the choices, their roots were in history, and the stakes were high. As Dickinson wrote, "Read me, do not let me die."

Writers

My work. It is only here on paper that I dare say it like that: "My work!"
Lorraine Hansberry, 1955

I never wanted to get married. The last thing I wanted was infinite security and to be the place an arrow shoots off from. I wanted change and excitement and to shoot off in all directions myself, like the colored arrows from a Fourth of July rocket.
Esther Greenwood in The Bell Jar, *a novel by Sylvia Plath, 1963*

[I] did not publish a book until I was fifty, raised children without household help or the help of the "technological sublime" (the atom bomb was in manufacture before the first automatic washing machine) . . . worked outside the house on everyday jobs as well (as nearly half of all women do now, although a woman with a paid job, except as a maid or prostitute, is still rarest of any in literature . . .)

Tillie Olsen, Silences, *1965*

Rage is to writers what water is to fish. A laid-back writer is like an orgasmic prostitute—an anomaly.

Nikki Giovanni

"The myth of Prometheus is well known. We should have a feminist version of that myth. Women, defying their fear of punishment, wrest from men that jealously guarded fire, the sacred right to work. No longer will we agree to protect the hearth at the price of extinguishing the fire within ourselves.

Celia Gilbert, 1977

Louisa May Alcott in the 1990s

A book written for the guards, not the inmates.

Biographer Martha Saxton on Little Women, *1995*

Daughter of a leading New England intellectual with "no talent for money," Alcott supported her entire family for ten years, from 1857 to 1867. Secretly, for money, she wrote sensational tales under a pseudonym: "Blood and thunder stories," she said, "easier to compoze" and "better paid than moral tales." Madeleine Stern and Leona Rostenberg, who met as college students in the 1930s and have lived together ever since, are responsible for uncovering the secret. Many of these stories, like "A Long Fatal Love Chase" (1866, republished in 1995), a tale about obsession, control, and terror, feature females who direct their own destinies, bad girls who have sex and take drugs.

Readers have always identified the author with her character, Jo, the girl who writes, in *Little Women*. Fictional characters are often confused with their female creators, as though, lacking the imagination to transform what they know into art, women are capable only of autobiography. Even so, as biographer Martha Saxton says, Jo is mistakenly idolized. Her journey is "far more problematic than it seemed. [Her] task was to dwarf herself cheerfully."

Little Women's renewed popularity, fueled by the 1994 film version, has, in an age of "family values" what Saxton calls "a sinister side. To read Alcott's story without caution, to read it as an inspiring depiction of reality, historical or contemporary, is dangerous, but to read it in the context of Alcott's embattled, even heroic, life can be a reminder of our unfinished struggle to make womanhood a bit less little."

Who Loves Scarlett O'Hara and Why?

Despite its length and many details, it is basically just a simple yarn of fairly simple people. There's no fine writing; there are no grandiose thoughts; there are no hidden meanings, no symbolism, nothing sensational—nothing, nothing at all that have made other best sellers best sellers. Then how to explain its appeal from the five year old to the ninety five year old? I can't figure it out.

Margaret Mitchell to a friend, October, 1936

Since its publication on June 30, 1936, figuring out the appeal of *Gone with the Wind* has been a cottage industry. Among explanations for the book's success was the idea that Scarlett's independent spirit was attractive to modern women, Eleanor Roosevelt among them. Roosevelt admired the book in her newspaper column and wrote to David O. Selznick requesting that her maid, Lizzy McDuffy, be tested for the role of Mammy in the film version. McDuffy was tested, but not cast. Franklin Roosevelt did not share his wife's view. "No book need be that long," he commented.

Margaret "Peggy" Mitchell had worked on her novel for ten years. It was published to good reviews, marred by gossip that Mitchell's husband, John Marsh, fellow reporter on the *Atlanta Journal*, had been her cowriter. The more acclaim her novel got and the more massive its sales— no book except the Bible has sold more copies, and Mitchell would win a Pulitzer Prize in 1937—the more puzzled Mitchell was.

She never wrote another book.

Women, Writing, Race, and Ethnicity

I have not written my experiences in order to attract attention to myself. I do earnestly desire to arouse the women of the North to a realizing sense of the condition of two millions of women at the South. . . . I want to add my testimony to that of abler pens to convince people of the Free States what Slavery really is.

Harriet Jacobs, preface to Incidents in the Life of a Slave Girl, *1861*

What we get in steerage is not the refuse, but the sinew and bone of all the nations.

Mary Antin, They Who Knock at Our Gates, *1914*

I was unmoved by the story of Washington's crossing the Delaware, nor was I inspired by his truthfulness and valor. My thin knowledge of history told me that the

sinister wisdom 37

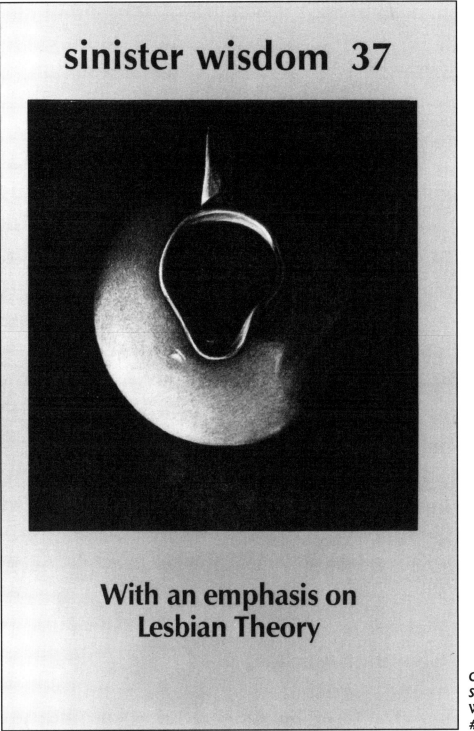

With an emphasis on
Lesbian Theory

*Cover of
Sinister
Wisdom,
#37, 1989*

George Washingtons and their kind had stolen the country from the American Indians, and I could lodge all my protests against this unforgivable piece of thievery.
Pauli Murray, Proud Shoes, *1956*

The New Paternalists have mistaken the oppression of the Negro for "the Negro." They have found in his color, not in his bondage, the source of his grace and wily speech.
Lorraine Hansberry on Norman Mailer's The White Negro, *1961*

✄ Frances Ellen Harper's novel *Iola Leroy, or Shadows Uplifted* (1892) ends with the heroine resolving to write a novel: "There are scattered among us materials for mournful tragedies and mirth-provoking comedies, which some hand may yet bring into the literature of the country, glowing with the fervor of the tropics and enriched by the luxuriance of the orient, and thus add to the solution of our unsolved American problem."

✄ Nella Larsen wrote to Gertrude Stein, praising her handling of the "mulatto" character in her 1909 novel *Melanctha*: "I never cease to wonder how you came to write it and just why you and not some one of us should so accurately have caught the spirit of this race of mine." Larsen more than caught the spirit two decades later in her novels. *Quicksand* (1928) and *Passing* (1929), about repression and its consequences, were important books in the Harlem Renaissance. The first black woman to win a Guggenheim Fellowship, in 1930, Larsen mysteriously disappeared from the literary world immediately afterward, working as a nursing supervisor until close to her death in 1963.

Zora Neale Hurston

Hurston had considerable experience with the double edge of patronage. Novelist Fannie Hurst, for whom she worked as a secretary, once took Hurston to a restaurant where she passed her off as an African princess. After the meal, Hurston said, "Who would think that a good meal could be so bitter?" Mrs. Rufus Osgood Mason, a major patron, would not allow her to publish while she was receiving Mason's money. Only after severing that tie did she write her first novel. *Jonah's Gourd Vine* (1934) was followed by, among others, *Their Eyes Were Watching God* (1937), a novel of black female independence, and her autobiography, *Dust Tracks on a Road* (1942).

> **"**
>
> Sometimes I feel discriminated against, but it does not make me angry. It merely astonishes me. How *can* any deny themselves the pleasure of my company! It's beyond me.
>
> **"**
>
> *Zora Neale Hurston,* How It Feels to Be Colored Me, *1928*

⤞ Ann Petry's novel, *The Street* (1946), is about the possibilities for female autonomy in a hostile environment. *The Narrows* (1953) is a novel about interracial love.

⤝ Alice Childress, a member of the American Negro Theatre, wrote *Gold through the Trees* (1952), the first play by a black woman produced off Broadway. *Trouble in Mind* won an Obie, the first awarded a woman playwright, in 1955. *Wine in the Wilderness* was produced on television in 1969. *Wedding Band*, (1973), subtitled *A Love/Hate Story in Black and White*, is about a black woman and her white lover in World War I's Charleston, South Carolina, where racial intermarriage is against the law.

Lorraine Hansberry

Hansberry came from a Chicago family friendly with Langston Hughes, W. E. B. Du Bois, and Paul Robeson. *A Raisin in the Sun* (1959) is about a family trying to decide between buying a house in a white neighborhood and sending their daughter to college and medical school or using their money to help their son invest in a liquor store and his own independence. Its Broadway success made Hansberry a celebrity.

The Sign in Sidney Brustein's Window was originally called *The Sign in Jenny Reed's Window* and was based on Hansberry's friend, photographer Gin Briggs. It was in production in 1965 when the playwright died of cancer at thirty-four.

The posthumously produced *Les Blancs* explores the making of a black revolutionary. *To Be Young, Gifted and Black*, based on a compilation of her writings, was the longest-running drama of the 1968-1969 season. Many believe that if Hansberry had lived to see women's liberation flourish, she would have been part of it and would have found the cultural encouragement to write plays in which women drive the action.

⤝ Maya Angelou's *I Know Why the Caged Bird Sings* (1970), the first of five autobiographical books, describes her young female black life in the South, especially the harrowing rape by her mother's boyfriend that left her mute for five years. It won the National Book Award. In addition to being an Alvin Ailey dancer and a civil rights worker, she has written four collections of poetry and read "A Rock, a River, a Tree" at President Bill Clinton's inauguration in 1993.

⤞ In 1987, African-American poet Rita Dove won the Pulitzer Prize for her poems in *Beulah and Thomas*. In 1993, she was named Poet Laureate of the United States.

Toni Morrison

Had she paints, or clay or knew the discipline of the dance, or strings; had she anything to engage her tremendous curiosity and her gift for metaphor, she might have exchanged the restlessness and preoccupation with whim for an activity that provided her with all she yearned for. And like any artist with no form, she became dangerous.

Sula, *1974*

Novelist Toni Morrison wrote *The Bluest Eye* (1972), *Sula* (1974), *Song of Solomon* (1977), and *Tar Baby* (1981) while holding a full-time job and raising a child by herself. She won the Pulitzer Prize for Literature in 1994.

Lydia Maria Child

Child's *The First Settlers of New England*, a nonfiction book about the Indians of her own region, was followed by *Hobomok* (1824), a novel about love between a "noble" Indian and a white woman. *An Appeal in Favor of That Class of Americans Called Africans* (1833) traced the history of slavery, rejecting African colonization as a solution, denouncing laws against race mixing, segregation, and unequal education.

In the vanguard of the abolitionist movement, in 1860 Child, a white woman, wrote pamphlets on "The Duty of Disobedience to the Fugitive Slave Act," "The Patriarchal Institution," and "The Right Way, the Safe Way," urging immediate emancipation. In 1861, she edited the recollections of ex-slave Harriet Jacobs.

Mary Antin, an immigrant from Russia at thirteen, wrote, "I was born, I have lived, and I have been made over." *The Promised Land* (1912), written at the urging of her friend Josephine Lazarus, sister of poet Emma Lazarus, whose words are inscribed on the base of the Statue of Liberty, might well have been called "The Making of an American."

✣ Fannie Hurst's novel, *Imitation of Life* (1933), is a tragedy by a white novelist about a black woman passing as white. The 1934 film with Claudette Colbert changed a crucial element of the story. In the novel, Peola, the passing woman, has herself sterilized so she will not have a black child when she marries a white man. In the less brutal film, the sterilization never happens.

✣ Lillian Smith's novel of interracial love, *Strange Fruit* (1944), was considered one of the most inflammatory books ever published. When the U.S. Post Office banned it from the mail on the grounds of obscenity, Eleanor Roosevelt personally intervened. Smith, a white Southerner, wrote a weekly column in the black newspaper, the *Chicago Defender*. In 1949, she published *Killers of the Dream*, analyzing how the role assigned the black mammy affected Southern male perceptions of the sexuality of black and white women, probably the first book to explicitly address what racism does to white people as well as black.

✣ Laura Z. Hobson read in *Time* magazine in 1944 that Representative John Rankin of Mississippi, addressing Congress, referred to columnist Walter Winchell as "the little kike." No one protested. In fact, "The House rose and gave him prolonged applause." Hobson, a former screenwriter, taped the item over her desk. In 1946, *Gentleman's Agreement*, a provocative novel about anti-Semitism among "nice" people, was published.

✣ Harper Lee's novel *To Kill a Mockingbird* (1960) is the tale of a white lawyer, raising two children alone, who defends a black man accused of rape in a small Southern town. It won a Pulitzer Prize for its white author, has sold 16 million copies in the United States, and has been translated into twenty-four languages. Gregory Peck, star of *Gentleman's Agreement* (1949) played Atticus Finch, the lawyer with a conscience, in the movie version of Lee's novel.

Like every young child, I was read fairy tales about Cinderella, Snow White and Little Red Riding Hood. But I also was told stories about growing up that had nothing to do with the experiences of the characters in those fairy tales. Mi abuelita and mis tias would tell me the tales of La Llorona, the weeping woman who wandered the river banks, howling for the children she had thrown into the waters. However, as much as I read, I never found their stories in the pages of a book you could order through school or on the shelves of the neighborhood library.

Tiffany Ana Lopez, Growing Up Chicana/o, 1993

>> Gloria Anzaldua says, "The joys of looking like a white girl ain't so great since I realized I could be beaten on the street for being a dyke." A dramatist and poet, her most important book is *Borderlands: La Frontera*, 1988.

>> Sandra Cisneros grew up in Chicago with a Mexican father and a Mexican-American mother, in a community that, with a fresh voice, forms the background for her novel, *The House on Mango Street* (1985) and the related stories in *Woman Hollering Creek* (1991).

>> Cherrie Moraga wrote in 1979 that she had "denied the voice of my brown mother—the brown in me. I have acclimated to the sound of a white language which, as my father represents it, does not speak to the emotions in my poems—emotions which stem from the love of my mother."

The Woman Warrior gave me permission to keep going with what I'd started.
Sandra Cisneros, 1992

>> Jade Snow Wong's *Fifth Chinese Daughter* (1945), her autobiography, describes the conflict between an American daughter (born and raised in Chinatown) and traditional parents who demanded unquestioning obedience. Against her parents' wishes, Wong went to college, supporting herself by working as a housemaid. She became a well-known ceramicist and writer.

>> Jeanne Wakasuki Houston is "the first member of our family to finish college and the first to marry out of my race." She wrote *Farewell to Manzanar* (1973), an account of life in the first permanent concentration camp built for people of Japanese ancestry by the U.S. government in 1941. For her, writing the book meant confronting the most hidden family secret.

>> Maxine Hong Kingston created a sensation with *The Woman Warrior: Memories of a Girlhood Among Ghosts* (1976), establishing the close connection between autobiography and fiction that was becoming a style for many women writers, but grounding it in the terrain of her ethnic identity. The book begins, "In China your father had a sister who killed herself. She jumped into the family well. We say that your father has all brothers because it is as if she had never been born." Kingston also wrote *China Men* (1980) and *Tripmaster Monkey: His Fake Book*.

Feminist Presses: A Revolution in Print

While some feminist writers were published by mainstream presses in the 1970s—especially after it became clear that the books had commercial appeal—the revolution was really carried by little magazines and small publishing operations created and run collectively by women in the movement. These included Daughters, Inc., which first published novelist Rita Mae Brown; Shameless Hussy Press; the Alice James poetry collective; The Woman's Press Collective in Oakland, California, which published Judy Grahn's poetry; Auntie Lute Books; Naiad Press; and Seal Press. The feminist literary underground created by these publishers and the bookstores that sold their wares became vital parts of a political network.

Sisters in Crime

It takes tough talk to write a convincing American detective story. The contributions of Raymond Chandler and Dashiell Hammett to the genre are mostly brilliant narrative voice and atmosphere. Not a conventional place for women's writing, one might think, but one would be wrong.

Women have been writing mystery and detective fiction all along, especially at the height of hard-boiled male fame in the 1940s and on the crest of the feminist wave since the 1970s. Sometimes, before Kinsey Millhone and V. I. Warshawski turned the category inside out forever, the detective was female and she told her own story; usually not. A male protagonist was *de rigeur*. Even today, the mysteries by Emma Lathen, set on Wall Street, feature male heroes. Behind the single pseudonym, the two authors, now in their sixties, are economist Mary J. Latsis and corporate financier Martha Henisart.

A younger generation of writers has brought the female sleuth front and center. In this genre, too, women push the envelope. A form of light entertainment, the crime story has become even more a vehicle for social criticism, especially sexism. See how the old-line men react to Sue Grafton's Kinsey Millhone going out on her own late at night. At the outer edges of the envelope but perhaps at the center of what is new in detective stories is the avalanche of formerly marginalized women characters setting the world right. An entire industry has been built on the lesbian detective story and a smaller one on the black female detective.

A female private eye not only gets her man in an entirely untraditional way, she also takes care of herself, is assertive, often physically strong, wily and cunning. She is rarely married or a mother; it's hard to chase bad guys to Rio when somebody needs you to change diapers.

It may well be the relative antidomesticity of crime novels—although, perhaps in reaction, a countertradition of housewife/detectives is emerging—that has made them so popular with modern women.

Sisters in Crime poster, 1991

Chandler's Ghost

Raymond Chandler would no doubt be aghast at the shape-shifting bloat of mystery novels today, and I don't just mean the proliferation of cat detectives and fussy-librarian sleuths (that's a given). Nowadays, it's all the rage to domesticate the private eye, to render her "ordinary," to show her wrestling with husbands and kids and mortgage payments and dinner parties . . .

This sisterly approach may jack up supermarket sales, but it does little for a genre that was chiseled on the margins, and whose best flatfoots still turn a jaded eye to the dominant culture rather than grapple for a toehold within it.

Elizabeth Pincus, Voice Literary Supplement, *November 1995*

It would never do for me to lose my wits in the presence of a man who had none too many of his own.

Anna Katharine Green, one of the first female detective writers, That Affair Next Door, 1897

Nor at that time could any power on earth have convinced me that I should find myself late one terrible night, sans my dress and my false hair, dangling from the eaves of the Richelieu Hotel in pursuit of a triple slayer.

Adelaide Adams, heroine of Anita Blackmon's 1937 novel, Murder à la Richelieu

Each husband gets the infidelity he deserves.

Zelda Popkin, creator of Mary Carner, department store detective, in No Crime for a Lady, 1942

If the dreams of any so-called normal man were exposed, there would be no more gravity and dignity left for mankind.

Vera Caspary, Laura, 1943

The tension in Iris' chest built up unbearably. By rights, the hooks on her bra ought to snap.

Mary Collins, Dog Eat Dog, 1949

Most full lives are filled with empty gestures.

Amanda Cross, No Word from Winifred, 1986

Murder is always good copy, particularly when it happens to the rich and venal.

Lucille Fletcher, Eighty Dollars to Stamford, 1975 (Fletcher wrote the screenplay, Sorry, Wrong Number)

Too much virtue has a corrupting effect.

Sue Grafton, A Is for Alibi, 1982

Rule number something or other—never tell anybody anything unless you're going to get something better in return.

Sara Paretsky, Deadlock, 1984

"I love you," I say anyway.
"Go to hell," she says, and slams out.

Sandra Scoppetone, Everything You Have Is Mine, 1991

I wanted to pay homage to working women because they are the bridge that got us over. [My work] is about the people who are assumed not to have a worldview.

Barbara Neeley, describing Blanche on the Lam (1992) and Blanche among the Talented Tenth (1994), featuring a crime-solving African-American domestic protagonist

Some important biographies of American women, written by American women since 1970:

Nancy Milford, Zelda, 1970

Gerda Lerner, *The Grimké Sisters from South Carolina: Pioneers for Woman's Rights and Abolition*, 1971

Kathryn Kisk Sklar, *Catherine Beecher*, 1973

Myra Friedman, *Janis Joplin: Buried Alive*, 1973

Martha Saxton, *Louisa May Alcott: A Modern Biography*, 1977, reissued 1995

Jean Strouse, *Alice James*, 1980

Millicent Dillon, *A Little Original Sin: The Life and Work of Jane Bowles*, 1981

Sharon O'Brien, *Willa Cather: The Emerging Voice* , 1987

Kathleen Brady, *Ida Tarbell: Portrait of a Muckraker*, 1984

Elisabeth Griffith, *In Her Own Right: The Life of Elizabeth Cady Stanton*, 1984

Patti Bosworth, *Diane Arbus*, 1984

Vicki Goldberg, *Margaret Bourke-White*, 1986

Marion Meade, *Dorothy Parker: What Fresh Hell Is This?*, 1987

Gloria T. Hull, *Color, Sex and Poetry: Three Women Writers of the Harlem Renaissance*, 1987

Kathleen Barry, *Susan B. Anthony: A Biography of a Singular Feminist*, 1988

Roxana Robinson, *Georgia O'Keeffe: A Life*, 1989

Emily Toth, *Kate Chopin*, 1990

Ann J. Lane, *To "Herland" and Beyond: The Life and Work of Charlotte Perkins Gilman*, 1990

Benita Eisler, *O'Keeffe & Stieglitz: An American Romance*, 1991

Diane Middlebrook, *Anne Sexton*, 1991

Ellen Chesler, *Woman of Valor: Margaret Sanger and the Birth Control Movement in America*, 1992

Blanche Weisen Cook, *Eleanor Roosevelt: Volume One, 1884-1933*, 1992

Carol Brightman, *Writing Dangerously: Mary McCarthy and Her World*, 1992

Barbara L. Michaels, *Gertrude Kasebier*, Abrams, 1992

Kay Mills, *This Little Light of Mine: The Life of Fannie Lou Hamer*, 1993

Nancy Mathews, *Mary Cassatt: A Life*, 1993

Deborah Baker, *In Extremis: The Life of Laura Riding*, 1993

Thadious Davis, *Nella Larsen*, 1994

Glenda Reiley, *The Life and Legacy of Annie Oakley*, University of Oklahoma Press, 1994

Brooke Kroeger, *Nellie Bly: Daredevil, Reporter, Feminist*, 1994

Joan D. Hedrick, *Harriet Beecher Stowe: A Life*, 1994

Carolyn Heilbrun, *Gloria Steinem: A Woman's Life*, 1995

Honor Moore, *The White Blackbird: A Life of the Painter Margarett Sargent by Her Granddaughter*, 1996

Nell Irvin Painter, *Sojourner Truth, A Life, A Symbol*, 1996

Susan Cayleff, *Babe, The Life and Legend of Babe Didrickson Zaharias*, University of Illinois Press, 1996

What Have They Done to Nancy Drew?

"Waiting was never one of my really strong points," Nancy smiled. "I crave action."
The Mystery of the Ivory Charm, *1930s*

The tight jeans looked great on her long, slim legs and the green sweater comple-
mented her strawberry-blond hair.
"You'll make the guys absolutely drool," her friend Bess sighed.
Secrets Can Kill, *The Nancy Drew Files, 1986*

There were teen girl detectives before and after her, but Nancy Drew is the champ, the longest-lived, the most popular. Conceived in 1930 by Edward Stratemeyer, whose syndicate also created the Hardy Boy books, her adventures always bore the byline Carolyn Keene, who didn't exist. Stratemeyer wrote the first three books himself; when he died, the job went to his daughter, Harriet Stratemeyer Adams, and a host of ghostwriters.

In the books, Nancy is one in a long line of motherless girls. Her handsome, romantic father treats her more like his wife than his daughter. She is spunky and independent and never gives a thought to marrying her football-playing boyfriend. A consummate WASP in a blatantly WASPy world, she cares little for blacks, Jews, Italians, Irish, or other "others." In later years, the books' racism was toned down.

In fifty years, she solved fifty-six mysteries. She also flew an airplane, drove her roadster, competed in a golf tournament, fixed her own car, and made her own decisions. Like most heroines, she could think her way out of any scrape and her thinking made the Hardy Boys look like dimwits. She was incredibly superior to everyone around her.

In Harriet Adams's lifetime, Nancy became less "bossy," but the real changes happened after her death in 1982. The new Nancy Drew books, written in the 1980s, were quite different from the originals. Nancy's looks, which had been called merely attractive in the original series, were given much elaboration. Her housekeeper, once a remote servant, behaves like a fussing mother. Adults supervise her in ways they never did before. Altogether, as *Ms.* magazine said in 1992, "The symbol of female independence was replaced by a Barbie doll detective."

Saving Women's Lives: Feminist Biography

Her choice was a life of her own making, just as that life of her youth and young
womanhood had been of her making out of whatever resources were available.
Thadious M. Davis on Nella Larsen

In 1915, Laura Howe Richards and her sister, Maude Howe Elliott, became the first women to win the Pulitzer Prize for biography for the life of Julia Ward Howe, their mother. They set quite a precedent.

Biography is part of the rescue mission and the rethinking of history. Simply to say a woman's life is worth writing about is itself a feminist act, but the volume of biographies in the past twenty years has gone beyond expanding what we mean by American history, just by putting women in the record. What has been taboo in the past is less so now. The new biographies include sophisticated understanding of sexism and racism, gender construction, the importance and range of women's connections with each other, the politics of sexual abuse, and madness. Some call it pathology; some call it truth.

Painters and Sculptors

"

This is so good you would not know it was done by a woman.

"

Painter Hans Hofmann to his student, Lee Krasner, late 1930s

Most women paint as though they are trimming hats . . . Not you.
Edouard Degas to Mary Cassatt, 1877

I have had to go to men as sources in my painting because the past has left us so small an inheritance of woman's painting that had widened life. . . . Before I put a brush to canvas I question, "Is this mine? Is it all intrinsically of myself? Is it influenced by some idea or some photograph of an idea which I have acquired from some man?"
Georgia O'Keeffe, 1930

When a woman decides to be a painter—a decision for which, until the past few years, there has been no precedent—she assumes the primary responsibility for her life. She becomes responsible for her perceptual, emotional and intellectual experience. . . . Every coffee cup she places on every table, every table on every rug, in relation to every floor, has meaning for her. Everything in her life becomes a part of her perceptual encyclopedia.
Miriam Schapiro, 1977

I'd rather risk an ugly surprise than rely on things I know I can do.
Painter Helen Frankenthaler

Lee Krasner, 1950

Sarah Miriam Peale

Peale supported herself for sixty years doing portraits. The daughter of a well-known painter father with progressive views about women, she moved in prominent circles, giving her access to portrait commissions. Never married, the first woman artist with an independent and successful career, she spent her last decades living with her sisters: Anna, a miniaturist, and Margaretta, a painter of still lifes. The female Peales showed their work at the Pennsylvania Academy of Fine Arts, which was clearly hospitable to women. Cecilia Beaux, another successful painter, was appointed the first female instructor there in 1895 and Mary Cassatt studied at the academy before moving to Paris.

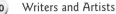
Lily Martin Spencer

Spencer's mother was a feminist and she grew up surrounded by political activists. Raised on the revolutionary talk of Stanton, Anthony, and their allies, it is not surprising, though certainly unusual in any time, that Spencer married a man who took over the domestic work of the household. This included the care of the seven children out of thirteen who survived. Famous as a painter of domestic scenes, her fresh take on homelife in *The Young Husband: First Marketing* (1854) is unique in its time.

"The White Mamorean Flock" in Rome

Europe mattered a lot in the nineteenth century; an art education depended on it. Expatriate American female sculptors gathered in Rome, drawn by the artistic treasures, abundant marble, and superb stonecutters, and perhaps also by a better attitude than they found at home.

Vicki Ream, whose statue of Abraham Lincoln was made when she was 17 (in spite of Mary Todd Lincoln's disapproval) was there.

So was Adelaide Johnson, who went home to be an active feminist and unofficial sculptor of the women's movement. Guides in the U.S. Capitol would refer, later, to Johnson's busts of Susan B. Anthony, Lucretia Mott, and Elizabeth Cady Stanton on a rough-hewn marble base as "The Ladies in the Bathtub." Soon after its donation to the government, the sculpture was stored in the Capitol's basement.

The famous cropped-haired, pants-wearing Harriet Hosmer was there, and the half-Chippewa half-black Edmonia Lewis.

Henry James called them a "strange sisterhood who at one time settled upon the seven hills in a white Marmorean flock."

Harriet Hosmer: Sculptor

I honor every woman who has the strength enough to step out of the beaten path when she feels that her walk lies in another. I honor all those who step boldly forward and, in spite of ridicule and criticism, pave a broader way for the women of the next generation.

Because his wife and three of their children had died of tuberculosis, Dr. Hiram Hosmer created a vigorous outdoor regimen to ensure his surviving daughter's health. "Hatty" developed "powers of great endurance" and became a fiercely willful tomboy. The local school declared her incorrigible, but the celebrated actress Charlotte Cushman, friend of Dr. Hosmer, admired the sculpting Harriet had begun and paid her way to study in Rome.

In 1856, she sold a piece to the Prince of Wales. Within ten years, she had her own palatial studio, a staff of male stonecutters, and as many commissions as she could handle.

She cropped her hair short to keep it free of marble dust, and wore a man's shirt and baggy trousers so that she could climb a scaffold. Nathaniel Hawthorne, in Rome writing *The*

Marble Faun, admired her lack of falseness and gave her "full leave to wear what may suit her best, and to behave as her inner woman prompts."

Her inner woman prompted heroic sculptures of female figures. Of *Zenobia in Chains*, Hawthorne said, the "high, heroic ode . . . revealed a soul so much above her misfortune."

1893: The Woman's Building and the Lost Murals of Mary Cassatt

The World's Columbian Exposition in Chicago in 1893 was a fair on a huge scale, literally a "White City," picketed for the very cultural whiteness it represented by Ida B. Wells, among others. The Woman's Building, run by a Board of Lady Managers, designed by architect Sophia Hayden, featured sculptures and architectural details by women inside and out, crafts of all kinds, painting, home design, and a library in the exhibition spaces.

Mary Cassatt's large mural, *Modern Woman*, hung high on the wall in the Great Hall, was nearly impossible to see. Its center section, "Women Picking the Fruits of Knowledge," done at a time of educational advances and a backlash claiming that knowledge would make women sick, shows remarkably robust female figures. Cassatt's work was disliked in the United States and this painting was not well received. It disappeared after the Exposition.

Janet Scudder: Sculptor

> I won't add to this obsession of male egotism that is ruining every city in the United States with rows of hideous statues of men—men—men—each one uglier than the other—standing, sitting, riding horseback—every one of them pompously convinced that he is decorating the landscape.

A tomboy, uninterested in female pursuits, Scudder worked her way through Cincinnati's Art Academy and worked as a woodcarver, but the carver's union, which forbade female members, forced her out. In Chicago, she was one of a small group of female assistants helping sculptor Lorado Taft prepare for the World's Columbian Exposition of 1893.

She made her way to Paris and then New York. An architect offered a phony commission for a lamppost design, but only wanted to seduce her. The father of a rich friend saved her by getting her hired to design the seal for the New York Bar Association. Other jobs followed. She began to specialize in the new, popular genre of garden sculpture. Stanford White, leading architect and taste-maker, used her work to adorn the estates of his clients, including John D. Rockefeller.

At the height of her career, when she was asked to create a memorial to the poet Henry Wadsworth Longfellow, Scudder refused, with her pithy words about male egotism.

In 1915, she began work on *Femina Victrix*, a sleek female figure modeled on dancer Irene Castle, poised on a globe, holding a laurel wreath. The statue honored the suffrage movement.

Sculptor Vinnie Ream Hoxie at work on statue of Admiral David G. Farragut, 1881

Edmonia Lewis in undated photograph

Lois Mailou Jones: Painter

The first known important black female painter, Lois Mailou Jones, spent summers in Martha's Vineyard, where she met sculptor Meta Warwick Fuller and other artists and began to paint furiously. In 1930, she joined the art department at Howard University, where Elizabeth Catlett and Alma Thomas would come to study with her.

Louise Nevelson: Sculptor

Nevelson's Russian Jewish family came to America when she was six years old. Under the WPA during the 1930s, like many women artists, she worked as an assistant to Mexican muralist Diego Rivera. Her work went unrecognized for three decades, although her assemblages were at least a decade ahead of their time. The disdain and discouragement of the conventional art world that she overcame has become legendary. One male artist told her, "You know, Louise, you've got to have *balls* to be a sculptor."

Learning from Louise

Some men seem to have much greater physical strength in their work than some women have. Yet . . . Louise Nevelson's large black sculpture, Transparent Horizon, [was] recently installed at MIT by this magnificent seventy-six-year-old woman, aided, of course, by machines and workmen. It is extremely important to learn not only to envision and obtain, but also to *direct* whatever aid—physical, mental, or technological—is available.

Most of my students at Wellesley College are definitely afraid of the physical aspects of trying to make sculpture. . . . If I have taught these girls anything, it has to be that "massive is not masculine."

Alice Atkinson Lyndon, 1977

Harriet Hosmer with her statue of Senator Thomas Benton, 1868

Mary Cassatt, detail of mural, **Modern Woman,** *Woman's Building, World's Columbian Exposition, Chicago, 1893*

Does Size Matter?

Writers and artists made similar revolutions. Like the Amazonian efforts of athletes and the ambitious literary undertakings of the time, a visual monumentality became almost common. Painter Helen Frankenthaler's canvases are often nine feet long. Nevelson's steel sculpture for the San Francisco Embarcadero is over fifty feet high. In Los Angeles, Judith F. Baca began a mural program in 1974 that would eventually involve 1,000 crew members making over 250 murals in a ten-year period.

Judy Chicago

Because we are denied knowledge of our history, we are deprived of standing upon each other's shoulders and building upon each other's hard earned accomplishments. Instead we are condemned to repeat what others have done before us and thus we continually reinvent the wheel. The goal of *The Dinner Party* is to break this cycle.

In 1970, at California State University at Fresno, Judy Chicago organized what is probably the first feminist art course. A year later, she and painter Miriam Schapiro created the Feminist Art Program at the California Institute for the Arts. In 1972, Chicago, Schapiro, and students showed the world *Womanhouse*, an abandoned Los Angeles house remodeled into a female fantasy environment, including a "menstruation bathroom."

For five years, she worked on what would become *The Dinner Party*, a feminist reinterpretation of *The Last Supper*, honoring great women who contributed to our cultural history but, instead of being cherished, were ignored, maligned, or obscured. The installation consists of an enormous triangular table and 39 place settings with round plates (many with labial connotations), a chalice, and a stitched runner. Hundreds of women and several men did the ceramics and embroidery.

May Stevens, Mysteries and Politics, showing the spiritual and political factions of the feminist art movement, including painter Buffy Johnson (kneeling) and Betsey Damon (dressed as 2,000-year-old woman, crouching), 1978

Tomie Arai and Lower East Side Women, Wall of Respect for Women, New York City, 1974

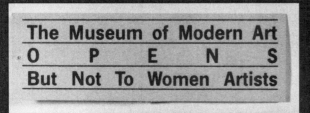

The Museum of Modern Art OPENS But Not To Women Artists

Badge worn by Women's Caucus for Art demonstrators in New York City to satirize the Museum of Modern Art's exclusion of women artists from its international show, 1984. Of 165 artists, only 14 were women.

Judy Chicago's collaborative,
The Dinner Party, *1979*

Lorraine O'Grady, performance piece, **Mademoiselle Bourgeoise Noire Goes to the New Museum,** *protesting exclusion of minority artists, New York City, 1981*

MLLE BOURGEOISE NOIRE GOES TO THE NEW MUSEUM TO REMEDY BEING OMITTED FROM THE NINE-WHITE-PERSONAE SHOW

No art event has aroused as much controversy. Thousands came to see it. Many exulted, others scoffed. In 1990, without looking at the work, the U.S. House of Representatives refused to authorize space for permanent housing of *The Dinner Party* in Washington, D.C., calling it a prime example of obscenity in art. A fundraising drive to house the project independently began in 1996.

Contesting Public Space

➣ In 1875, prominent New England sculptor Anne Whitney won an anonymous competition to sculpt Senator Charles Sumner. When the jury learned the winner was female, they withdrew the commission. She persisted, and her statue was eventually unveiled in Harvard Square.

◅ In 1987, architecture professor Dolores Hayden, noting that 98 percent of the landmarks in the City of Los Angeles honored Anglo-American history and 96 percent of them honored men, created a space of public tribute to former slave Biddy Mason. Having sued for her freedom in the early nineteenth century, Mason became a midwife, one of the first African-American landowners in the city, and cofounder of the local First African Methodist Episcopal Church. Two permanent installations honor her: Betye Saar's work in a window frame and an eighty-foot-long, eight-foot-high black concrete wall of graphics by Sheila de Bretteville.

➣ Amid much controversy, twenty-one-year-old student Maya Ying Lin won a national competition to design the Vietnam Veteran's Memorial in Washington, D.C., which was unveiled in 1982. Her acclaimed Civil Rights Memorial in Montgomery, Alabama followed.

◅ The Vietnam Women's Memorial in the capital, the first to honor military women, took a decade to bring to fruition. With money raised by a former army nurse, the Santa Fe artist Glenna Goodacre dedicated her monument on Veterans Day, 1993.

Race and the Female Artist

◅ When Meta Vaux Warwick, who trained at the Pennsylvania School of Industrial Arts, got to Paris in 1899, her work impressed Auguste Rodin, but not the American Girls Club, which prevented her staying there because she was black. Warwick overcame and caused a stir when she returned home and began showing work described as "morbid," "strong," and "grim and terrible," work apparently about racial agony. Her sculptures were destroyed in a fire in 1910.

➣ Lois Mailou Jones had a white friend submit a painting she did to a competition at the Corcoran Gallery in Washington, D.C., in 1941. When the work won a prize, the white woman picked it up. Jones waited two years to claim the credit.

◅ White critic Lucy Lippard and black artist Faith Ringgold started the Ad Hoc Committee to confront women's exclusion from the official art world. In 1970, to protest the all-white-male annual show at the Whitney Museum in New York, the group spilled eggs and tampons all over the museum's clean floors and staged a sit-down in the middle of the opening.

➣ Forty percent of the artists in the 1993 Whitney Biennial were female and more than a third were people of color.

Sylvia Sleigh, **The Turkish Bath,** *with naked male art critics including Laurence Alloway (reclining) and John Perrault (cross-legged), 1973*

Photographers

I went to Europe because I had to.
Berenice Abbott

I implore you to believe this is true.
Note to her editor accompanying Margaret Bourke-White's photographs of survivors at Buchenwald, 1945

If anybody gets in my way when I am making a picture, I become irrational. I'm never sure what I am going to do, or sometimes even aware of what I do—only that I want that picture.
Margaret Bourke-White

There are things which nobody would see unless I photographed them.
Diane Arbus

Landmarks of Art Activism

1969: When women learn that the radical Art Workers' Coalition in New York, which protests museum policies, U.S. intervention in Southeast Asia, and racism, is planning to demonstrate over the exclusion from major art institutions of minority males only, they leave to form Women Artists in Revolution.

1970: Demonstrations at New York art museums.

First feminist art class organized by Judy Chicago at California State University at Fresno.

Artist Faith Ringgold and her daughter, Michele Wallace, launch Women, Students and Artists for Black Art Liberation, an early step in the black arts movement.

1971: The African-American Store Front Museum is founded in Jamaica, New York.

La Raza Graphic Center opens in San Francisco.

Feminist Art Program starts at California Institute of the Arts.

Because of feminist pressure, the usual five percent representation of women artists in the Whitney Museum annual rises to 22 percent.

1972: *Womanhouse,* a collaborative exhibition/installation and the first West Coast Conference of Women Artists A.I.R., a cooperative women's gallery, forms in New York, followed by one at the Women's Interart Center in New York and women's galleries in Chicago, Rhode Island, Philadelphia and elsewhere.

The Feminist Art Journal begins publishing.

1973: "Women Choose Women" show in New York.

Woman's Building opens in Los Angeles, housing, among other groups, the Feminist Studio Workshop and the Center for Feminist Art Historical Studies.

Women's cooperative galleries Artemisia and ARC open in Chicago and Soho 20 in New York.

1974: Women's Caucus for Art forms as an offshoot of the College Art Association

1976: Great Wall of Los Angeles, mural project, begun by Judy Baca.

Women Artists: 1550-1950, the largest exhibit of its kind in history, opens at the Los Angeles County Museum of Art and travels to other mainstream institutions, including the Brooklyn Museum in New York City.

1977: First issues of *Heresies* and *Chrysalis,* journals of art and politics.

Alice Austen: the Female World of Love and Ritual

Unlike the other women pioneers, Alice Austen did not leave home or make money, but she did make the most accomplished and daring pictures of her era, developing and printing them herself, using the outdoor pump to wash prints.

Beginning in the 1880s, she photographed the wealthy Staten Island, New York, world around her: horse races, tennis matches, and most particularly what historian Carol Smith-Rosenberg would later call, in the context of social history, "the female world of love and ritual." Austen's playful rituals caught on camera—pictures of female courtships, cross-dressing and masquerades—show nothing less than the very modern awareness of gender construction.

Good Guy: Oliver Jensen Rescues Alice Austen

In 1951, a young editor named Oliver Jensen found eighty-five-year-old Alice Austen confined to a wheelchair in a poorhouse ward. She had struggled since the stock market crash

1979: *The Dinner Party* opens at the San Francisco Museum of Modern Art.

1981: Whitney Annual has eighty-one artists, fifteen of them female.

1984: Museum of Modern Art in New York reopens with a major international show of 169 artists, 13 of whom are women.

1985: The Guerrilla Girls form in response to the Museum Of Modern Art show. "The conscience of the art world," they wear gorilla masks in public to protect their identities and answer to the names of women artists of the past, like Frida Kahlo or Romaine Brooks. Their witty informational posters and protests add a new twist to art activism and members say that channeling their anger keeps them from turning it back on themselves.

1991: SisterSerpents, a Chicago collective, presents the "Rattle Your Rage" exhibit. The opening poster says: "For all you folks who consider a fetus more valuable than a woman: Have a fetus cook for you; Have a fetus affair; Have a fetus clean your house. . . ." The show includes images like Off with Their Heads: Revenge for Rape, by Maria Epes, in which three figures with exposed penises are shown, heads cut off.

Sixteen Asian-American artists form an activist group named Godzilla Girls, after the monster that ravages Tokyo in a classic Japanese movie.

1992: Many artists are among the founders of The Women's Action Coalition, an activist political group created in response to women's anger over the Anita Hill–Clarence Thomas confrontation in the Senate. Starting in New York, WAC spreads to other cities and to

Europe. WAC and Guerrilla Girls protest the Guggenheim Museum's Soho branch, which includes no women in its inaugural show. At the last minute, museum officials agree to include Louise Bourgeois along with the male artists.

1994: Two-part "Bad Girls" exhibition of feminist art at New Museum of Contemporary Art, New York.

1995: The Museum of Modern Art invites painter Elizabeth Murray to organize a show of modern women artists. Among the Americans included are: Lee Krasner, Barbara Chase Riboud, Elaine de Kooning, Grace Hartigan, Anne Ryan, and Jennifer Bartlett. Murray calls the show "a payback" for women artists whose struggles paved the way for her work. "The gender thing," she claims, "doesn't play any more. It's just about making art. People are interested in what women have to say."

Alice Austen, **Trude Eccleston and I Masked, Short Skirts,** *photograph taken at St. John's Rectory on Staten Island, New York, 1891*

of 1929, when all her family money was lost, losing the battle against poverty in 1945, when she was evicted from the house her grandparents had bought a century before. Jensen salvaged 3,500 photographs languishing in the basement of the local historical society. He also salvaged the photographer, publishing her work and using the money to move her to a comfortable nursing home. She died there in June 1952.

Frances Benjamin Johnston

Frances Benjamin Johnston, perhaps the first in a line of women artists better known for her personal notoriety than she was for her work, published her pictures in popular magazines in the 1890s and wrote articles urging women to enter the field of photography. Her contemporaries noted that she drank beer, smoked, and daringly showed her ankles. At the turn of the century, the slightly notorious Johnston was photographing in coal and iron mines, in fac-

Frances Benjamin Johnston, Self-Portrait, 1897

tories and among poor black families in the south. Her work knew no class boundaries: Mrs. Grover Cleveland, cabinet wives, student carpenters at the Hampton Institute. One of the first women to do architectural photography, she infuriated the customers at the estates of Morgans, Whitneys, and Astors by ushering them out of their own homes while she was working. Her eccentricities included taking a woman named Mattie Edward Hewitt as her working partner—perhaps more; nothing is known of Johnston's private life. In her sixties and seventies, she became the foremost recorder of early American architecture.

Gertrude Kasebier

The leading female photographer in the first decade of the twentieth century, Kasebier didn't take up photography until her three children were grown. After claiming for herself the freedom to travel and earn money independent of her husband, she eventually set up a successful portrait photography business in New York in 1897. Her best known works are portraits of mothers and children, but the sexual politics of taste might well have determined their popularity. She also was drawn to photographing talented women like the Native American activist Zitkala-Sa and the heiress-reformer Theodate Pope, friend of Mary Cassatt. Kasebier made advanced, unstereotyped pictures of Native Americans, whom she had known in her youth. Many of her sitters were provided by Buffalo Bill's Wild West Show.

Kasebier was encouraged by the most powerful person in the early days of the fledgling art form. Edward Stieglitz admired and publicized her work, along with that of many other female photographers. She, in turn, became a mentor to Laura Gilpin, America's first female landscape photographer, who, at the age of eighty-eight, flew low over the Rio Grande Valley in a small plane, leaning out the window to make her final photographs.

Kate Cory and the Hopi

From 1905 to 1921, photographer Kate Cory did what no one had done before or since. Daughter of an abolitionist family, former student of painting, she lived in Hopi villages on the Arizona mesas, achieving an intimacy and trust with the people there that make her pictures unique. Working in isolation, she developed her negatives in a primitive darkroom, using rainwater. Unlike Edward S. Curtis, who dressed and posed his subjects, Cory's camera recorded people as they really were.

Contesting Public Space: Berenice Abbott

Abbott left a visual record of the circle of American lesbians, like bookstore owner Sylvia Beach, who exiled themselves to Paris in the 1920s to build a culture of their own that was the bedrock of avant-garde art and literature. Abbott's excursions with her camera in New York in the 1930s violated as many social restraints as Georgia O'Keeffe's paintings of the urban landscape did: "The men thought I'd lost my mind," O'Keeffe said, about the work of the late 1920s, "but I did it anyway."

Kate Cory photograph of Hopi women playing Ya-ha-ha, the ritual chase of a man, from Hopi series, 1905–12

Bourke-White: The Glamor Girl's Conversion

The glamorous Margaret Bourke-White, with a unique reputation for architectural and industrial photographs, was converted by a 1935 *Fortune* magazine assignment to cover the Dust Bowl. The suffering she saw and captured in the drought-ridden Midwest convinced her to use her camera as an agent for social change. "I could never again face a shiny automobile stuffed with vapid smiles," she said, leaving commercial work to travel among Southern sharecroppers with writer Erskine Caldwell, producing the book *We Have Seen Their Faces* in 1937.

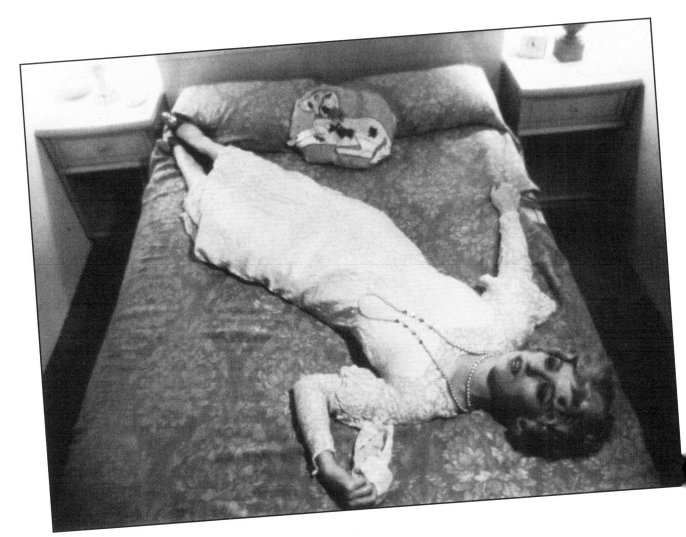

Cindy Sherman, **Untitled Film Still #11,** *1978*

The "Muses": Women Who Made Art Possible

Lilla Cabot Perry: Introducing Impressionism

Born to the socially prominent Lowell and Cabot families of Boston, married to a scholar, Lila Cabot Perry met Claude Monet in 1889 and spent the next ten summers in a house beside his, becoming his informal pupil. She was a respected American painter, but when she brought the first Monet home, no one liked it. She began an eventually successful campaign of public lecturing and private pressuring to publicize the new art.

Dorothy Dunn: Preserving Tradition

Dorothy Dunn founded the Art Studio at the Santa Fe Indian School in 1932. Contrary to attitudes about what constituted real art, she encouraged the Native Americans working there to retain their indigenous traditions.

Abby Aldrich Rockefeller: Valuing Americana

In 1929, Abby Aldrich Rockefeller, Lizzie Bliss, and Mary Quinn Sullivan, spirited, rich partisans of the modern art first revealed at the Armory Show of 1913, created a gallery that became the Museum of Modern Art.

Although connoisseurs valued European artists above all others, Abby Aldrich Rockefeller also cared for American "folk art": "primitive" paintings, signs, weathervanes, and ceramics. She not only collected it herself, but founded the Folk Art Center in Williamsburg, Virginia, which has the most extensive collection in the country.

Monroe, Anderson, Heap: Making Modernism

Chicago poet Harriet Monroe was the founding editor of *Poetry* magazine (1912) and Margaret Anderson started *The Little Review* (1914), two publications responsible for promoting what was then avant-garde writing (H. D., T. S. Eliot, Ezra Pound, Mina Loy, Robert Lowell, William Carlos Williams) and is now simply American modernism. By 1916, Anderson was sharing editorship of *The Little Review* with her lover, writer Jane Heap. They moved to Paris, where *The Little Review* serialized James Joyce's novel *Ulysses* from 1918 until 1920, when the magazine was seized and they were arrested and tried for obscenity.

Gertrude Whitney: Antiestablishment Art

Gertrude Vanderbilt Whitney, serious sculptor and art patron, ran a gallery specializing in American moderns with her secretary, Juliana Force, in the 1920s. When the stalwart Metropolitan Museum turned down the offered collection, they opened a museum of their own—the Whitney Museum, in 1931. Force, who had no training, became a major crusader for the moderns and taste-maker in the art world.

Gertrude Stein, flanked by Claribel and Etta Cone, collectors of Mary Cassatt's painting, among others, June 26, 1903

The Pleasure of Isabella Stewart Gardener

"*C'est mon plasir*" was Gardener's motto, emblazoned over the doorway of her museum. A flamboyant figure in 1880s Boston, a billionaire bohemian, she competed ferociously to buy artwork and ranked with the Morgans and Fricks in the scope of European masterpieces she acquired. Although she belonged to a ladies' club that included painters like Cecilia Beaux, she mostly patronized young male painters. When she decided to house her impressive collection in a public museum, she took a strong hand in its design and construction and was the only woman of her time to direct every phase of its operation, even post-mortem. After her death in 1924, her will revealed that any change in her arrangement of furniture and displays would cause the entire collection to be dissolved. The only other female collector with such sureness of taste was Gertrude Stein.

Jesse Fauset: Renaissance Woman

As literary editor of *The Crisis* from 1912 to 1926, Jesse Fauset was responsible for bringing the literature of the Harlem Renaissance to a broad public and to recognizing the talent of Jean Toomer, Langston Hughes, and others before anyone else did.

Peggy Guggenheim and the Power of Money

She was an heiress in love with artists and although most of those she befriended were men, in the early 1920s, Guggenheim did help poet Mina Loy, photographer Berenice Abbott and some other women. During World War II, she arranged passage for painters, poets, and writers from Europe to America, changing the intellectual climate of New York. Her most extraordinary accomplishment was her gallery, Art of This Century, which opened in 1942. The series of exhibits of American art made history and so did the gallery itself, with its curved ultramarine blue canvas walls on which the paintings were suspended in air. When Guggenheim returned to Europe in 1947, the walls were sold to a Fifth Avenue department store.

Barbara Smith: What Can Happen at a Kitchen Table

In 1980, writers and activists Barbara Smith and Audre Lorde formed Kitchen Table Press, named for Smith's kitchen table, where it was conceived. *Home Girls: A Black Feminist Anthology* (1983), edited by Smith, and *This Bridge Called My Back: Writings by Radical Women of Color* (1981, 1983), edited by Cherrie Moraga and Gloria Anzaldua, published by the collective, gathered unpublished writing and presented what amounts to a new literature to the world. As the only source of this material, the books became critical in women's studies courses.

Josephine Baker, 1927

CHAPTER 6

Entertainers

Women of the stage all desire to vote.
Billboard headline, 1909

You don't own me. Nobody does. My life belongs to me.
Joan Crawford in Possessed, *1931*

Consider, if you can bear to imagine it, what might have been the result if singing, too, had been forbidden by law. Listen to the voices of Bessie Smith, Billie Holliday, Nina Simone, Roberta Flack and Aretha Franklin, among others, and imagine those voices muzzled for life.
Alice Walker, In Search of Our Mothers' Gardens, *1974*

Instead of saying "Do this," I say, "Darlings, Mother has a problem." Often I pretended to know less than I did. That way I got more cooperation.
Ida Lupino on her directing methods in the 1950s, on television shows Have Gun Will Travel *and* Gunsmoke

You Don't Own Me.
Song by Lesley Gore, 1963

I can play a heterosexual. I know how they walk. I know how they talk. You don't have to be one to play one.
Lily Tomlin

I've never seen a stuntman working who wasn't in black Reeboks, but women get thrown down stairs in a negligee and high heels. No room for kneepads there.
Linda Howard, President, Stuntwomen's Association of Motion Pictures, 1994

Madonna, 1987

" It is better to be looked over than overlooked. "

Mae West

Mae West and Edward Arnold in I'm No Angel, *1933*

A woman could always sing for her supper, no? She could kick in the chorus line, bat her mascara on celluloid, pass a hat on a street corner, or preen at a Los Angeles drugstore counter, waiting to be discovered. Show business has been a beacon for women, poor women in particular, for whom the star on the dressing room door represented the pot of gold and the promise of freedom and power.

But only certain women have qualified and only in certain ways. To make a living and/or a name as an entertainer, a woman needed a particular look, a way of appealing to "the male gaze." For most of American history, she had to be young, white, and "feminine" or an easy fit into an awaiting stereotype: a black mammy, a dragon lady, a vamp, a good girl.

Internally, she needed whatever it took to get along in the system, for as long as there has been a Broadway or a Hollywood, there has been a system. From Mary Pickford to Roseanne Barr, women have fought for the power to define entertainment, to hire and fire, to choose material, and dole out money. Mae West was one of the few to achieve autonomy, writing her own lines and making her own choices. "If he can talk, I'll take him," she said, seeing Cary Grant. Although she meant business, not romance, in the casting couch world of Hollywood, women who said what they would take were trouble.

> *B*ette Davis claimed to have invented the name Oscar for the Academy of Motion Picture awards. On seeing it for the first time, she said that it looked like her Uncle Oscar.

Female entertainers are mostly remembered for what they looked like, and usually confused with the roles they played: devil-may-care Clara Bow was actually tormented, frosty Grace Kelly was actually hot. Feminists, particularly in cultural studies and biographies, have begun to supply dimension to a cardboard history, revealing complexities and contradictions, writing a history in which performers know what they are doing, are makers, not just participants in culture. A performer now can be "read" as a text—the cross-eyed gestures of dancer Josephine Baker or the sexual strategies of Madonna.

Entertainment is serious business and women have been serious about it. As the quip goes: "Don't forget. Ginger Rogers did everything Fred Astaire did, backwards and in high heels." Many women did everything men did, under more difficult circumstances. They wrote, directed, and produced movies and plays, organized concerts, started unions. They used their celebrity and their art forms to stand up to demagogues, fight racism, and subvert sexism.

Theda Bara in Cleopatra, *1917*

Women, particularly tough, working-class girls and the daughters of immigrants, thrived in new forms of twentieth-century entertainment. The Ziegfeld Theatre sign said "Celebrating The American Girl" and the show was a stepping-stone to the movies for Barbara Stanwyck, Irene Dunne, and Paulette Goddard. Comedian Fanny Brice played Ziegfeld's Follies with her unique brand of singing and Yiddish schtick. Dancer Martha Graham made her debut in the Greenwich Village Follies of 1923.

After World War I, popular culture pushed the envelope about race and gender. Lesbian entertainers performed in Harlem, where sexual permissiveness and uptowners out "slumming" went hand in hand. The word *bulldaggers* entered the language in clubs where the blues were played. For a while, the doors seemed wide open for women. In 1920, there were as many women working as actresses as there were graduating from college.

Anita Loos advised readers in *How to Write a Photoplay* that the new form was "the most lucrative of all the various forms of literary effort." In a new business, its hierarchies scarcely defined, women moved from script girls or actors to directors and producers in ways unthinkable afterwards. It was not unusual to have a female writer-director-star team.

Throughout the Jazz Age, Hollywood blossomed with vamps and flappers, girls like Clara Bow who had what screenwriter Eleanor Glyn described as "It." Broadway tittered at raunchy plays written by and starring Mae West, who went to jail, silk underwear and all, for her transgressions. Blues singing divas like Bessie Smith, with real female sexual authority, transformed American music.

Glamor dust obscures the fact that entertainers were working women. Mary Pickford, the first movie star, won a part the day she arrived at D. W. Griffith's Biograph Studios in 1909 and negotiated a raise that afternoon. Gloria Swanson, a Mack Sennett bathing beauty in silent films, had Joseph Kennedy's money behind her when she set up her own production company. She was clever enough to maneuver around the industry's censorship code and courageous enough to film the shocking *Rain* (1927) in which an ex-prostitute exposes a clergyman's moral hypocrisy.

Unlike women in other jobs, who were laid off in the 1930s, entertainers worked. In the new medium of radio, women invented the enduring form of the soap opera. Betty Crocker's Cooking School of the Air was a hit on the radio for a decade. In clubs, all-women bands, invented as public relations gimmicks, turned out consummate musicians. The bands were hot until the end of the Second World War, when jazz pushed them out.

Just as Rosie the Riveter could work in factories during World War II, Sally the Screenwriter turned out the "women's pictures" that characterized the dream factories and Tillie the Trumpeter blew her horn without censure. Women together—in bands, in movies, in movie audiences—made a culture of their own while large chunks of the male population were away. Mary Margaret McBride became a celebrity with her daily morning show on the radio, mixing chatter, interviews, and plugs for sponsors.

When the men came home, the career girl movies starring Katharine Hepburn, Tallulah Bankhead, or Bette Davis stopped being made, tough vamps like Gloria Grahame and Barbara Stanwyck were pushed aside, and the Joan Crawford classics with their vicious daughters and vile husbands became history. Women were sent home again, in life and on the screen.

Hollywood women lost their power on the printed page at the same time they lost it on celluloid. It is no accident, film critic Julie Burchill says, that "The first films of the fifties— *Sunset Boulevard* and *All About Eve*—had the hatchet out for women, especially actresses." The women were still big, but the pictures got small.

In a country with strong roots in Puritanism, becoming an entertainer in any medium meant fighting against and changing what was considered the domain of prostitutes. Even classical musicians faced this obstacle. Although upper-class white women in the nineteenth

" How Can You Play a Horn with a Brassiere? "

Headline in Downbeat *magazine, April 1938*

century learned keyboards and instrumentals as part of their education, performing in public was out of the question. "Lady" orchestras played popular music in "disreputable" places like beer gardens and theaters. In 1888, Caroline B. Nichols founded a women's orchestra; there were thirty by the turn of the century.

Popular music was always more open to female performers, but less willing to give women any power. There were no female-owned record companies until lesbian-feminist Olivia Records set up to promote women's music in 1972, the same year Helen Reddy won a Grammy for her song, "I Am Woman." In the 1990s, obervers were saying it was more likely a woman would be President of the United States before one would run Sony Music.

For black women, however, whose musical education was often in church, show business was an option as early as the Civil War, when they were piano players in minstrel bands. By the early twentieth century, black female musicians appeared in theatres and cabarets as vocalists or pianists. The woman's blues in the 1920s added a new vocabulary to American popular music and offered an image of female sexuality never seen before. A woman who wanted to drum or blow the trumpet, a woman "born to swing," in Lil Hardin Armstrong's words, was something of an anomaly, but she would finally be able to swing in public and for money throughout the 1940s.

A white woman brought black women's music into the white mainstream, establishing, along the way, a tenuous place for women in the rock and roll counterculture of the 1960s. When Janis Joplin sang "Ball and Chain," written earlier in the decade by Big Mama Thornton, in the same year Diana Ross and the Supremes were appearing in wigs and evening dresses, she offered an alternative vision, a female performer with a lack of conventional visual and musical prettiness not heard in thirty years.

There has always been a counterculture, and women have always been part of it. Nineteenth-century feminists praised the theater for providing equitable pay for women, and actresses were among the first women to reveal and protest sexual harassment. In the early twentieth century, suffrage plays were an important part of the campaign for the vote. The radical political theater of the 1930s was almost entirely the work of women, especially Hallie Flanagan, a Vassar theater professor who transformed American theater in 1935 by designing and heading the Federal Theater Project. Giving out-of-work theater professionals needed jobs, Flanagan also produced some of the most relevant political dramas of the American stage, a heritage continued in the avant-garde of the 1960s by Judith Malina at the Living Theater and Ellen Stewart at LaMama.

Still, twenty-five years after the women's movement was reborn, women in Hollywood are told that making too many films about women will brand them as lesbians, a bad idea. And the crass sexual harassment of early years has merely changed shape. Paula Weinstein, producer of *The Fabulous Baker Boys*, says today's sexual harassment is subtle, not "a guy jerking off at your desk," but "a constant peeling away of one's sense of authority, position and responsibility."

Peeling away, perhaps, in all entertainment media, but not erasing. Performers who began in the feminist counterculture have appealed to increasingly large audiences—from Roseanne Barr's domestic goddess stand-up comedy to Lily Tomlin's monologues to Laurie Anderson's performance pieces.

Movies

Kiss me, you fool.
Theda Bara in A Fool There Was, *1915*

She made a pass at me.
Louise Brooks on Greta Garbo

Irving Thalberg used to tell me: "When you write a love scene, think of your heroine as a little puppy dog, cuddling up to her master, wagging an imaginary tail, and gazing up at him as if he were God."
Anita Loos, Kiss Hollywood Goodbye

I can be smart when it's important, but men don't like it.
Marilyn Monroe in Some Like It Hot, *1959*

We must have naked breasts in this movie four times. I don't care how you do it. I just want naked breasts.
Producer Irving Azoff to director Martha Coolidge, about Valley Girl, *1983*

I have a head for business and a bod for sin. Is there anything wrong with that?
Melanie Griffith in Working Girl, *1988*

The Good Old Days

More females worked at all levels in the early days of movies, radio, and television than they do today. Although no woman producer won an Oscar until Julia Phillips in 1973 for *The Sting* and no female director has yet won, from the turn of the century until 1920, pioneer

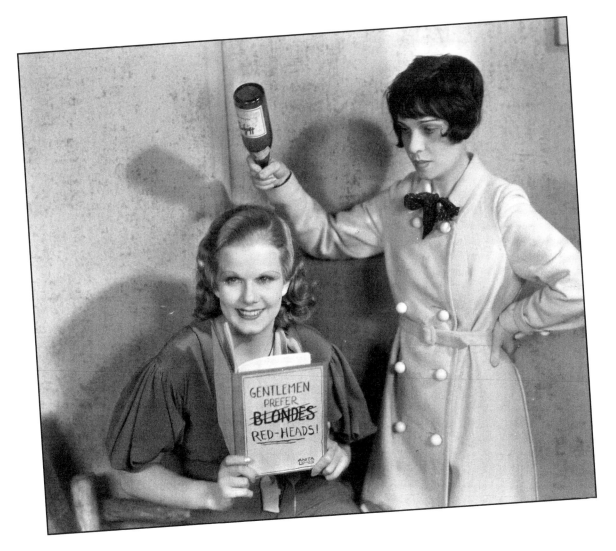

Jean Harlow and Anita Loos in "stunt" photo for Loos's film, Red-Headed Woman, *in which blonde Harlow plays the title role, 1932*

female producers and directors crowded the silent film lots and women outnumbered men as screenwriters ten to one. Today, the ratio of male to female screenwriters is four to one.

When Hollywood Was Female

Florence Lois Weber, the first female director and the highest paid one in silent films, was a former street evangelist. With her husband, she experimented in sound twenty years before the first talking picture. Most of her films were about controversial social issues.

June Mathis, at twenty-seven, ran the scenario department at Metro Pictures by 1918. She discovered Rudolph Valentino. *Blood and Sand* (1922), adapted by Mathis and edited by Dorothy Arzner, made him a matinee idol. By 1923, she was the highest paid woman in the industry. She produced *Sea Beast* (1926), writer Bess Meredyth's interpretation of *Moby-Dick*, and was the only person able to adapt Eric Von Stroheim's *Greed*, reducing seven hours to two, as the studio wanted. She died at thirty-five.

> Sally: You dropped your fur.
> Lil: Oh, it's only a silver fox.
> Sally: Haven't you got a gold one?
> Lil: No. Well, I might have this one plated.
>
> *Red-Headed Woman,* film script by Anita Loos, 1932

Adele Buffington, a former Fort Wayne, Indiana, movie theater cashier, wrote more than 150 Westerns, including the Tom Mix series, starting in 1919.

Ida May Park, a director at Universal, started her own production company in 1920. Most of her output is lost.

Lillian Gish, the biggest star of the silents, directed her sister Dorothy in *Remodeling Her Husband* in 1920 and campaigned to lift the ban on filming *The Scarlet Letter*.

Lotte Reiniger, a twenty-four-year-old producer, made the first fully animated feature, *The Adventures of Prince Achmed* (1923).

Frances Marion wrote over 130 movies, including most of Mary Pickford's films, winning the second and third Oscars ever presented for screenwriting. One of the first female war correspondents, she returned to Hollywood after World War I to start her own company, making the transition to talking pictures with *Anna Christie, Dinner at Eight,* and *Camille.*

Clara Bow, a poor teenager from Brooklyn, completely captured the spirit of the time between 1922 and 1930. She was *Flaming Youth*, a wisecracking cross between a tomboy and a vamp.

Anita Loos wrote over 100 movie scripts, beginning with *The New York Hat* (1912), starring Mary Pickford and Lionel Barrymore, and the titles for D. W. Griffith's *Intolerance* (1916). She wrote five of Jean Harlow's films and, with playwright Jane Murfin, did the screen adaptation of Claire Booth Luce's *The Women*, a classic. Edith Wharton called Loos's book *Gentlemen Prefer Blondes* (1926) the great American novel.

Dorothy Arzner directed Clara Bow in *The Wild Party* (1927), a female buddy movie that was Paramount's first talkie. On this set, she invented the boom microphone. The longest-working and most-respected female director in Hollywood, she had short hair and mannish attire. Her career, only recently unearthed by feminist researchers, included Katharine Hepburn's *Christopher Strong* (1933), major films with Rosalind Russell and Joan Crawford, and training films for the Women's Army Corps during World War II.

Constructing a Star: Gender as Performance

> I had played a manicurist in 500-dollar beaded evening dresses; a salesgirl in 300-dollar black satin afternoon dresses; and a schoolgirl in 250-dollar tailored suits.
> *Silent film star Louise Brooks*

Little Girls: An American Institution

Although early Hollywood had ambitious, hardworking, complex, interesting women around, they didn't show up on screen. Fueled by the predilections of men like D. W. Griffith and Charlie Chaplin, whose preferred love objects were young girls, the image of women in the movies was shaped by the 1914 *Perils of Pauline*, financed by William Randolph Hearst.

Mary Pickford played children until she was in her thirties. The first generation of vamps and flappers, like Clara Bow, were teenagers. Shirley Temple, top star in the late 1930s, debuted at age four. Elizabeth Taylor, Judy Garland, Brooke Shields, and Jodie Foster were preadolescent when they started working and each had to fight to be allowed to grow up, to become women, on-screen. Pickford and Taylor had their breasts bound for filming.

On radio and television, women acting like silly children were stock figures, but some performers turned the act into a lucrative and subversive career. Comedian Fanny Brice played the imaginative, mischievous, and decidedly unnymphetlike Baby Snooks on the radio throughout the 1930s and 1940s. In her hands, the child role allowed a freedom of expression that was denied adult females. Lily Tomlin's Edith Ann could well be Baby Snooks's granddaughter.

Lily Tomlin as Edith Ann on **Laugh-In,** *c. 1968*

Elizabeth Taylor in
Courage of Lassie, 1946

Fanny Brice as Baby
Snooks, 1930s

≪ Fanny Brice's nose straightening in 1923 was front page news. One of the most ethnic early performers, she would appear in a gorgeous Madame Du Barry costume, wave a fan, then say in a thick Yiddish accent: "I'm a bad voman, but I'm demm good company." Brice, who had learned the accent, not having grown up with Yiddish, wasn't as happy with her Jewish nose as observers wished she had been. Dorothy Parker said Brice "cut off her nose to spite her race."

≫ When little Mary Pickford cut off her long golden curls in 1929—she was thirty-six years old—leaving a modern, grown-up, Jazz Age bob, her public nearly rioted in anger. "You would think," she said, "I had murdered someone—and in a sense, I had."

≪ Marilyn Monroe often talked candidly about how she constructed the character called Marilyn. Her sashaying walk was created by sawing a piece off the heel of one shoe.

≫ Joan Crawford had her back teeth removed to make her cheekbones more prominent.

≪ Rita Hayworth was nothing special as a screen presence until she dyed her hair red. Jean Harlow's platinum hair was her trademark, but when she died of uremic poisoning, many people believed that the chemicals used to bleach her hair had killed her.

≫ Big band horn players worried about smearing their lipstick until they discovered Mercurochrome.

≪ Judy Garland first got addicted to drugs when the studio gave her diet pills to keep her thin. "I always swore I wouldn't end up like Judy," Elizabeth Taylor said.

≫ Louise Beavers was always being told to gain more weight so she could play black mammys in the movies.

≪ Lauren Hutton had trouble getting modeling jobs because of the gap between her front teeth. Eventually, she used undertaker's wax to seal it up. When she let her teeth go natural, the gap became her trademark, seen by advertisers as an all-American look.

Women, Race, and Movies

Some people hurl themselves in front of a train. I hurled myself in front of another white man.
Dorothy Dandridge

Beulah, peel me a grape.
Mae West

Nobody's going to turn this thing into a minstrel show.
Lorraine Hansberry, holding out for some artistic control when she sold Raisin in the Sun *to Hollywood*

Hattie McDaniel and Bette Davis in The Great Lie, 1941

⊰ D. W. Griffith adapted *Ramona*, a romantic novel by Helen Hunt Jackson about the California mission Indians, into a silent film starring Mary Pickford.

⊱ The bee-stung lips of glamorous film stars in the 1920s, which have returned in the collagen-enhanced lips of some stars today, were clearly influenced by black women's looks.

⊰ Sophie Tucker sang in blackface, as did Eddie Cantor and Al Jolson in the 1920s. At the end of Tucker's stomping blues act, she would peel off her glove and wave to the crowd to show she was white.

⊱ Hattie McDaniel, who occasionally played drums with Kansas City bands, was the first black actress to win an Academy Award, for her role as mammy in *Gone with the Wind*. She refused to go to the film's premiere in segregated Atlanta.

⊰ For all her liberated sexual assertiveness, Mae West did not use her wit to turn the tables on racial stereotypes. In *I'm No Angel* (1933), she gets laughs by saying imperiously to her black maid, "Beulah, peel me a grape."

⊱ In 1943, Lena Horne signed a contract with MGM, becoming the first black performer to have a long-term contract with a major studio.

⊰ In 1937, *The Good Earth* had white stars made up to look Chinese. Katharine Hepburn played a Chinese woman in *Dragon Seed* (1944). Glenn Close and Meryl Streep play Chileans in *The House of the Spirits* (1995).

⊱ In her 37-year career, in over 100 films, Chinese-American actor Anna May Wong played mainly China Dolls and Dragon Ladies. In 1935, turned down for the central role of O-lan in *The Good Earth*, which went to white actor Luise Rainer, Wong refused the offered role of a vindictive concubine.

Anna Mae Wong guards the door against a villian's advances, 1930s

≫ Nancy Kwan starred in *The World of Suzie Wong* (1960), and *Flower Drum Song* (1961).

≪ Powerful Harry Cohn at Columbia Pictures refused to groom Judy Holliday for stardom, shouting, "You're joking! Films are made for Jews and by Jews—not WITH JEWS."

≫ Until well into the 1960s, blacks who didn't play servants were cut out of films for the Southern market.

≪ Dorothy Dandridge was the first African-American nominated for Best Actress, for her work in *Carmen Jones*, an all-black musical released in 1954. She starred in three interracial love stories, including *Island in the Sun* and, in 1958, *Porgy and Bess*.

≫ Cicely Tyson made *Sounder* and *The Autobiography of Miss Jane Pittman* in the 1960s, breaking out of the stereotypes that limited black women for six decades and becoming a movie star for the civil rights generation.

≪ Anita Loos talked about writing a black version of *Gentlemen Prefer Blondes*, to be called *Gentlemen Prefer Bronze*, starring Flip Wilson as Dorothy Shaw.

Dorothy Dandridge in Carmen Jones, *1954*

What El Colon (the Spanish-speaking movie theater) gave us was passion, another form of possibility and way of living. Crying with Dolores [Del Rio] or Pedro [Infante], laughing with Cantinflas, I embraced my mother and her dreams, as well as those of all my people, the Mexicans and Mexican-Americans of La Frontera. . . . We were brothers and sisters united in our world away from the Plaza Theater, with its stately red carpets and elegant balustrades, where red-costumed blond ticket-takers greeted you in crisp English and promised you, at least momentarily, the great American dream. Somehow in Spanish, our dreams seemed purer.
Denise Chavez, The McCoy Hotel, *1991*

In the eyes of many Anglos, the diverse Latino cultures are interchangeable. Thus, Hollywood will create absurdities such as Cubans eating tacos or Anglo actors cast in Latino roles only because they have dark hair and a tan.
Delia Poey and Virgin Suarez, Iguana Dreams, *1992*

KATHARINE HEPBURN: TROUBLEMAKER

Her mother was a suffragist and birth control activist. In 1934, the Philadelphia Social Register dropped Mrs. Ogden Ludlow, as Katharine Hepburn was then known, for performing in movies. She had taken her career into her own hands, optioning the rights to *The Philadelphia Story*, doing it as a play and then a smash movie. Her films, featuring strong, independent women—usually tamed by the story line—coupled with her fights with the studios over her right to wear pants in public, have made Hepburn one of the most popular screen women of all time.

The Hepburn Canon

In *Little Women* (1933), she plays Jo with the spunk that made her famous.

In *Sylvia Scarlett* (1935), she is a young woman disguised as a man and forced to reexamine her sexuality. The daring film, written by feminist Gladys Unger, was toned down during rewrites. Nobody toned down the scene in which Hepburn is kissed by a woman who thinks she is a man.

In *Christopher Strong* (1933), she is an aristocratic daredevil aviatrix reminiscient of Amelia Earhart. In love with a married man, she crashes her plane rather than tell him she is pregnant.

In *A Woman Rebels* (1936), Hepburn plays an unmarried mother and fighter for women's rights in Victorian England.

In *Woman of the Year* (1942), Spencer Tracy is a sportswriter, she is a journalist, and she gets tamed.

In *Adam's Rib* (1949), she and Tracy are husband and wife lawyers on opposite sides of a murder trial.

Pat and Mike (1952) opens with her boyfriend saying, "You're not going to wear pants, are you?" and sending all-around athlete Hepburn into the arms of small-time but supportive sports manager Tracy.

Mae West

As George Raft's girlfriend in *Night After Night* (1932), she sashays into a nightclub, stopping at the coat check, where the girl says, "Goodness, what beautiful diamonds." She replies: "Goodness has nothing to do with it, dearie."

She wrote the line herself, as she would do for most of her movies—and as she had done for the plays that brought her notoriety before she got to Hollywood. In the 1920s, her Broadway play *Sex* got her sent to jail, where she was allowed to keep her silk underwear. Released

Katharine Hepburn in **Christopher Strong, 1937**

for "being good" before her ten days had been served, she wrote a series of articles about prison, donating the money to her sister inmates.

Unlike the simpering girls tied to railroad tracks waiting to be rescued, the characters West played never suffered. She made men suffer. Some said she was a man, a female impersonator, or that she had learned her exaggerated mannerisms from a drag queen. She was forty, an older woman, when she started making movies, seducing young boys and old men on the screen.

Not everybody thought her wonderful or even acceptable. In 1936, when West criticized Marion Davies, the public girlfriend of William Randolph Hearst, his newspapers called her "a menace to the sacred institution of the American family." The following year, a radio skit about Adam and Eve caused an uproar, particularly her delivery when she called the serpent "swivel hips." She was barred from radio.

In the 1960s, she turned down an Elvis Presley picture because she would not be allowed to write her own lines. Close to eighty, she appeared in the film *Myra Breckenridge* (1970). One of the last lines she wrote was addressed to a room full of eager young men: "I'm a little tired tonight. One of you boys will have to go home."

Blondes and Brunettes

∽ At the height of the Silent Era, as the country worried about foreigners undermining the republic, a Jewish-American girl named Thodosia Goodman appeared as the screen's first sexpot. Theda Bara, they called her, passing her off as French-Egyptian. (Her last name is *Arab* spelled backward.) An entirely contrived exotic, she starred in forty films in four years, playing up her fake exoticism off-screen by conducting all her interviews in black velvet rooms with incense burning.

∽ Blonde Jean Harlow played urban, working-class girls. In *Red Dust* (1932), she is a stranded prostitute, played off against the dark Clark Gable and the good girl/wifey Mary Astor.

∽ Before the fifties, there was no blonde fever. Fifties blondes include the innocent Doris Day and the classy but frosty Grace Kelly.

∽ Critic Julie Burchill says that "Hitchcock spiritually spawned the current crop of Americans to whom women are things to be hurt, hunted and hacked to death." Mostly, these are blondes. The bad blondes who get punished in Hitchcock films are Tippi Hedren in *The Birds*, Janet Leigh in *Psycho*, and Kim Novak in *Vertigo*.

∽ In 1954, Dorothy Dandridge, the first black woman nominated for an Oscar, lost the Best Actress competition to Grace Kelly, who won for her role in *The Country Girl*.

∽ During the 1953 making of *Gentlemen Prefer Blondes*, the brunette Jane Russell (paid $100,000 for the role) befriended Marilyn Monroe (paid $18,000 for her role) in life as well as on-screen. When actor Tommy Noonan complained that Monroe "kissed like a vacuum cleaner," Russell stepped in to comfort her. Director Howard Hawks said that the film might never have been made if Russell hadn't taken care of Monroe.

∽ The pivotal scene in *Sabrina* (1954) hinges on the contrast between the brunette, elegant, gamine Audrey Hepburn and her nemesis, the blonde Martha Hyer, ostentatious, overdone, wearing a fussy dress with a plunging bodice.

∽ Madonna is the first performer to live and work equally successfully as a switch-hitter, blonde and brunette.

Kim Novak and Rita Hayworth surround Frank Sinatra in Pal Joey, *1957*

Jane Russell and Marilyn Monroe in
Gentlemen Prefer Blondes, 1953

Carole Lombard on wartime
cover of Photoplay, 1940s

Lauren Bacall and other actors on Capitol Hill protesting the tactics of the House Un-American Activities Committee's investigation into alleged Communism in Hollywood, 1947

Movie Star Scandals: Cherchez la Femme

⤜ In 1949, Norwegian-born Ingrid Bergman had an out-of-wedlock child with Italian director Roberto Rossellini. There was an outcry across America, including denunciation on the floor of the U.S. Senate. Her films were withdrawn from release and she was barred from working in the United States.

❧ When Kim Novak fell in love with Sammy Davis, Jr., practically the only black entertainer in Hollywood, Harry Cohn, head of Columbia Pictures, stopped it by threatening to use his connections to make sure Davis would never work in a nightclub again. In January 1957, Davis married Loray White, a black Las Vegas dancer.

❧ Eddie Fisher left Debbie Reynolds for Elizabeth Taylor. "What do you expect me to do? Sleep alone?" Taylor said to columnist Hedda Hopper in 1958.

❧ Jean Seberg's involvement with a prominent Black Panther and a miscarriage drove her to Paris in 1970. Reportedly hounded by the U.S. government, she never worked again and was found in a car overdosed on sleeping pills in 1979.

Women and the Blacklist: Crimes against the State, 1950s

> Frankly, I was going through change of life then. How would you have felt?
> *Dorothy Parker to FBI agents asking how she felt about various left-wing groups*

❧ Women who suffered from or stood up to the search for Communists in the entertainment industry in the 1950s:

❧ Dorothy Parker, a lifelong radical, who worked regularly as a screenwriter, told FBI agents who asked if she had conspired to overthrow the U.S. government, "Listen, I can't even get my dog to stay down. Do I look to you like someone who could overthrow the government?" Nonetheless, Parker got no screenwriting work in the 1950s.

❧ Blacklisted producer Hannah Weinstein started her own studio in London in 1950, making a television series about Robin Hood that was very successful and employed many blacklisted Americans.

❧ Playwright Lillian Hellman refused to cooperate with the HUAC Committee, agreeing to talk about herself, but refusing to discuss anyone else. She wrote about the events in her best-selling book, *Scoundrel Time* (1976).

❧ Actor Gale Sondergaard took the Fifth Amendment and was immediately blacklisted. Her husband, director Herbert Biberman, was one of the Hollywood 10, who went to jail.

❧ Lauren Bacall led the Committee for the Fifth Amendment, formed after the House Un-American Activities Committee hearings, to enforce the constitutional guarantee against self-incrimination.

Performers and Politics: Helen Gahagan Douglas

The first of many Hollywood women to take up serious politics and enter public life, fighting images of scatterbrained actresses with trivial motivations, was Helen Gahagan Douglas. Daughter of one of Ohio's first feminists, Helen Gahagan defied her father, who thought the theater only a step above the street. Educated at Barnard College, she debuted on Broadway in 1922. In 1930, she married actor Melvyn Douglas and moved to Hollywood.

By 1940, she had gone from actor and amateur political activist to working with the California Democratic party to organize women in Franklin Roosevelt's presidential campaign. In 1944, Douglas went to Congress, where she distinguished herself as a militant liberal, refusing attempts to bait her into a cat fight with Republican Claire Booth Luce. In 1950, her opponent for a Senate seat, Richard Nixon, viciously attacked Douglas as a Hollywood Commie, calling her "pink right down to her underwear." She lost the election.

Marilyn Monroe

The concept of "woman" which fashioned, warped, and destroyed a human being such as Marilyn Monroe . . . is HIDEOUSLY WRONG—and she, in repudiation of it, in trying tragically to RISE ABOVE IT by killing herself is (in the Shakespearean sense)—right. Such a life as hers was an affront to her humanity. [Arthur Miller] is incapable of indicting the social order which did that to her—choosing to wallow around in her "self destructive" will as if it were some kind of metaphysical lollipop she couldn't stop sucking.
Lorraine Hansberry, on After the Fall, *a play about Monroe by her husband, playwright Miller, 1964*

Actresses before Marilyn Monroe did not make an asset of their ineptitude by turning faltering misreadings into an appealing style. It is one of the uglier traditions of movie business that frequently when a star gets big enough to want big money and artistic selection or control of his productions, the studios launch large-scale campaigns designed to cut him down to an easier-to-deal-with size or to supplant him with younger, cheaper talent. Thus, early in movie history the great Lillian Gish was derided as unpopular in the buildup of the young Garbo (by the same studio) and in newspapers all over the country Marilyn Monroe, just a few weeks before her death, was discovered to have no box office draw.
Pauline Kael, I Lost It at the Movies, *1965*

She played stupid girls who thought they were smart but she was a smart girl who thought she was stupid. She played gold-diggers while giving blank checks to the Actor's Studio. She played girls to whom everything came easily, but she had things hard, even when her beauty was evident.
Julie Burchill, Girls on Film, *1986*

I don't really hate Marilyn. I just hate the way she colluded with those who were belittling and objectifying her. In fact, I understand her motives all too well. She wanted love, didn't believe she deserved it, and took what she considered the next-best thing—lust. At least she got attention, but to believe that this attention was a good, positive thing, she had to bludgeon her consciousness with every drug she could find.
Cynthia Heimel, 1991

Marlee Matlin

Left almost entirely deaf by a childhood disease, Matlin grew up in a supportive family atmosphere. Her mother helped establish the Center on Deafness in Illinois, where Matlin made her stage debut at 9, playing Dorothy in *The Wizard of Oz*. The 1986 film, *Children of a Lesser God*, the first in which deaf characters were played by deaf or hearing-impaired actors, won Matlin an Academy Award. She has used her prominence to make a stand for deaf rights, supporting protesters at Gallaudet University in 1988, when officials tried to install a hearing president who could not sign, and refusing to be interviewed on television programs that are not close-captioned.

From the Page to the Screen

The Children's Hour. Lillian Hellman insisted that her play, filmed in 1962, was not about lesbians, but about the power of a lie. Nonetheless, as director William Wyler pointed out, the "lie has to have such a devastating effect that to be credible, it must be appalling."

The appalling lie is that Shirley MacLaine loves Audrey Hepburn. MacLaine's character becomes the first in a long series of self-hating film homosexuals who kill themselves. In the play, as critic Vito Russo says in *The Celluloid Closet*, "It is not a lie that destroys Martha; it is the truth." But the movie buries the lesbianism. "The innuendos about child molestation are more explicit than those about the sexuality of the teachers."

The Color Purple. The 1985 premiere of the film based on Alice Walker's novel was picketed by a group protesting its "savage and brutal depiction of black men." (A similar protest had greeted Ntozake Shange's *For Colored Girls* on Broadway in 1976.) Whatever else they disagreed about, most readers of Walker's novel knew that the story of an abused girl growing into womanhood with a sense of worthiness gained through bonding with other women was not exactly what appeared on the screen.

Michele Wallace said director Steven Spielberg used "film clichés and racial stereotypes" to banish and ridicule Walker's black feminist agenda. Barbara Christian felt that Spielberg made the novel less harsh and made "the purple pink."

Many people defended the film. "You have never seen black women like this put on the screen before," said critic Donald Bogle. "When you see Whoopi Goldberg in a loving close-up . . . you know that in American films in the past, she would have played a maid."

Women Watch Movies

If *The Group* had had a woman scriptwriter and director, it might have been much more satirical. But, ultimately, [screenwriter] Buckman and [director] Lumet have betrayed women in a more basic way: by treating the girls as poor, weak creatures, as insignificant "little women." For this, of course, is their way of being sympathetic.

Pauline Kael, 1966

Women Write Movies

State Fair (1933) by Sonya Levien, a Russian immigrant who practiced law and wrote for the suffragist publication *The Woman's Journal*. She also wrote *Oklahoma!* (1955).

A Star Is Born (1937) by Dorothy Parker, with her husband, Alan Campbell. The last remake, in 1976, starring Barbra Streisand, was written by husband and wife team Joan Didion and John Gregory Dunne.

Dance, Girl, Dance (1940) by Tess Slesinger with husband Frank Davis.

The Little Foxes (1941) by Lillian Hellman, with added dialogue by Dorothy Parker.

Sudden Fear (1952) by Lenore Coffee, who also wrote vehicles for Bette Davis and Joan Crawford.

Rebecca, Foreign Correspondent (1940), *Suspicion*, and *Saboteur* (1942) by Joan Harrison, Alfred Hitchcock's longtime assistant.

The Big Sleep (1946) by Leigh Brackett, with William Faulkner. Her last film was *The Empire Strikes Back* (1980).

Hud (1963) by Harriet Frank, Jr.

Funny Girl (1968) by Isobel Lennart, adapted from her own play.

Five Easy Pieces (1970) and *The Fortune* (1975) by Carole Eastman.

American Graffiti (1973) and *Indiana Jones and the Temple of Doom* (1984) by Gloria Katz.

Slap Shot (1973) and *Coming Home* (1978) by Nancy Dowd.

Heaven Can Wait (1978) by Elaine May and others. May was also an uncredited cowriter on *Tootsie* (1982) and a credited one on *The Birdcage* (1996).

Silkwood (1983) by Nora Ephron and Alice Arlen. Ephron also wrote *When Harry Met Sally* (1989) and *Sleepless in Seattle* (1993).

E.T. The Extraterrestrial (1982) by Melissa Mattheson.

The Big Chill (1983) by Barbara Benedek.

Outrageous Fortune (1987) by Leslie Dixon.

I left the theater haunted by this tragic tale of forbidden love. Not the love of a woman for a man. The love of a woman for baseball. [Annie Savoy] was forced to settle for the great feminine trade-off: If you can't be it, sleep with a man who can. Hence her long career as a glorified groupie of the hometown team. They wouldn't let her pitch balls, so she balled pitchers instead.

Kathi Maio on Bull Durham *in* Sojourner: The Women's Forum, *1992*

The Ballad of Little Jo [written and directed by Maggie Greenwald]—based on the true story of a young society woman from Buffalo expelled from her family for having a child out of wedlock who headed west to make a new life, disguised as a man—is a unique and sorely needed subversion of the western mythology. In Hollywood's telling of the frontier story, women . . . were the saintly wives and mothers or the whores with (or without) the hearts of gold. How refreshing to see a woman, who takes no bullet for anyone, take the lead in a western. Too bad she had to be a man to do it.
Kathi Maio in Sojourner, *1993*

Feminist Film Criticism

In the 1970s, feminists analyzed images of women in film, pointing out their disparity with women's actual lives. By 1975, a more academic vocabulary arrived with Laura Mulvey's writing on *Visual Pleasure and Narrative Cinema*, which described how "the determining male gaze projects its fantasy onto the female figure, which is styled accordingly. In their traditional exhibitionist role, women are simultaneously looked at and displayed, with their appearance coded for strong visual and erotic impact so that they can be said to connote 'to-be-looked-at-ness.'"

Writing on film now includes analysis of genres like film noir, defined as critic Sylvia Harvey says, by the presence of two types of women: "the exciting, childless whores, or the boring, potentially childbearing sweethearts. If successful romantic love leads inevitably in the direction of the stable institution of marriage, the point about film noir, by contrast, is that it is structured around the destruction or absence of romantic love and the family."

> **"**
> Motion picture writing is as practical a profession as plumbing, only the plums are bigger.
> **"**
>
> *Anita Loos,* How to Write a Photoplay, *1920*

The "Business" of Show Business

I've been pinched, patted, and kissed. I've fought my way out of cabs, bars, and hotel rooms. But I've learned this business—and I'm going to the top!
Susan Hayward in I Can Get It for You Wholesale

Hollywood's first star was also one of its smartest businesswomen. By 1917, Mary Pickford was earning $350,000 a week, plus bonuses. "America's sweetheart" was a multimillionaire before she was thirty, partly because she fought to be valued in the terms movieland valued. Every time Charlie Chaplin got a raise, she insisted on and got one for herself. In

According to Marina Warner in *Six Myths of Our Time* (1995), the ancient she-monster, once represented by Medea, Medusa, and the Sirens, is reincarnated in the current passion for female predator movies. Among these: *Fatal Attraction* (a desperate single woman stalking a man), *Thelma and Louise* (duo out-guns male pursuers), and *Jurassic Park* (matriarchal set of dinosaurs wreaks havoc on human civilization). These images derive, Warner says, from the perception that "women in general are out of control and feminism in particular is to blame."

1919, she, Chaplin, and Douglas Fairbanks, whom Pickford married, formed the United Artists studio. In 1920, she bought up all her child films to keep them off the market. She reportedly directed all her own pictures after 1921 but refused credit because it would ruin her childlike image.

⚞ Bessie Smith was the highest paid black entertainer of the 1920s. Her success was said to have saved the Columbia Phonograph Company from bankuptcy.

⚞ Mae West was credited with single-handedly saving Paramount Pictures from financial ruin in the 1930s. Shirley Temple did the same at Twentieth Century Fox, as did Deanna Durbin at Universal.

⚞ In 1936, Mae West had the highest declared income in the country, except for William Randolph Hearst. She invested most of her earnings in California real estate and died a multimillionaire.

⚞ Women were heavily involved in all the unions and guilds organized to protect writers and performers. Adele Buffington was an early member of the Screenwriters Guild. Theresa Helburn was a founder of the Theater Guild. Lillian Hellman helped organize the Writer's Guild and Mary McCall was its three-time president.

⚞ When Howard Hughes deserted RKO, it was bought by Lucille Ball, who had once been fired there, and turned into a television lot for Desilu Productions.

⚞ Dawn Steel became the first woman in history to head a motion picture corporation when she took over Columbia Pictures and Tri Star in 1987.

Good Guy: Mike Nichols

In the 1960s, Mike Nichols and Elaine May were a brilliant comedy team. In the 1970s, Nichols brought an unknown Whoopi Goldberg to national attention by producing her one-woman show. In 1983, Nichols directed Nora Ephron's screenplay for the movie *Silkwood*, based on the real story of whistle-blower Karen Silkwood, who died mysteriously in 1974 as she was on her way to give a *New York Times* reporter documents proving contamination inside the plutonium factory where she worked. "The lucky thing," Ephron said, "was that Mike Nichols identified with Karen. Normally on a movie, the director, who is usually a man, identifies with the male character and you're constantly having to fight to preserve the line with the female character."

Feminism versus Hollywood

You wouldn't know women were part of the human race from most of the films.
Eleanor Perry, producer and screenwriter, 1974

Screenplay idea: Two women go on a crime spree.
From the notebook of Callie Khouri, whose script for Thelma and Louise *won the Academy Award in 1992*

Between 1968 and 1974, according to feminist groups monitoring the industry, of 200 films, 98 to 99 percent were written, produced, and/or directed by men; 80 percent of all roles were male, and 90 percent of the speaking roles were male.

In 1972, Eleanor Perry, screenwriter of *Diary of a Mad Housewife* (1970) and *David and Lisa* (1971), for which she received an Oscar nomination, led a protest at the Cannes Film Festival. Women spread red paint over the three breasts of a nude woman in a poster advertising Fellini's *Roma*. They carried signs that said "Women are people, not dirty jokes."

Perry, who wrote *The Man Who Loved Cat Dancing* later described a story conference that went like this: "The coproducer said, The first time he screws her is right after she's raped. I said, Rape? There's no rape in the script. And he said, Oh, what do you know about it, that turns men on. She's raped and she's sitting there and she has no reaction. Suddenly, she's in bed with Burt Reynolds and all is well."

The organization Women in Film began in 1974, honoring seven women directors who made films that year.

When Martha Coolidge applied to film school at New York University, the man who interviewed her said, "You can't be a director, you're a woman." He told her she was wasting her time and her parents' money. In fact, it was her money. One of Coolidge's first films was *Not a Pretty Picture*, a documentary about date rape. In Hollywood, she made *Valley Girl*, *Rambling Rose*, and *Lost in Yonkers*.

Marcia Nasatir, vice president at United Artists in 1975, the only woman present at company meetings, was treated like "one of the boys" so thoroughly that when a secretary came to take dictation, one of the men let out a curse word and then apologized to the secretary.

> **"**
> Maggie: I let him lie to me.
> Sandra: You're smarter than I thought you were.
> Maggie: All women are smarter than other women think they are.
> **"**
>
> *The Great Lie, 1941, by Lenore Coffee, starring Bette Davis and Mary Astor*

> Women's roles in Hollywood are easily identifiable types like bimbos, whores and nagging wives. I wanted, as a woman, to walk out of the theater not feeling dirty and worthless, for a change, not feeling like I had compromised the character of women. So many times you go to the movies, and what woman up there would you want to be? None of them.
>
> *Callie Khouri*

The Year of the Woman?

> Welcome to the Year of the Woman. We've come a long way. Not too long ago, we were called dolls, tomatoes, chicks, babes and broads. We've graduated to being called tough cookies, foxes, bitches and witches.
>
> *Barbra Streisand, 1992*

> So this is the Year of the Woman. Well, yes, this has been a very good year for women. Demi Moore was sold to Robert Redford for $1 million. Uma Thurman went for $40,000 to Mr. De Niro. While just three years ago Richard Gere bought Julia Roberts for . . . what was it? . . . $3,000? I'd say that was real progress.
>
> *Michelle Pfeiffer, 1992*

In 1993, the year after The Year of the Woman, women were 75 percent of Hollywood production office coordinators, 86 percent of script supervisors, 60 percent of costume designers, but 20 percent of directors, 15 percent of producers, 25 percent of writers, 9 percent of sound technicians, and 4 percent of lighting technicians.

Theater

Pathbreakers

≫ Laura Keene managed her own theater in New York City before the Civil War. She changed the rules of popular entertainment by inventing matinee performances and long runs for individual plays.

≫ In 1926, Eva Le Gallienne was a powerful Broadway actress with her own theater company. The Civic Repertory, created and maintained by women, brought the first Chekhov plays in English to the American stage and produced several of Susan Glaspell's plays. Later, Le Galliene played the title role in *Hamlet* with Uta Hagen as her Desdemona.

≫ At the turn of the century, famous actor Minnie Maddern Fiske insisted on rights for actors and playwrights, fighting a syndicate that operated like a plantation, its workers pow-

*Louise Bryant and Eugene O'Neill in Provincetown Players' production of O'Neill's **Thirst**, 1916 (unidentified third party)*

erless to choose their roles or their material. She introduced the controversial plays of Hendrick Ibsen to American audiences.

➠ Alice Gerstenberg, early Bryn Mawr graduate, adapted *Alice in Wonderland* for the stage in 1915. Some say she was America's first expressionistic playwright, using the technique of inner and outer characterization a decade before Eugene O'Neill. She founded the Playwrights Theater in Chicago, where she was also a director.

Lillian Russell: The American Beauty Wants to Vote

If it is true, as we Americans try to make ourselves believe, that "the hand that rocks the cradle is the hand that rules the world" why not let that be one of the hands which places the ballot of intelligence in the voting repository.

1911

She was blonde, tall, and elegant, an embodiment of all the values of the 1890s. A comic opera singer, Russell, known as "The American Beauty," gave out beauty hints, advocating exercise, especially bicycle riding. Her mother was a novelist, organizer, friend of Susan B. Anthony, suffragist, feminist, and socialist who ran for mayor of New York in 1884. Lillian was very much her daughter. She became a fixture at suffrage meetings and marches. Her greatest value to the suffrage movement was as living denial of the idea that women in it were mannish and ugly.

Susan Glaspell: Heroines Who Rebel

Susan Glaspell and her husband started the Provincetown Players in 1915, which first produced Eugene O'Neill's plays. Edna St. Vincent Millay and Paul Robeson were among the members. The theater turned Glaspell, a well-known journalist and novelist, into a playwright. Her one-act play *Trifles*, one of the first American dramas about spousal violence, is about a woman who murders her husband and is protected from the law by two other women. Inspired by the life of Emily Dickinson, *Alison's House* is about a family's attempts to suppress the writing of a recently deceased poet. Produced by Eva Le Gallienne's Civic Repertory Company, it won the Pulitzer Prize in 1930.

Margaret Webster: Daring Othello

Margaret Webster, leading director of Shakespeare's plays in America, cast Paul Robeson to play Othello on Broadway. Every New York management she approached was afraid of a production in which a black man made love to and murdered a white woman. The Theater Guild, led by Theresa Helburn and Lawrence Langner, brought it to New York on October 19, 1943. Black actress Fredi Washington, who, for lack of decent roles, had become a drama critic for the Harlem newspaper *The Peoples Voice* wrote, after the triumphant opening, that a film of Robeson in the role would enlighten "all the small-minded unjust elements of our country" and called upon "the dynasties of the far-reaching picture world" to make it happen. They never did.

Judith Malina: Troublemaker

In 1947, Judith Malina, a young actor, read Hallie Flanagan's book about the Federal Theater and wrote in her diary: "She describes how she created a nationwide theater movement to speak to the people, to the workers. A theater using all the forms, new and traditional, verse and prose, in all the languages that are spoken in the USA; in every city and village, and on wagons for the country people and the poor. . . . And I look at the scope of the book and I think pridefully: 'It can be done. She did it. So can I.' "

That year, Judith Malina and Julian Beck started The Living Theater, using improvisation, collectively created productions, rituals, and ceremony. Theirs is a theater aimed at breaking down walls and conventions and their productions have as often been played in the streets as they have indoors. Continually closed by the government, once for tax reasons, they were the heart of the avant-garde and the standard-bearers of a political theater found nowhere else.

The Tony behind the Tonys

Antoinette Perry grew up traveling with a theatrical aunt and uncle and debuted as an actress in Chicago at the age of seventeen. Two years later, she married and gave up acting, but when her husband died in 1922, she returned to the theater. She made her reputation as a director, first with a Preston Sturges play in 1929 and then with thirty more successes. She was a tireless supporter of young talent and one of the founders of the American Theater Wing, which entertained military personnel on leave during the Second World War. In her honor, the ATW established the Tonys a year after her death.

Ellen Stewart: Muse

In 1961, an unemployed black fashion designer, Ellen Stewart, rented a basement room very far off Broadway. LaMama was a coffeehouse theater and Stewart, with no theatrical experience, became a prominent avant-garde theatrical producer and director in a field previously closed to black women. In its first decade, drawing more and more audiences interested in experimental theater, which sometimes involved nudity and often involved radical politics, Stewart was continually harassed by city authorities trying to close her down. By the 1970s, she began to get recognition and support. Today, LaMama, having presented nearly a thousand new plays and launched the careers of many writers and actors, is still downtown. There are four buildings instead of the original basement, and its scope has expanded to a virtual center for international progressive theater.

Feminist Theater

In the 1970s, political theater became viable on a scale not seen since the 1930s. Feminist theater dissolved the conventional line between politics and art, performers and playwrights, actors and audiences, and made drama of women's lives. Most feminist theater groups operated as collectives, with decisionmaking shared among performers, writers, and directors, who were often the same people. A counterculture activity, these new works were put together on shoestrings and produced in bookstores, cafés, and women's arts centers, as well as on little theater stages.

In 1972, Megan Terry, who had been working with the Open Theater in New York, and five other playwrights formed the Women's Theater Council to direct, produce, and encourage the plays of women. Terry said: "Jane Austen wrote under her embroidery. My grandmother wrote and no one knew it until she died. The fact that we exist will give other women a chance to come out."

Chicanas and black women created the choreopoem, a theatrical form like Ntozake Shange's *For Colored Girls*, performance pieces consisting of loosely related poems performed by ensembles.

> I was once asked if I would be interested in directing a feminist version of Shakespeare's *King Lear*. . . . It's an absurdity to think that anyone would think feminism is about women "liberating" themselves to play the "great themes," rooted in roles originated by and for men. If there is one play of genius in the Western world which exclusively deals with the utter calamity of patriarchy, it is *Lear*.
>
> Eleanor Johnson, Notes on the Process of Art and Feminism, *1979*

Radio

The First Crooner

In 1919, Vaughan de Leath, a young concert singer, came to seek her fortune in New York and went to see the owner of a radio station atop the World Tower. She sang "Suwannee River" very softly, murmuring for fear of shattering a transmitter tube. She not only got on the air, but was so popular that she was known as "the first lady of radio." She composed songs, sang on Broadway, and in 1939, sang and played the piano, taking phone requests, as one of the earliest television shows went out over the airwaves.

Good Night, Gracie

When Gracie Allen and George Burns started in vaudeville, he intended to be the funny one while she, true to type, would be the dumb straight woman. But, whatever her lines were, Gracie got the laughs. Burns got the point. For eighteen years, Burns and Allen delighted audiences with Gracie's brilliant undermining of male logic:

> George: Gracie, let me ask you something. Did the nurse ever happen to drop you on your head when you were a baby?
> Gracie: Oh no, we couldn't afford a nurse. My mother had to do it.

Irna Phillips: Soap Radio

In 1930, a young woman teaching speech and drama at local schools and volunteering at a Chicago radio station was asked to create a family drama for the airwaves. Irna Phillips wrote a ten-minute serial called *Painted Dreams* about a widowed woman, her grown daughters, and her neighbors. In the years to come, she would create others, including *The Guiding Light*, paving the way for stories about multiple love affairs, amnesia victims, murder trials, and domestic betrayals. By 1943, she had five serials running concurrently and was earning $250,000 a year.

When television came, she moved *The Guiding Light* into the new medium in 1952 and in 1956 invented the most successful daytime serial, *As the World Turns*, which featured soapland's first illegitimate baby. "My greatest asset," she often said, was "my limited vocabulary."

A husband and wife team, Frank Hummert and Anne Ashenhurst, wrote *Stella Dallas*, based on the 1923 novel of mother love and sacrifice, by Olive Higgins Prouty and *The Romance of Helen Trent*, which proved that romance exists after thirty-five. In these scripts, critics note, men seem strong, but are weak, lack confidence in themselves, and are in need of practical help from women.

The Nightbird

Alison Steele became the first female DJ at a major radio station in 1966. When FM radio became an independent operation, paying much less than AM radio, station WNEW in New York hired an all-female staff. They lasted a year, but Steele survived. She was a knowledgeable promoter of progressive rock, and her show remained one of the most popular radio programs until 1979.

Television

Put down the baseball bat and pick up the lipstick.
Mother to daughter, Father Knows Best, *1959*

Television does not provide human models for a bright thirteen-year-old girl who would like to grow up to be something other than an ecstatic floor waxer.
Caroline Bird, 1971

Ida Lupino directed *Gunsmoke* for money while her production company made independent features about rape, unwed motherhood, and bigamy.

Ida Lupino directing a scene from **Mother of a Champion,** *1940s*

Lucy and Ethel (Lucille Ball and Vivian Vance) in I Love Lucy, 1950s

Is Television Better Than the Movies for Women?

⋘ Unlike movies, television was full of women: mothers and daughters, housewives, female buddies.

⋙ In the late 1940s and early 1950s, even the moms were transgressive, defying the complaint housewife stereotype. Lucille Ball, Audrey Meadows as Alice Kramden on *The Honeymooners*, Imogene Coca on *Your Show of Shows* all refused to stay in their place. As more women in public life developed the hushed, little-girl voices of Marilyn Monroe and Jacqueline Kennedy, these mutinous, loud-mouthed women stood out.

⋘ Carol Burnett, the "Queen of Comedy," had a weekly television show for eight years, from 1967 to 1975. Other funny ladies with more exposure on television than in films are

Lucille Ball, Mary Tyler Moore, Joan Rivers, Lily Tomlin, Gilda Radner, Roseanne Barr, Paula Poundstone, and Ellen De Generes.

➤ It took television to showcase black actresses: Cicely Tyson in *Roots*, Leslie Uggams, Irene Cara, Diahann Carroll, and *Star Trek*'s Nichelle Nichols.

➤ Television, like the Ziegfeld Follies half a century before, was a stepping-stone for women's careers.

➤ Mary Tyler Moore started on the *Dick Van Dyke Show* in 1961, creating the character of Laura Petrie and stretching the medium's conventions about wives as extensions of their husbands. *The Mary Tyler Moore Show* made network executives nervous, with its very Jewish Rhoda Morgenstern and its central character, Mary Richards, a woman who had a job, no husband, and talked about birth control. It ran successfully from 1969 to 1979, produced by the production company she ran with her husband, MTM Enterprises, which she called "the little empire that could." MTM also produced *Hill Street Blues* and *Rhoda*.

➤ Lily Tomlin started on *Laugh-In* in the 1970s and went on to one-woman shows.

➤ Penny Marshall began on *The Odd Couple*, went on to do *Laverne and Shirley*, and then became a movie director.

The State of the Art: Television, 1996

➤ No woman regularly anchors the news alone.

➤ No woman ever successfully hosted a game show.

➤ The only woman ever to headline a musical show remains Dinah Shore.

➤ The upper echelons of network decisionmaking are white and male.

> Roseanne Barr is four things tv women are not supposed to be—working class, loud-mouthed, overweight and a feminist. Roseanne became a success because her mission was simple and welcome: to take the schmaltz and hypocrisy out of media images of motherhood.
> *Susan Douglas,* Where the Girls Are: Growing Up Female with the Mass Media, *1994*

Music

Jeannette Thurber: Troublemaker

Jeannette M. Thurber tried to establish a National Opera Company in the 1880s with native conductors, performers, and scene designers. It was unheard of. In 1888, she tried to get support for the arts from the federal government, which shared the opinion of the Boston newspaper that called her "a half-educated woman, possessed with a bank account but very little brains." Thurber was fifty years ahead of her time.

The (Woman's) Blues

➣ The theme of women's blues, a black woman's form popular in white culture after World War I, is generally the balance of power in sexual relationships. These songs are about sex and domination, slavery to no-good men, submission to physical violence or its mirror, and fantasies of becoming violent. The singer's text is submissive but cynically so, or it has a tenuous bravura. For musical genius, richness of drama, and poetic language, classic women's blues had no counterpart in our cultural heritage. Black feminists point out the power and authority of the singers. The struggle within the blues, says critic Hazel V. Carby, is "to reclaim women's bodies as the sexual and sensuous subjects of women's song, to manipulate and control their construction as sexual subjects."

➣ **Mamie Smith,** the first black woman to record the blues, was a cabaret singer in New York in 1918, when an agent convinced Victor Records to make a test of her singing "That Thing Called Love." The company didn't release it, but bootlegged copies flooded the market. At the height of the Jazz Age, she was selling seventy-five thousand copies of her records and performing with her band, the Jazz Hounds, for up to three thousand dollars a night.

➣ **Gertrude "Ma" Rainey** appeared in a local talent show in Georgia when she was fourteen and ran away with Will "Pa" Rainey and his traveling minstrel show. She left him. In the 1920s, Paramount recorded her, bringing her inimitable voice to people outside the rural black South. Arrested in 1925 for holding a lesbian orgy in her home, she got an outlaw image that made her a culture hero. "Prove It on Me Blues," in which she sings, "They say I do it, ain't nobody caught me," was advertised with a picture of a woman in mannish clothes talking to two ultra-feminine flappers.

➣ **Bessie Smith** learned her first blues from Ma Rainey and spent her youth traveling with the Rabbit Foot Minstrels. Recordings brought her fame and fortune and she began appearing in theaters and nightclubs instead of tent shows. When sales of race records declined in the Depression, Columbia records dropped her. Trying for a comeback in 1937, she was killed in a car accident outside Clarksdale, Mississippi.

➣ **Ida Cox** played with the Rabbit Foot Minstrels most of her life and did not appear outside the Deep South. She formed her own touring company and was still on the road until late in the 1950s.

➣ **Memphis Minnie,** one of the few singers to play her own accompaniment, usually on the guitar, was discovered by a record company scout while she was singing for dimes in the barber shops on Memphis's Beale Street. In the 1930s, she left the South for Chicago. It was said that she sang and played like a man.

➣ **Thomas "Fats" Waller** learned to play piano by hanging around Mazie Mullins, organist at the Lincoln Theater.

➣ **Arizona Dranes,** a blind church singer and pianist recorded between 1926 and 1928, brought a rocking beat to the sanctified music, combining gospel, blues, and boogie woogie.

➣ In the 1970s, **Rosetta Reitz** almost single-handedly got the recordings of the great female blues singers reissued.

Serious Music in an Age of Flappers

Women's breakthroughs in the 1920s extended to the classical music world. Minna Lederman Daniel started *Modern Music* magazine in 1924, the first to give serious coverage to new American music in all forms: concerts, jazz, theater, film, radio, and dance music. That year, composer Amy Beach became the first president of the Society of American Women Composers, dedicated to advancing music written by women. In 1925, a brilliant 100-player women's symphony orchestra was formed in Chicago. Its radio performances made it the best known American women's group.

Ina Ray Hutton and Her Melodears

The most popular all-woman swing band of the 1930s was led by Ina Ray Hutton, "The Blonde Bombshell of Rhythm," who was not a musician but a glamorous front woman recruited from the Ziegfeld Follies. Promoters pressured her to begin every set with "A Pretty Girl Is Like a Melody," but Hutton resisted. "I wanna sound like Basie and Goodman and everybody else," she said.

She was a consummate businesswoman. When television arrived in the early 1950s, she brought a fourteen piece all-female band to the small screen with a weekly show out of Los Angeles.

Lil Hardin Armstrong: Born to Swing

> I was sort of standing at the bottom of the ladder holding it and watching him climb.
> *Lil Hardin on Louis Armstrong*

Lil Hardin grew up playing organ at her Memphis church and being glared at by the pastor for putting "a definite beat" into "Onward Christian Soldiers." In her teens, she got a job playing piano at a Chicago music store, which led to performances her mother didn't care for, with some of the great jazz bands of the day. In King Oliver's band, she met the new trumpeter, Louis Armstrong, and married him in 1924.

She encouraged Armstrong to strike out on his own. When he couldn't get work, she took club jobs, insisting he be hired, too. For his first records, she was pianist and music director. She

> " If more girl drummers had cradle-rocking experiences before their musical endeavors, they might come closer to getting on the beat. "
>
> Downbeat *magazine, 1938*

At Harlem's Cotton Club, blacks were performers, but barred from being patrons. Female entertainers had to be light-skinned until 1932, when the rule was relaxed to accommodate Louis Armstrong's second wife, Lucille Watson.

Ina Ray Hutton and the Melodears, 1943

ETHEL WATERS: BREAKING THROUGH

Ethel Waters was originally a blues singer, the first black woman to do serious monologues on stage. The highest paid woman on Broadway, she appeared in the Irving Berlin show, *As Thousands Cheer,* introducing "Supper Time," a song about a woman learning that her husband has been lynched. As an actor, in 1939, Waters played in *Mamba's Daughters,* the first serious role for a black woman on Broadway. She played Hagar, a woman she said "was all Negro women lost and lonely in the white man's antagonistic world."

In movies, her roles were more limited. Critic Hazel V. Carby says that Waters—and Hattie McDaniel, who also sang blues before she got into movies—on-screen "occupied not a privileged but a subordinate space and articulated not the possibilities of black female sexual power but the 'Yes, Ma'ams' of the black maid."

wrote Armstrong's compositions down as fast as he played. She went back to school, getting graduate and postgraduate degrees in music.

Separating from Armstrong in 1931, she formed The Harlem Harlicans, an all-woman band, with Leora Mieux, Fletcher Henderson's wife, on trombone and Alma Long Scott, Hazel Scott's mother, on reeds. For three decades, she worked in bands, as the house pianist at Decca Records, in her own dressmaking operation, and as a restaurant owner. In 1971, she performed at a Chicago tribute to her ex-husband, six months after his death. Halfway through one of her numbers, she collapsed and died of a massive heart attack.

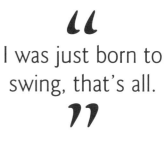

“
I was just born to swing, that's all.
”

Lil Hardin Armstrong

Lil Hardin with Louis Armstrong's Hot Five, c. 1927

Tina Turner and Janis Joplin, Madison Square Garden, New York City, 1969

Helen Oakley Dance, writer and producer, close friend of Billie Holiday, produced America's first jazz concert in Chicago in 1935: the Benny Goodman trio, with Teddy Wilson and Gene Krupa. It was the first public appearance of black and white musicians together.

The International Sweethearts of Rhythm

The most popular swing band of the 1940s started at the Piney Woods School in Mississippi, attended mostly by poor black Southern students who participated in work/study programs in exchange for their education. In 1937, a jazz band for girls was added to the curriculum. The band performed locally, becoming the school's top fund-raiser. In 1938, eighteen band members left the school and went out on their own.

When they played New York's Appollo Theater—the sixteen-piece band had a strong brass section, heavy percussion, and strong rhythm—unconvinced men were sure they were only pantomiming and insisted on looking backstage for the male band that was really playing.

Outstanding among many outstanding players was trumpeter Ernestine "Tiny" Davis, known as the "female Louis Armstrong." The white women wore blackface onstage and trumpeter Roz Cron said the makeup turned her skin orange. In the mid-1940s, they added Jewish and Asian musicians. In the segregated South, they slept on their bus to avoid arrest.

Until the 1960s, there were no female instrumentalists in the New York Philharmonic, except for harpists, who were always ladies in chiffon dresses. In 1966, Orin O'Brien was hired to play bass. The following year, cellist Evangeline Benedetti joined.

Rock Sluts and Mothers

Rock and roll has always preferred its women subservient and sluttish. For many years, record companies thought that their male artists could only relate to women in that role, that they in fact needed women like that in order to strut.

When the occasional female voice breaks through with a vengeance, it's invariably a Janis Joplin or a Tina Turner. When you look at the history of rock-and-roll, "clone" male voices abound, but every female voice is singular.

Rock and roll is built on the bones, and stands on the shoulders of, Ma Rainey, Bessie Smith, Victoria Spivey, and a host of women who gave birth not just to the blues but to the men who sing the blues.

Songwriter Janis Ian, letter to the New York Times, *1996*

> When you went to an audition for a fellows' band, they'd look down their noses and they'd think, "Oh, God, here comes a girl." You felt just like ice was thrown over you. But you'd get in there and you'd prove yourself to them and they'd be marvelous to you. . . . You had to put them at ease. If I missed a note, I'd quickly call that four letter word out and the fellows would say, "Hey, she's a regular! She's not a silly girl!"
>
> *Jane Sager, trumpeter*

The Women's Philharmonic in San Francisco is the only orchestra in the country dedicated to promoting women composers, conductors and performers. Since 1981, the orchestra has performed the works of fifty-seven women composers under the artistic director Miriam Abrams, who began to dig up the lost works of women composers in 1975, while still a college music student.

In 1983, Ellen Taaffee Zwilich became the first woman to win a Pulitzer Prize for music. Today she holds the first appointment to the Carnegie Hall Composers Chair.

Last Words

We should insist that there is nothing inherently superior about Elvis or James Dean in relation to the Shirelles or Natalie Wood. The ridiculing and erasing of our cultural history is nothing less than a ridiculing of our past selves and of who we are today, and while flying nuns and watusi-dancing beach bunnies were pretty revolting, they were also, simultaneously, metaphors for our incipient jail break and for efforts to keep us behind bars.

Susan J. Douglas, Where the Girls Are: Growing Up Female with the Mass Media, *1994*

Selling **The Woman's Journal***, Boston, Massachusetts, 1911*

Nicole Hollander cartoon, 1991

CHAPTER 7

Media

*J*ust as long as newspapers and magazines are controlled by men, every woman upon them must write articles which are reflections of men's ideas. As long as that continues, women's ideas and deepest convictions will never get before the public.

Susan B. Anthony

Peace is not a passive but an active condition, not a negation but an affirmation. It is a gesture as strong as war.

Mary Roberts Rinehart, Saturday Evening Post, *1919*

Gathering news in Russia was like mining coal with a hat pin.

Mary Heaton Vorse, labor journalist and Moscow correspondent for Hearst newspapers, 1921

I was a slave. I was part of the "paper bag brigade," waiting patiently for someone to "buy" me for an hour or two, or, if I were lucky, for a day.

Marvel Cooke, Daily Compass, *1950*

This is not only a fight for courteous and equitable treatment, this is the first organized and disciplined revolt against a cruel and inhuman custom.

Ethel Payne, Chicago Defender, *1956*

This is a case where . . . highly paid women, who have been well treated by the Times, now assert for some reason . . . that they have suffered discrimination because of their sex.

New York Times *attorney, 1973*

It's like they believe that once you make over $17,000 a year you give up your constitutional rights.

Harriet Rabb, attorney for New York Times *women, 1973*

Godey's Lady's Book *masthead, 1852*

L ois Lane lives. Born in 1938, two years before Brenda Starr, three years before Wonder Woman, she had no time to worry about Clark or the red-caped wonder. Instead, she gets through police lines to report on a fire, writes inflammatory editorials, and observes the front in wartime. She's good. She's "a newspaperman." They don't like her much in radio or television.

The real Lois Lanes of American history have been on the scene since before the American Revolution. Newspaper publishing was, and still is, a family business, so women had access to it through the men in their families. Out of nine colonial printers, seven were printers' widows, called "deputy husbands." Intrepid souls who wrote books also found their way to newspapers. In the early nineteenth century, Anne Newport Royall published ten travel journals and started her own periodical in Washington, D.C., which survived twenty-three years. In 1846, Margaret Fuller, author of the monumental *Woman in the Nineteenth Century*, became the first female foreign correspondent, reporting from a Europe on the brink of revolution.

American newspapers had no official correspondents abroad until after 1870, but women went anyway, writing freelance for newspapers that refused to hire them at home. When being a foreign correspondent became a serious, lucrative career, papers hired only men.

At home, the walls fell slowly. In 1850, Jane Grey Swisshelm, publisher of a Pittsburgh antislavery newspaper, was hired by the foresighted Horace Greeley to report for the *New York Tribune* from Washington, D.C. She forced the government to admit her—and all women after her—to the Senate gallery, where she could hear and report on the great debates of the time. Access matters. In 1868, Jane Cunningham Croly, *New York Graphic* writer, organized newswomen into a club to compensate for their exclusion from the boys' clubs of mainstream journalism.

But the boys' clubs were never women's best means of acquiring information. Informal networks were often better. Women learned from each other what newspapers never told them. In more formal and less congenial circles, this sharing of information was called gossip.

Yet the gossip was often more accurate than the news. In newspapers run by powerful white men, the women's rights movement was of minimal interest and treated with hostility or ridicule, if at all. The 1848 Seneca Falls meeting was "the most shocking and unnatural event" according to the papers. "Women unsexed in mind," held an 1853 "women's wrongs convention." By 1893, in a fit of wishful thinking, a Western paper reported that Elizabeth Cady Stanton was dead and Susan B. Anthony suffering from insanity.

The women's movement itself moved from concentrating on conventions to concentrating on publishing. Between 1870 and 1890, thirty-three suffrage papers appeared, along with other journals of reform in which women had a strong hand. These periodicals helped identify and create not only a political movement, but its leaders. Stanton and Anthony, Lucy Stone, Amelia Bloomer, Frances Wright Davis, Abigail Scott Duniway—all were organizers, speakers, activists, and publishers.

A media of one's own is not to be confused with media aimed at women, which became big business by the end of the nineteenth century. As the population doubled between 1890 and 1900 and public education turned out increasing numbers of literate Americans, it became clear that female consumers were an untapped resource. To tap it, countering the message of the women's rights media, male publishers, editors, and advertisers turned their sights on women as they understood (and constructed) women.

Enter magazines, a word that originally meant *storehouse*. Journals directed specifically to women had been around since the 1790s. In the West, in the 1820s, *Masonic Miscellany* and the *Ladies Literary Cabinet* depended heavily on fiction and book reviews, with no household columns and minimal attention to public events. Editor Sarah Hale and *Godey's Lady's Book*, the most popular magazine of the nineteenth century, changed the formula. And Mrs. Frank Leslie, publisher of weekly and monthly tabloids in the 1880s, became the first media glamor queen, paying herself $100,000 a year, often pictured beautifully dressed, writing at her white oak desk with her long black quill.

By the 1880s and 1890s, with the women's rights movement in full swing and publishing periodicals of its own, a counterrevolution set in. In defense of "traditional" values, especially home and motherhood, the *Ladies' Home Journal* entered the fray, followed by *McCall's* (1870), *Good Housekeeping* (1885, bought by Hearst in 1912), and *Harper's Bazaar* (1904). These magazines, however conservative their politics, were a boon to women writers and photographers, paying decent fees, copyrighting material, publishing quality work, and encouraging authors to use their real names. They set the mold for ladies' magazines—aimed at a white, urban, in-need-of-help "lady"—that remained remarkably unchanged for a hundred years.

By 1917, the women's press was gone. Mainstream newspapers had been forced by popular opinion to cover the movement, although women working for the straight press had to battle hard to wrest coverage away from male reporters. Mainstreaming the movement, ostensibly making feminist media obsolete, would recur in the 1970s.

But "the woman's angle," as men defined it, had become a crucial component of journalism. Newspapers had a woman's page, and some token women had jobs there and were forced to stay there. A female reporter eager to cover politics could be told to stick to her knitting.

The woman's angle might be what Lily Tomlin later called the "meatballs and mending" angle. It might be the crusading social reform angle of Ida B. Wells, who used print to expose and organize against the crime of lynching, or of Ida Tarbell, whose magazine series about corruption and chicanery in the oil business brought down the Standard Oil Company.

"The woman's angle" widened with every war, when ingenuity, daring, and ambition made up for the limitations on getting media jobs. To get the story, women broke the rules, especially the military rules that prohibited their presence in combat. Peggy Hull went with U.S. forces, pursuing revolutionary Pancho Villa into Mexico in 1916, then to Europe as World War I exploded. Mary Roberts Rinehart reported from France in 1918 and from the disarmament conference at the war's end. The Russian Revolution and the Spanish Civil War had outstanding female eyes, ears and voices sending the news home. Dorothy Thompson covered Hitler's rise to power from Berlin until her reporting so angered the Fuhrer that he had her expelled.

More than 150 female correspondents were accredited during the Second World War. Marguerite Higgins, hired by the *New York Tribune* in 1944, assumed that jobs for women were only possible because newspapermen were fighting the war, and called herself "a war profiteer." Even more women went to report on the conflict in Korea. By the 1960s, in Vietnam, for the first time in history, the Defense Department officially allowed women to cover combat on an equal footing with men.

Whatever the woman's angle was, Eleanor Roosevelt had enlarged it. Beginning with her husband's 1933 presidential inauguration, the First Lady insisted that female reporters be assigned her, forcing the news services to scurry around hiring women. Eleanor Roosevelt's weekly all-female press briefings featured distinguished women from all fields as experts, bringing them press attention. Her network of women in media functioned as a support system.

The history of radio is the history of progressively diminishing opportunities for women. The new media, heralded as a fresh frontier in the 1920s—when Judith Waller in Chicago put play-by-play coverage of the Cubs games at Wrigley Field on the air and Louella Parsons reported Hollywood "news"—soon became a field with isolated, "exceptional" women.

On the serious side of radio, women's voices were considered too high and thin to command interest or attention. Still, throughout the 1930s and 1940s, Mary Margaret McBride's daily show, mixing homemaking tips with celebrity interviews, drew six million faithful listeners. The "manpower" shortage of World War II allowed women in jobs unthinkable before and after, but the jobs mostly ended when the war did. In 1972, Susan Stamberg brought women's voices to serious radio reporting when she began hosting *All Things Considered* on National Public Radio.

In television news, there was room for one (white) woman, generally the "weather girl," sometimes trotted out to interview a candidate's wife. In the 1950s and 1960s, women owned daytime, men owned the night. Cooks Julia Child and Dione Lucas, Hollywood reporter Virginia Graham, and actor Arlene Francis had successful daytime shows. Aside from entertainments, where they couldn't very well be avoided, women were notably missing from the serious side of television. As news reporters or commentators, they didn't exist.

Print was always most hospitable to women. *Seventeen*, the magazine for socializing young women, staked out a new market in 1944. While radio and then television challenged the dominance of the women's magazines, their formula remained essentially the same until Helen Gurley Brown brought the then-fresh air of her best-selling book, *Sex and the Single Girl*, to magazines by revamping *Cosmopolitan* in 1965, making it the most successful in the field. *Essence*, the first mass magazine for black women, started in 1970, and Gloria Steinem and others created *Ms.* magazine in 1972.

Thirty-five years after Eleanor Roosevelt's all-female press corps, some less famous women were redefining the woman's angle again. When women's liberation finally became of interest to the media, in the late 1960s, its members would only speak to female reporters. Newspapers rummaged for such creatures in their research departments and women's pages, thereby launching many mainstream careers.

Perhaps because so many feminists worked in the media—and because its influence on American life had become so pervasive—the media was analyzed and criticized more during the 1970s than it had ever been before. It was also changed. Litigation exposed and somewhat redressed illegal gender discrimination in all the institutions that prided themselves on objectivity, fairness, and even-handedness.

Communication was no less important to feminism's second wave than it had been to the first. This time, it was bigger: hundreds of newsletters, newspapers, magazines, a few radio and television shows. Like its predecessors, feminist media did more than convey information, offering support and encouragement to isolated readers as well as activists. Depending on bonds between writers, editors, and readers that mainstream media never entertained, it built a cultural and political community.

Much as the nineteenth-century feminist media folded after women won the vote, when "women's issues" appeared to be part of general public news, the concerns of women appeared satisfied by mainstream media in the 1980s. In fact, they had only been suppressed.

The 1990s saw not only an upsurge in activism and organizing, but media suited to its time. One of the first things the punky/feminist Riot Grrrl group did was publish a 'zine, a computer-generated underground magazine. Black feminists, lesbian feminists, Chicanas, Asians—are linked by journals. The next frontier, feministically being breached, is technological—cyberfeminism lives on the Internet.

Who Owns the News?

> Perhaps a woman editor is resented because an editor is supposed to possess wisdom, and something in the masculine mind objects to the suggestion that a woman can know anything except what she has already been told by a man.
> *Cissy Patterson, on taking over the Washington, D.C., newspaper,* The Herald, *1930*

✄ Anna Zenger may or may not have had the idea to start a newspaper opposing the Colonial government in New York City. She did, however, defiantly keep that paper going in 1734, printing her husband's inflammatory letters from jail, while John Peter Zenger, accused of libel, languished in prison for ten months. After his death, it clearly was her newspaper and she added women's news to its contents.

✄ Ann Franklin, sister-in-law of Benjamin Franklin, took over a Newport, Rhode Island, paper and became the first woman to print in New England. Elizabeth Timothy, whose husband had been in business with Franklin, published the *South Carolina Gazette* from 1739 until 1746, when she turned the paper over to her son.

✄ Mary Katherine Goddard's mother published the *Providence Gazette*. Her brother ran the *Maryland Journal* and *Baltimore Advertiser*, where Mary worked. When he left in 1774, she took over. Many newspapers were forced out of business during the Revolution, but hers survived. In 1776, she printed copies of the Declaration of Independence.

Mary Ann Shadd Cary: Breaking Ground

> How it can be more indelicate for a female doctor to attend a sick man than for a male doctor to attend a sick woman is beyond our humble ken.
> *Editorial,* Provincial Freeman, *1854*

Mary Ann Shadd Cary, the first black woman journalist in North America, was born free in Delaware, but joined former slaves in Canada and founded the *Provincial Freeman* in 1854. Widely distributed, her editorials urged slaves: "You have a right to your freedom and to every other privilege connected with it and if you cannot secure these in Virginia or Alabama, by all means make your escape, without delay, to some other locality in God's wide universe."

Opposition to a woman expressing opinions in public forced her to resign, although she kept a behind-the-scenes hand in the paper. After the Civil War, Cary wrote for black newspapers in Washington, D.C., became the first female law student at Howard University in 1869, practiced law, and campaigned for women's rights.

Eliza Nicholson

Eliza Nicholson became the only woman publisher of a major metropolitan newspaper in 1875 when she took over the *New Orleans Daily Picayune*. The former literary editor, she had married the paper's publisher and run it after he died. She introduced the Sunday funnies, columns on household hints, and discovered and started advice columnist Dorothy Dix on her newspaper career. Nicholson opposed women's suffrage because it would give black women the vote. She founded the Women's International Press Association in 1887 and hired many white women to work at her paper. When the Spanish-American War broke out in 1898, Picayune correspondent Fanny B. Ward was there to report the sinking of the battleship *Maine* in Havana harbor.

Mrs. Frank Leslie: Working Wife, Secret Feminist

The highly unconventional Miriam Follin of New Orleans knew several languages, was a published writer at fourteen, and traveled with the actress Lola Montez, who had run off with Follin's half brother. When her husband became editor of the tabloid *Frank Leslie's Illustrated Newspaper* in 1861, she ran *Leslie's Ladies Magazine*, bringing a fresh touch to fashion news.

Woman Suffrage in Wyoming Territory
from **Frank Leslie's Illustrated Newspaper,**
November 24, 1888

She also, apparently, took over Mr. Frank Leslie. For a decade, she lived and traveled with both her employer and her husband until her heavy-drinking, older husband was judged insane. Then she became Mrs. Frank Leslie. As the country's most famous working wife, she wrote accounts of a Pullman car journey across the country, Mormon leader Brigham Young and two of his many wives, an opium den, and a San Francisco brothel.

At Leslie's death in 1880, she inherited seventeen lawsuits, but within a year, the creditors were paid. She encouraged American talent—and women—at a time when English writers were favored. After ten successful years, she sold out and married, briefly, Oscar Wilde's alcoholic brother.

Although she never publicly advocated women's rights, her death in 1914 revealed a nearly $2 million bequest to Mrs. Carrie Chapman Catt for suffrage work. After a bitter contest, Mrs. Catt got less than half of Mrs. Leslie's gift.

Helen Rogers Reid

Suffragist Helen Rogers Reid married into the *New York Tribune* family and became vice president of the newspaper. Because of her feminist influence, the *Trib* led the way for women. Helen Reid was responsible for hiring women as food critics, book critics, and news reporters, including Dorothy Thompson in the 1920s. During World War II, when she became the paper's publisher, she convinced the War Department to allow Sonia Tomara to cover China, Burma, and India. Later the War Department changed its policy and gave Marguerite Higgins a job reporting from Europe.

Eleanor Patterson

Eleanor (Cissy) Patterson grew up in a newspaper family. In 1930, at forty-nine, she persuaded William Randolph Hearst to let her run the *Washington Herald*. In 1932, she went out to see how the poor lived, well aware of her own playacting and how different the reality was for the people she met. The series she wrote was followed by one on hungry children and another on the Bonus Army. When she built the paper into the city's largest morning circulation, Hearst made her publisher.

Feminism and Media: The First Wave

Maria Stewart in *The Liberator* (1831–1833)

> How long shall the fair daughters of Africa be compelled to bury their minds and talents beneath a load of iron pots and kettles?
>
> *1831*

Maria W. Stewart, who wrote the "Ladies Department" created for her in William Lloyd Garrison's newspaper, was a famous black abolitionist speaker. Her words were published as pamphlets also, but the violent reactions of black men, who threw tomatoes at her when she spoke, forced her to leave Boston. In New York, she published a book and taught in the public schools, raising money for Frederick Douglass's newspaper, *The North Star*, in the 1860s.

The Lily *masthead, February 15, 1854*

The Lily (1849–1856)

Who knows, perhaps some day mankind may learn to be *charmed* with truth—may not need to be mauled and ground to powder by it.
1854

The lady drops her glove and a dozen cavaliers would sacrifice theirs, how white and well fitted soever, in the dust, to spare her the fatigue of even glancing at it where it lies; but the cavalier who drops his glove on a staircase will allow any waiting-maid in the house to descend and pick it up for him.
1856

The first newspaper owned, operated, and edited by a woman for women was Amelia Bloomer's *Lily*, published first in Seneca Falls, New York, then in Iowa. It started as a temperance journal, but quickly evolved to advocate for women's equality. Contributors included Stanton, Anthony, and Swisshelm. It carried many stories about role models: the first issue had examples of sixteen women who wrote and published during the Revolutionary War. At its peak in early 1854, it had 6,000 readers.

The Una (1853–1855)

You have swallowed up a thousand household workshops in every great factory and we demand our place at the power loom with wages up to the full value of our services.
1853

Striking shirtwaist makers selling **The Call,** *New York City, 1909*

Pauline Wright Davis of Providence, socialite, young widow, abolitionist, and spiritualist, was the first woman to lecture on female anatomy and physiology, providing the only available information about female bodies. Her magazine, *The Una* (the mystical name means truth) was plagued by money worries. Aimed at immigrant and working-class women, offering "stronger nourishment" than the light fare of other ladies' magazines, it carried articles on child labor and a serial, "Stray Leaves from a Seamstress' Journal," largely written by seamstresses themselves.

The Folio: A Plea for Women's Rights (1855)

Published in Hawaii, once only, *The Folio* was a four-page newspaper produced and written by women, the first in the Pacific region.

The Sibyl (1856–1861)

We believe, and hope to prove it, that there is nothing that has such a false and narrowing influence over woman as her servility to fashion.

1856

The Sibyl *masthead, April 1, 1859*

In The Sibyl I learn that I am not alone in the world; that I have brothers and sisters of kindred sentiments and feelings with my own, scattered here and there over the country.
Reader's letter, 1858

Edited by Lydia Sayer Hasbrouck, *The Sibyl* was primarily a dress reform weekly, ridiculing fashion magazines: ". . . senseless ninny faces and forms deformed and horrified by a redundancy of paints, puffs, bows, flounces and laces." It also advocated medical training for women, female education, and suffrage, and ran a continuous campaign supporting Hasbrouck's refusal to pay taxes until women could make the country's laws.

The Revolution (1868–1872)

Principle, Not Policy; Justice, Not Favors—Men, Their Rights and Nothing More; Women, Their Rights and Nothing Less.
It is our intention to turn the State, the Church and the Home inside out, and let the people see the utter rottenness of our political, religious and social life.
1868

The Revolution was an uncompromising, controversial weekly that established women's political journalism. Devoted to issues broader than the vote, Elizabeth Cady Stanton and Susan B. Anthony, who edited it for its first two years, believed that the women's movement reforms would benefit working-class women. They wrote openly and controversially about prostitution, divorce, venereal diseases, forced maternity, racism, and direct action by women against men's laws. At its peak, the magazine had 3,000 subscribers and, presumably, a large pass-along rate.

Emily A. Pitts bought an interest in the *California Weekly Mercury* in 1869, became coeditor, then gained control of the paper, changing its name to *Pioneer* and making it the first voice for women's suffrage in the West.

The Woman's Journal: Torchbearer of the Woman Suffrage Cause (1870–1917)

Women were spat upon, slapped in the face, tripped up, pelted with burning cigar stubs and insulted by jeers and obscene language too vile to print or repeat.
Report of 1913 suffrage march in Washington, D.C.

The Woman's Journal was started by Lucy Stone and Henry Blackwell, targeting women who resented the triviality of women's publications, but also as a conservative response to the more radical *Revolution*. More focused on suffrage, more solid financially, more mainstream, the paper recruited experienced editors like Julia Ward Howe. One of its readers called it "a paper that would corrupt you gradually." After 1910, it featured cartoons regularly. In 1917, it became *The Woman Citizen*.

Woodhull and Claflin's Weekly: Upward and onward (1870–1876)

> Suppose the admission of women in politics should, as some objectors predict, increase the ratio of insanity among them . . .
> *1870*

The most radical publication, advocating free love and women's rights, including abortion, it was the first periodical in the United States to print "The Communist Manifesto." In 1870, Victoria Woodhull used it to announce her candidacy for president. In 1872, when the paper broke a scandal about the Reverend Henry Ward Beecher's affair with the wife of his friend, Woodhull was arrested and tried for obscenity. Although not convicted, she stopped publishing.

THE ANTIS

True Woman, the first antisuffrage journal, was published in Baltimore, then in Washington, from 1870 to 1873. A longer-lived antisuffrage periodical, *Remonstrance*, existed from 1890 to 1920. The official journal of the National Association Opposed to Woman Suffrage, founded in 1911, was the *Woman's Protest*.

The New Northwest Free Speech, Free Press, Free People (1871–1887)

> The senior editor has often encountered a narrow, puritanical, blue-law churchanity, which bars its doors against her work and, with an over-pious and super-holy air, turns its priestly back upon her mission.
> *1881*

Published and edited by Abigail Scott Duniway in Portland, Oregon, *The New Northwest* was "not a Woman's Rights, but a Human Rights organ." It was the most important factor in the area's women's movement for sixteen years, exposing frauds, defending mistreated women, reporting on business and cultural events, and keeping track of legislatures and law courts. Duniway encouraged young women to write for the paper and learn typesetting.

The Suffragist *on sale in Boston, 1919*

The Woman's Tribune (1883–1909)

Clara Bewick Colby's influential newspaper reported news events related to many kinds of reform, reprinted speeches from conventions, and left a record of the movement and its past which, by the time she was publishing, reached back nearly forty years to Seneca Falls. Headquartered in Nebraska, Colby also published in Washington, D.C., while Congress was in session.

The Woman's Era (1890–1897)

Think of this, you colored women whose money and efforts are going to support in luxury the writers of that paper, while you hesitate to give ten cents toward the encouragement of writers of your own race!

1895

The exclusion of colored women and girls from nearly all places of respectable employment is due mostly to the meanness of white women.

1896

The Woman's Era, a national monthly, was the first newspaper by and for African-American women. Josephine St. Pierre Ruffin, founder, publisher, and editor, had been a charter member of the Massachusetts Suffrage Association; she started the Woman's Era Club in 1894, and her paper became the club movement's organ. "Womanliness is an attribute," she wrote "and not a condition. It is not supplied or withdrawn by surroundings." Since the *Ladies' Home Journal*, the largest women's magazine in the country, refused to accept articles by African-American women, her readers, she said, should be insulted, cancel their subscriptions, and subscribe to the *Era*. Ruffin had, perhaps, invented aggressive marketing techniques that included promotions, giveaways, traveling to club meetings to solicit subscriptions, and selling ads.

The Suffragist (1913–1921)

We declare that suffrage has reached its political stage.
1913

Those who hold power are responsible not only for what they do but for what they do not do. Inaction establishes just as clear a record as does a policy of open hostility.
Editorial, December 1913

The Suffragist, in Washington, D.C., started by Alice Paul and the Congressional Union women who devoted themselves entirely to getting a federal amendment passed, had Nina Allender as its official cartoonist and journalist Rhete Childe Dorr as its first editor. At least one staff member resigned when Allender went so far as to satirize President Woodrow Wilson in her drawings.

The Woman Citizen (1917–1920)

Men come and men go, but a truth goes marching on. Not a banner will be furled, not a marcher will break step, not a friend will desert, not a political party will falter, not a newspaper will lapse into silence.
1919

The Woman Citizen was the official organ of The National Woman's Suffrage Association until the vote was won. After the 19th Amendment passed, it became the paper for The League of Women Voters until 1932.

Nina Allender illustration, Equal Rights, *newspaper of the National Woman's Party, April 7, 1923*

Who Writes the News?

I think the greatest thing my generation of women accomplished was the freeing of younger women to go farther than ourselves.
Rheta Childe Dorr, 1924

Anne Newport Royall: 95 Years of Crusading

Anne Newport Royall, once a servant in West Virginia, married her employer. Widowed and impoverished, she wrote travel books that involved enterprising reporting, such as going into convents to interview nuns. In the 1820s, nearing sixty, Royall settled in Washington, D.C., as a crusading newspaperwoman. She reportedly interviewed thirteen presidents in her long lifetime. As publisher of a political journal for twenty-three years, she advocated free public education and supported the causes of Indians and immigrants.

Nellie Bly: The Original Stunt Girl

Nellie Bly, born Elizabeth Cochrane, got her first job by writing to protest a Pittsburgh newspaper's editorial saying a woman's place was in the home. The editor didn't print her letter, but hired her. Sent to Mexico, she was expelled. She became the model for "stunt girls" on newspapers by getting herself committed to the insane asylum at Bellevue and writing an exposé for the *New York World*. Although some reporters thought the stunt girl approach was self-exploitation, others understood that women's ability to "pass" in many ways was a boon for journalists.

Reporter Nellie Bly ready to travel, 1889

In 1899, in her biggest stunt, she set out to break the record of Jules Verne's hero in *Around the World in Eighty Days*. After seventy-two days, six hours, and ten minutes, Bly got a hero's welcome: the last lap of her trip was on a private train from San Francisco to New York, where she was serenaded by brass bands at every whistle-stop. In 1936, Dorothy Kilgallen picked up the challenge and beat Nelly Bly's time.

Ida Tarbell: Bringing Down Standard Oil

Ida Tarbell, the only girl in the freshman class at Allegheny College, taught in a seminary, worked for a magazine, and went to France, where she started sending columns to American papers. In 1893, she started writing for *McClure's Magazine*, covering early aviation experiments.

She made her name in 1902 by taking on Standard Oil, the first and largest oil trust, a Rockefeller company manufacturing 86 percent of the nation's oil. Congress had held a fruitless investigation, but Tarbell's voluminous research and a cooperative "deep throat" documented corrupt deals between refiners and railroads, also largely Rockefeller-owned. Tarbell's series ran for two years, causing a sensation and leading to government action four years later that disbanded the trust into smaller companies.

Ida B. Wells-Barnett: Lynching, Race, and Sex

There are many white women in the South who would marry colored men if such an act would not place them at once beyond the pale of society and within the clutches of the law. The miscegenation laws of the South leave the white man free to seduce all the colored girls he can, but it is death to the colored man who yields to the force and advances of a similar attraction in white women.
Ida B. Wells, editorial, Memphis Free Speech, *1892*

She knows nothing about the colored problem in the south. . . . A reputable or respectable negro has never been lynched and never will be.
The New York Times, *1892*

Ida B. Wells-Barnett, a former slave, taught at age sixteen to support seven brothers and sisters after their parents died. A part-time writer, she was the only woman at an African-American editors' convention in 1887. Two years later, she bought an interest in a Baptist weekly paper in Memphis, Tennessee, using it to criticize hiring practices in the school system. She lost her teaching job and became a crusading activist journalist. When three friends were shot, she urged blacks to "save our money and leave a town which will neither protect our lives and property." Two thousand people left.

Ida Wells-Barnett in undated photo

Ending lynching was her lifetime mission. The evidence told her that the alleged sexual crime at the heart of lynching often hid an economic motivation. White women, she wrote in her blistering editorials, were actually attracted to black men. As her campaign escalated, so did the criticism and the danger. Her paper destroyed by a mob, herself threatened with death, she went North to work for the leading black paper, the *New York Age*.

Jovita Idar: Mexican Feminism

One of the most prominent journalists in Spanish-language newspapers in south Texas, Jovita Idar founded *La Liga Femenil Mexicanista* in 1911 to oppose lynching and promote equal education for women. In 1914, during the Mexican Revolution, she wrote an article criticizing President Wilson's ordering troops to the Texas-Mexico border. The Texas Rangers were sent to close the paper down, but Idar stopped them by blocking the doorway. She lived until 1946, continuing to write about Mexican-American issues.

Marvel Cooke: Apollo Girls Are "Dogged Around"

Marvel Cooke was one of five African-American women in the student body of 20,000 at the University of Minnesota. In 1925, she went to work at W. E. B. Du Bois's magazine *The News*, New York's leading black paper. Her stories included an exposé of the working conditions of dancers at the famed Apollo Theater in Harlem ("Apollo Girls are 'Dogged Around'; Work Like Slaves"). In the 1950s, at the liberal *Daily Compass*, she wrote hard-hitting stories about heroin in the black community and prostitution. A lifelong activist, she coordinated activities for the Angela Davis Defense Committee in 1969.

Ethel Payne: Witnessing the Revolution

Mrs. Parks' act of rebellion touched off one of the most amazing reactions in the turbulent history of racial relations in the South. The young, the old, the middle aged, the lame and the halt, housewives, maids and cooks, bellhops, janitors and laborers, school teachers, doctors and lawyers—they were all taking to the road.

Chicago Defender, *February 1956*

THE GIRLS ON THE BUS

Before the new breed of New Age stiffs came on the campaign bus in the last few years, things were different. I could go out and have a couple of pops at an after-hours joint with my pal Alessandra Stanley of the *New York Times*. I could play blackjack on the campaign plane with Ann McDaniel of *Newsweek*. I could stop by an OTB parlor with Ann Devroy of the *Washington Post* and we could pick a good horse in the eighth. . . . Now the road is filled with a bunch of 30-something, touchy-feely guys, tying up all the cellular phone circuits trying to call home to talk baby talk to their wives and kids.

Maureen Dowd, New York Times reporter, 1993

Ethel Payne was frozen out of press conferences by President Eisenhower for rudeness, but Payne was only refusing to be polite about racial discrimination. As Washington correspondent for the *Chicago Defender*, she witnessed the major events of the Civil Rights movement and reported them all. She also participated, marching with Dr. Martin Luther King and was the only woman among civil rights leaders with President Lyndon Johnson as he signed civil rights legislation in 1965. Her reports from war-torn Vietnam were among the first mentioning Agent Orange. In her sixties, she became the first African-American woman news commentator on national radio and then on local television. Toward the end of her life, she syndicated her columns to the black press, covered civil war in Nigeria, and became an early advocate for Nelson Mandela's release from prison.

Janet Flanner: Letter from Paris

For over half a century, from 1931 until 1976, Janet Flanner reported from Europe for *The New Yorker* magazine. She wrote a prophetic profile of Adolf Hitler in 1936 and vivid coverage of the Nuremburg trials in 1945, but her most remarkable journalism was about Paris, especially the culture of American women living there, the "diehards," she called them, "to whom Paris during the 1920's and 30's seemed liberty itself."

Eleanor Roosevelt Meets the Press

Eleanor Roosevelt brought women into government and brought their ideas to bear on how the country was run. She also changed the role of women in journalism. Her insistence that the reporters covering the First Lady be female, forced major newspapers and wire services to hire at least one woman. Women's by-lines were no longer confined to small town journals. Early in her tenure, she gave women reporters a tour of the private living quarters at the White House. At her news conferences, usually crammed with seventy-five female reporters, Roosevelt assured press coverage for female experts in science, aviation, health, and education. In 1936, she invited the wives of fifty reporters attending the exclusively male Gridiron Club dinner to the White House, where they were entertained by members of the Women's National Press Club.

MASQUERADES: PASSING TO GET THE STORY

➤ In 1914, Emma Bugbee, who later covered Eleanor Roosevelt for the Tribune, stood at a street corner collection pail dressed in a Salvation Army costume, ringing a bell. Her Trib story lamented the cold-heartedness of the New Yorkers who just passed by.

➤ In the 1920s, Evelyn Seeley, working for a San Francisco newspaper, moved into a tenement in North Beach owned by a rich corporation to expose conditions there. The office boy posed as her husband.

➤ In 1921, Genevieve Forbes Herrick of the Chicago Tribune disguised herself as an immigrant and traveled from Ireland to America, publishing a thirteen-part series on immigration corruption and cruelty.

➤ During Herbert Hoover's administration, Beth Furman, working for the Associated Press, disguised herself as a member of the Girl Scout troop caroling inside the White House.

➤ In 1929, Esther Hamilton, Ohio newspaper reporter, managed to get access to a factory where there had been an explosion. Since no one was being admitted to the scene, she climbed into the hearse carrying the priest and, posing as a nurse, copied the list of dead and injured.

➤ In the 1930s, Beth Campbell, in Springfield, Missouri, put herself on a meager depression diet to see how her readers were faring. For ten days, she allowed herself twenty-five cents a day for meals.

➤ Cissy Patterson, editor of the Herald in Washington, D.C., went to a Salvation Army shelter in 1932 with only a comb, toothbrush, and eleven cents. In the days that followed, she was offered work as a cleaning woman at six dollars a week and as caretaker for a deaf couple at four dollars a week. "The Grand Canyon of Colorado," she wrote, "yawns no more dizzily than the pit of gold between the lives of the rich and the poor."

➤ In the early 1940s, Mary Ellen Leary posed as single woman on welfare seeking an abortion in order to expose the police corruption in California that allowed abortion rings to flourish. During World War II, she covered the state capitol in Sacramento, California.

➤ In the 1950s Marvel Cooke went undercover to write about the traffic in "Negro" maids at "the Bronx Slave Market, where Negro women wait, in rain or shine, in bitter cold or under broiling sun, to be hired by housewives looking for bargains in human labor."

➤ In 1963, Gloria Steinem went undercover as a Playboy Bunny for Show magazine when the Playboy Club opened in New York. Her trenchant article concluded, among other things, that all women are Playboy Bunnies.

Cartoon of Eleanor Roosevelt and female reporters, 1934

Reporting from the Front

Margaret Fuller: Witnessing the Revolution

They had counted the cost before they entered on this perilous struggle; they had weighed life and all its material advantages against liberty and made their election. . . . I saw the wounded, all that could go, laden upon their baggage cases. . . . The women were ready, their eyes too resolved, if sad.

Rome, 1849

Margaret Fuller served without pay as the first editor of *The Dial*, wrote a book about Indian tribes, and attacked the social order with *Woman in the 19th Century* (1845), which called for equality of the sexes. At his wife's suggestion, Horace Greeley hired Fuller as literary editor of the *New York Tribune*. Before Greeley sent her to report on the European literary scene in 1846, she wrote about imprisoned prostitutes and life in an insane asylum. In Italy, she became a partisan in the revolution, as well as an observant reporter.

Peggy Hull: Crashing World War I

Peggy Hull, a Kansas typesetter, moved to Hawaii, where her husband worked as a reporter and she wrote for the women's page. She left, alone, for Texas, where she got a job with El Paso newspapers in 1916, just as the United States was organizing an expedition into Mexico to capture revolutionary Pancho Villa. Hull went on training marches with the troops. When World War I broke out in April 1917, she went to Europe, writing "the woman's angle," although she was refused official credentials. The War Department relented in 1918 and made her the first woman authorized to cover a war zone.

> ## COVERING ELEANOR ROOSEVELT
>
> ⊰ Lorena Hickok, former servant, society news writer, then serious reporter, covered the kidnapping of the Lindbergh baby, the decade's biggest story, in 1932. That year, she was the only woman reporter traveling with Franklin Roosevelt's campaign. She convinced the Associated Press to assign independent coverage of Eleanor Roosevelt.
>
> ⊱ Beth Campbell worked at a Springfield, Missouri, paper edited by George Olds, who had encouraged Sigrid Arne, an early AP reporter. With seven years of experience, she came to Washington in 1936.
>
> ⊰ Emma Bugbee had been working for the New York Herald Tribune since 1910, when she was given a desk in an alcove on another floor because the men were too uncomfortable in her presence in the newsroom.
>
> ⊱ Ruby Black, hired as the first woman by the United Press, was also Washington correspondent for *La Democracia*, a Puerto Rican paper.

Dorr, Beatty, Vorse: "Red" Reporting

Rheta Childe Dorr became determined to make her mark in the world as a journalist the day she read a tombstone inscription that said: "Also Harriet, wife of the above." She covered World War I battlefields for *The New Mail* and freelanced from England, where she covered the suffrage movement in 1912 and 1913, once carrying $20,000 sewn into her corset to jailed leader Emmeline Pankhurst. In 1917, she and Bessie Beatty of the *San Francisco Bulletin* traveled with the Russian Women's Death Battalion, reporting their defeat of German troops and their loss of half their number in the battle.

Bessie Beatty covered Russia for the *San Francisco Examiner* in 1917 and left Petrograd on the last train out with Louise Bryant in 1918. In New York, she became editor of *McCalls*

Louise Bryant in the new
Soviet Union, c. 1919

magazine, where she published Bryant's journalism and wrote *The Red Heart of Russia*, her own eyewitness account of the revolution. After 1940, she worked in radio.

Mary Heaton Vorse was the Moscow correspondent for the Hearst papers in 1921, several weeks before male reporters for American dailies were admitted to the country. Almost single-handedly inventing labor journalism, from 1912 until the late 1940s, she wrote about international events for *Harper's*, *Scribners*, *The Atlantic*, and the radical magazine *The Masses*, where she was an editor. Central to the Bohemian life of Greenwich Village and Provincetown, Massachusetts—the Provincetown Players had started on her wharf in 1915—she lived to be the oldest official war correspondent during World War II.

Louise Bryant: "I Believe in Equality, Even in My Own Country"

Louise Bryant campaigned for suffrage in Oregon and left her dentist husband for radical writer John Reed, going to Russia with him in 1917. She wrote many articles and a book, *Six Months In Russia* (1918). While she lectured across America, explaining the revolution, she also joined suffragists picketing the White House, hanging Woodrow Wilson in effigy, going to jail, and staging hunger strikes in 1919.

When a Senate Committee investigating "Bolshevik propaganda" called her to testify, Bryant denied advocating the violent overthrow of the American government. She believed in self-determination, she said, and if the Russians wanted the government they had, America should not intervene. Questioned about the suffrage pickets, she replied, "I believe in equality . . . even in my own country."

After Reed's death in 1920, she was a Hearst correspondent in Europe, holding exclusive interviews with Lenin and, later, Benito Mussolini, the future fascist dictator of Italy.

Josephine Herbst in Spain

> More than once I wondered at what we had assumed to be the vaunted independence of the American woman: when I saw the proud authority of the Spanish woman . . . when I saw women of sixty come proudly home, erect, mangnificently wrathful as they shook their fists at far distant towers of enemy smoke piercing the sky, or burst out into gorgeous obscenities oddly mixed with symbolic religiosity, which reduced my memory of fashionable ladies back home, with their little stereotyped lavender curls and their mincing high heels, to a parody of a potential they had forfeited.
>
> *1937*

Josephine Herbst left Iowa for New York in the 1920s and became a well-known fiction writer. In the 1930s, she wrote for several magazines about farmers' strikes in the Midwest, an uprising in Cuba, German resistance to Hitler, and the Spanish Civil War.

Dorothy Thompson on the radio, 1939

Martha Gellhorn: Spain, Dachau, Vietnam

"The war is over," the doctor said. "Germany is defeated."

We sat in that room, in that accursed cemetery prison, and no one had anything more to say. Still, Dachau seemed to me the most suitable place in Europe to hear the news of victory. For surely this was was made to abolish Dachau, and all the other places like Dachau, and everything that Dachau stood for, and to abolish it forever.

Colliers Magazine, May 1945

Martha Gellhorn, born in St. Louis, raised by a suffragist mother, worked in New York, then went to Spain for *Colliers* magazine. She never stopped covering wars. During World War II, she reported the Russian invasion of Finland, the Japanese invasion of China, and, stowing away on a hospital ship, the American landing at Normandy. In 1966, angered by her reporting from Vietnam—"We were hated in Vietnam and rightly"—the American military denied her a visa to return there.

Dorothy Thompson: "The Only Female Newspaperman of Her Time"

Dorothy Thompson, equal in national prestige only to Eleanor Roosevelt, broadcast World War II for NBC radio, but first made her reputation in print, where "the only female newspaperman of her time," as her (male) colleagues called her, reported from Berlin until Hitler expelled her in 1934. In 1936, Helen Reid, vice president of the *New York Tribune*, whom Thompson knew from suffrage work, got her a column in the *New York Tribune*. The column appeared three times a week for twenty-two years, pioneering the modern column on world affairs. In 1937, she added a monthly column in the *Ladies' Home Journal*. Moving from a recorder to an analyst and interpreter of events, she wrote searingly against Fascism and was an early champion of Arab rights.

Thompson's real fame came on the radio. In 1935, she debated "Is woman happier in the home?" with a male "expert." By 1936, she was the leading voice against fascism in America. In 1938, having witnessed and written about the concentration camps in Germany, she broadcast the truth in German to the German people.

Cowan and Higgins: Daredevils

Patton: What is the first law of war?

Cowan: You kill him before he kills you.

Patton: She stays.

General Patton to Ruth B. Cowan, Associated Press Correspondent, recently arrived in Algeria, 1943

Ruth Cowan covered Chicago crime for the Associated Press in the 1930s, sneaking into a gangster's funeral for a story. She replaced Beth Campbell on the Eleanor Roosevelt beat in

Marguerite Higgins in Korea, 1950

1940. Based in London during World War II, she went to Algiers with the Women's Auxiliary Army Corps. Until she retired in 1956, she covered politics in Washington.

Marguerite Higgins went to Europe for the *New York Tribune* in 1944 (while writing fashion stories for *Mademoiselle* magazine on the side) and was present for the liberation of Dachau, the Nuremberg trials, and the Berlin blockade. She covered the Korean War, enhancing her daredevil reputation. Opposed to American involvement in Vietnam, she wrote about the "arrogance of seeking to impose our own values on a country that resents our demands."

What Do Women Want? Advice!

To the coyness of a kitten, let a girl add the friskiness of a colt.
Pittsburgh Playground Journal, *c. 1910*

Since times are hard now and my father earned only five dollars this week, I began to talk about giving up my studies and going to work in order to help . . . but my mother didn't even want to hear of it.
1907

My daughter has fallen in love with a Gentile. . . . I'm trying with goodness to influence my daughter to break up with this boy. . . . True, it could happen that she could marry a Jewish man and after the wedding not be able to stand him. But with a Jew it's still different.
1928

When we come to the children on Sunday, the only entertainment is television. . . . And, as often occurs with young American women, our daughter in law is not a great cook. It seems that the dinner is almost always from cans.
1950s

When my younger daughter took me to the beauty parlor and had me get my hair tinted black as it used to be before it turned gray [my husband] didn't like it. When I got home, he stared at me with a hurt look, then began to shout that I shouldn't have done it.
1960s

I could have married an American girl, but I was drawn to a girl from the old country because I had been told that American girls were spenders and bossed their husbands.
1970s

The Bintel Brief

From 1881 to 1925, *The Jewish Daily Forward*, a Yiddish newspaper, served the community of immigrants from Eastern Europe. "Bintel Brief," an advice column, was a forum for airing the confusions of American life for the new arrivals, particularly the women.

Dear Dorothy Dix

A young girl who lets any one boy monopolize her simply shuts the door in the face of good times and her chances of making a better match.

Men are a selfish lot.

Love is only the dessert of life. The minute you try to live on dessert, you get sick of it, and you can get sicker of love than you can of anything else in the world.

Dorothy Dix, one of the first personal advice columnists, wrote for the *New Orleans Picayune* from 1896 to 1901, when she was hired by the *New York Evening Journal* to replace "Beatrice Fairfax," who abandoned the column to work for suffrage. Dix's became the longest-running feature in a newspaper written by its original author. She counseled women to take charge of their lives and campaigned for suffrage, women's education and employment.

Magazines

Sara Hale and Godey's Lady's Book: Pushing the Envelope, but Not Too Far

Remember that woman must influence while man governs, and that their duties, though equal in dignity and importance, can never be identical. Like the influence of the sun and air on the plant, both must unite in perfecting society, and which is of paramount value can never be settled.
Editorial, 1846

Sara Hale, the most famous nineteenth-century editor, is credited with writing "Mary Had a Little Lamb" and with persuading President Lincoln to make Thanksgiving a national holiday. Widowed at thirty-four, left with five children to support, she went to work editing *Ladies Magazine*. In 1837, a Philadelphia publisher named Godey merged his magazine with hers, establishing the first important woman's magazine—named after a man.

Hale made *Godey's Lady's Book* a huge success, its circulation reaching 150,000 before the Civil War. She published the literary stars of the day—Emerson, Hawthorne, Longfellow—and important consumer information on the sewing machine, the washing machine, a model home, and the typewriter. For forty years, Sara Hale and the magazine pushed for women's education, campaigning for female seminaries to train women for the professions and for earning their own livings. She was a pioneer in getting women into teaching and medicine.

Like women's magazine editors after her, Sara Hale walked a thin line, advocating reform but never upsetting the status quo. Keeping "disturbing" events like the 1848 Seneca Falls convention and the Civil War out of her pages, she also eliminated nearly all the women in the abolition movement from her *Woman's Record*, a book with 1,800 biographical sketches, which retold world history as the history of women. She was antisuffrage, believing women would become less attractive to men if they demanded the vote and that it was better to stay in the domestic realm and exert indirect power.

The Ladies' Home Journal: "Never Underestimate the Power of a Woman"

The 1883 magazine, *Ladies' Journal* became *Ladies' Home Journal* when a printer's error inserted, consciously or not, the crucial extra word: *home*. Columns included "Domestic Happiness," "Hints for Housekeepers," and "Fashion Annex," and Louisa May Alcott sold many stories there.

By 1889, with a circulation over 100,000, Edward Bok, a Scribner's book editor, took over, stamping his personality on *LHJ*'s pages for thirty years. With more articles about events and issues of public interest, Bok also made a concerted effort to shape American taste with coverage of American fashions, interior design, and architectural plans.

His biggest bugaboo was fraudulent advertising and among the home-brewed "cures" he exposed was Lydia Pinkham's pills. After 1892, the magazine refused ads for patent medicines.

Women's Work

Vogue didn't have a terribly professional atmosphere. It was genteel. You made virtually no money at all and never discussed it—just as you didn't discuss whether the magazine did, either.

Grace Mirabella describing the 1950s

Ten years ago, I dreamed about becoming editor-in-chief of a woman's magazine. Accordingly, I went to work at one of the largest in the country, only to find that all the Katharine Hepburn roles were filled by short men.

Pamela Howard, Saturday Review, 1972

Ms. Magazine: Never Underestimate the Power of a Women's Movement

The premiere issue of the first national feminist glossy hit newsstands in 1971 and the magazine began monthly publication in 1972. The founders were journalists: publisher Patricia Carbine had been editor-in-chief of *McCall's*; Gloria Steinem worked at *New York* magazine, whose editor, Clay Felker, helped launch Ms. Steinem said that her feminist journalism began at a speak-out on abortion rights, where she "first heard women stand up and say what it was like to have to get an illegal abortion. . . . I never in my life heard women telling the truth in public, and it really was a kind of cataclysmic event for me."

First issue of Ms. *magazine, December 20, 1971, introduced as an insert in* New York *magazine*

For some readers, Ms. magazine represented a voice in the wilderness, while others saw it as a sell-out of the feminist revolution. Its impact on the culture, in addition to giving encouragement, space, and payment to writers who couldn't say what they wanted to in the mainstream, was to make Ms. an acceptable term of address. This did not come easily. The New York Times did not adopt Ms. to refer to women until 1986.

The magazine thrived through the 1970s, but faltered in the 1980s, as the women's movement became more scattered and diverse and mainstream magazines began covering what had once been the exclusive province of Ms. In the 1990s, it freed itself of commercial advertising and appointed Marcia Gillespie, former editor-in-chief of *Essence*, as executive editor.

Visual Media

In 1870 there were 418 female artists and art teachers; in 1910 there were 15,583 women working in art-related fields. Part of this explosion was caused by the proliferation of new media, as well as the developing fields of advertising and public relations, where illustrators, cartoonists, and photographers found markets for their work.

Jessie Tarbox Beals: A Little Lady with a Big Camera

Beals prided herself on her "hustle" and advised other women to get some. The first female news photographer, she was seen around town in Buffalo, New York, dragging her 8 x 10 camera to fires and floods and standing on ladders to peer over transoms and photograph courtroom scenes. By the 1920s, inspired by her, New York was flooded with camera-toting women.

Cartooning for Suffrage

The nineteenth-century women's movement press, like the rest of the country's, was primarily devoted to words. After 1910, feminists paid more attention to visual messages, planning marches and actions full of theatrical effects and striking back against the enemy's ridiculing cartoons and images by printing visual statements of its own. *The Woman Voter* in New York City was the first to have an art editor to manage the illustrations.

Did You Know?

Novelist Pauline Hopkins edited *Colored American Magazine*, the first African-American journal established in the twentieth century, between the two world wars. Hired to head the woman's department, she turned it into a forum for black writers and scholars.

Rose O'Neill's Kewpies

In 1893, Rose O'Neill came to Greenwich Village, bobbed her hair, published a novel, and started drawing illustrations. She sold *The Ladies' Home Journal* and other magazines her cartoons featuring Kewpies, androgynous figures, named after Cupid, often naked, their hair in topknots, their behavior communal and caring. The figures, combining the New Woman and the emancipated New Man, became the best known characters in American pop culture until Mickey Mouse.

O'Neill drew posters for the suffrage cause and opened a shop on Madison Avenue in New York that sold suffrage dolls. In 1915, the National Woman's suffrage Association issued postcards of Kewpies carrying "Votes for Women" placards. When they were made into dolls by a commercial manufacturer, the androgynous boys O'Neill designed became bashful girls.

Comic Strips: Why Brenda Starr Never Married

The story of comic strips is a complex saga of coded messages, male visions of women, and very little input from women themselves. The earliest ones show women in domestic, family roles. After 1920, female figures increase, many supposedly with jobs (as "stenogs" or actresses), but while they have the glamorous trappings of work, they never actually work. The lives of women in the Jazz Age comics are about romance. A small exception is Gladys Parker, one of the few women cartoonists, who drew two "girl strips": *Flapper Fanny* and *Mopsy*.

Rosie O'Neill's Kewpies, 1915

The 1930s introduced the vamp Betty Boop. First drawn for animated films, her body and sauciness were modeled on Mae West. The censors kept Boop from surviving past the end of the decade. There were also a lot of heros' girlfriends (Dick Tracy's Tess Trueheart), some assertive undercover cops, and newspaper "gals" like Lois Lane, who appeared in 1938. The 1940s featured a stunning array of strong, determined females like Wonder Woman and Brenda Starr. Mega-busty Daisy Mae and L'il Abner presided over the 1950s.

In the 1960s and 1970s, mainstream comics reflected the reaction to women's liberation. Bad guy R. Crumb created Angelfood McSpade, an African Amazon with an unbridled sexual appetite and Lenore Goldberg, an obnoxious, brassy, ugly feminist. Good guy Gary Trudeau drew Joanie Caucus in *Doonesbury*, a fortyish dropout from marriage ("For me, the role of little homemaker was stifling") who went to law school.

Women scarcely penetrated mainstream comics. In 1940, Dale Messick drew the flamboyant reporter Brenda Starr, torn between career and romance, who managed to avoid marriage until 1976. Messick, the first female cartoonist to be syndicated, changed her name from Dalia to Dale and mailed her work to newspapers so no one would know she was a woman.

Lois Lane and Wonder Woman were male creations. By the 1970s, feminism entered the comics, but underground, with Wimmen's Comix and Tits & Clits. Although the 1980s saw crossovers like Nicole Hollander and Lynda Barry, the bulk of feminist cartooning—with the notable exception of Roz Chast, a regular in *The New Yorker*—remains underground, in comic books like Slutburger Stories and in 'zines.

Jessie Tarbox Beals, photographing, Buffalo, New York, 1903

Feminism and Media: The Second Wave

> We are tired of Bellowing and Rothing, Mailoring and Malamuding and prepared to give an outlet to the feminine consciousness.
> *Preamble to* Aphra, *the first feminist literary magazine, 1969*

The first medium of communication in the Women's Liberation movement was talk. Small consciousness-raising groups formed the basis of building the earliest days of the movement. The next medium was what Russians called *samizdats*, short position papers, mostly group-written, sometimes only a page long, that were hand-circulated. At the same time, the underground press, including the antiwar press, and most leftist publications, where young, politicized women were writing, began to publish articles about the movement.

When *Ms.* magazine published its first issue in 1972, an entire feminist print culture already preceded it. Between 1968 and 1973, more than 560 feminist publications appeared. Three-quarters were newsletters, many sponsored by the National Organization for Women, which had been founded in 1966, or its local chapters, and other groups that were decidedly more revolutionary.

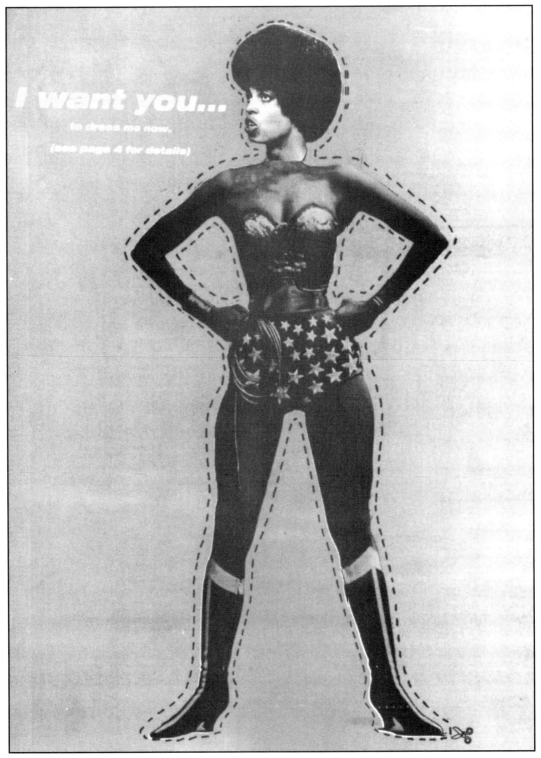

Angela Davis as Wonder Woman, montage in the "'zine" Bust, fall, 1993

Television

Television must show a new image of a woman as a doer, as an educated, serious-minded individual person.
CBS internal memorandum, 1970

Take Linda Ellerbee. Or Oprah Winfrey for that matter. If one of them were half of a 6:00 news-team, you can be darn sure that neither would respond to a treacly news story with a kneejerk chuckle and a suddenly serious "Thanks, Bob."
Jane Hanauer, "Mary Hart Sucks,"
Bust (*'zine*), 1993

The First Female Newscaster
In 1936, as NBC prepared its inaugural broadcast, veteran announcer George Hicks walked off just before airtime because he couldn't stand the chaos in the studio. Former newspaper feature writer Betty Goodwin Baker stepped in and did the twenty-minute show. Not long afterward, she married and was fired.

Notes from the Third Year: Women's Liberation, *1970*

Another First Female Newscaster
The first woman to anchor a television news show was Dorothy Fuldheim in Cleveland, Ohio, in 1947. A former network radio commentator, she stayed on the air anchoring the six o'clock news for more than thirty years, longer than any other newscaster.

Barbara Walters: Finally There?

Barbara Walters of the *Today* show has been allowed out of the house (including the schoolhouse), but, as is proper for a woman, she has not gone out unescorted. She is flanked by two men: Hugh Downs and Joe Garagiola.
Critic Winnie Stark in New York *magazine, 1964*

Media Activism: A Time Line

1850: Jane Grey Swisshelm, newspaper publisher, first official female Washington correspondent, strikes the first blow for equal access by insisting that women be admitted to the Senate press gallery.

1852: Mathilde Franziska Anneke establishes a German language feminist woman's journal in Milwaukee, Wisconsin, using women compositors. Male printers form a union to protect themselves against the encroachment of females. When the women back down, she moves to New York and keeps it going for two years.

1868: Jane Cunningham Croly and other women organize a dinner for the New York Press Club honoring Charles Dickens, but are not allowed to attend. Croly, reporter and columnist, responds by creating Sorosis, the first women's club, a forum for education and the exchange of ideas. In 1889, she founds the Women's Press Club of New York.

1880s: Delilah Beasley is the first African-American woman to write for a white newspaper, as part-time correspondent for the *Cincinnati Enquirer.* She writes a column for the *Oakland Tribune* from 1923 to 1934.

1965: Charlayne Hunter-Gault, who made front-page news desegregating the University of Georgia, becomes the first African-American woman on the staff of *The New Yorker* magazine. She moves to the *New York Times* in 1968; in the mid-seventies, she convinces her editors to use the word *black* instead of *Negro.* She makes the transition to television as a reporter on the *McNeil-Lehrer Report* for the Public Broadcasting System.

1970: Feminists take over the offices of the *Ladies' Home Journal*, criticizing the home-and-hearth focus of the magazine. The group demands that the (male) publisher allow them to create their own feminist issue of the magazine. Eventually they win an 8-page supplement.

Feminist actions are also directed against the CBS stockholders meet-

Charlayne Hunter Gault, 1961

ing, the *San Francisco Chronicle*, and the Washington, D.C., daily newspapers for their failure to hire women.

1972: Women at the *New York Times* present grievances to the publisher, including pay disparities (men are paid an average $59 more a week); lack of women on the editorial board; and the general white male voice of the paper.

NOW documents sex discrimination in the media, calling it a "wasteland for women": 90 percent of the voice-overs in television commercials are male; women are almost always shown working in the home and worrying about their appearance, 90 percent of the news stories are about men. The organization asks the Federal Communications Commission to deny renewal of licenses to stations discriminating against women. An avalanche of female hires is the direct result.

1973: The Associated Press has no female bureau chiefs. A rejected applicant is told she doesn't "look like a bureau chief" and should "fix herself up" and lose weight before she can be considered.

1974: Architecture critic Ada Louise Huxtable joins the editorial board of the *New York Times* and Charlotte Curtis becomes an editor of the "Op Ed" page. Neither has taken part in the brewing legal case.

Women's liberation members sit-in at the Ladies' Home Journal, New York, March 18, 1970

LATE 1970S: The Equal Employment Opportunity Commission finds reasonable cause for sex discrimination at the Associated Press. Suits are filed against *Newsday, Newsweek, The Readers Digest,* and NBC. None ever reaches court. NBC pays a $2 million out-of-court settlement in 1977. The following year, *The New York Times* agrees to a stepped-up affirmative action plan and pays $233,500, euphemistically called "annuities," to the women in the lawsuit.

1981: Pulitzer Prize to Shirley Christian, the *Miami Herald*'s chief Central American correspondent, who left the Associated Press because they refused to let a female cover Central America.

1983: The AP women's lawsuit is settled out of court for more than $800,000 in back wages.

1992: Lesbian Avengers occupy the offices of *Self* magazine in New York to protest its participation in an upcoming convention in Colorado, which had passed antigay legislation. The magazine agrees to join the boycott of that state.

The Detroit News starts the Deb Price column, "Say Hi to Joyce," the first gay column ever to run regularly in a daily newspaper.

Barbara Walters, the first female anchor on network television, moving from secretary to writer, became cohost of NBC's *Today* show in 1964. Before that, the only roles for women were the "Today girls," who smiled and read commercials. Walters finally was made cohost of the *ABC Evening News* with Harry Reasoner in September 1976. The job paid $1 million a year, making her the highest-paid TV news personality of the time.

Was Big Bird a Male Chauvinist Pig?

On New York's public television station, Joan Ganz Cooney rose through the ranks until, in 1969, she created and produced the innovative children's series, *Sesame Street*. While Cooney's advancement in the field was celebrated, the show was initially criticised for its sexism. Over the years, female characters have been given larger, more active roles to play and positions of authority to occupy.

Linda Ellerbee: Troublemaker

We call them Twinkies. You've seen them on television acting the news, modeling and fracturing the news while you wonder whether they've read the news—or if they've blow-dried their brains too.

Behind the camera, editing the pictures, producing the programs and running the networks, there were damn few, if any, women—and that situation continued for many years after the first rush to hire women in television news. You can count the number of women executives on both hands and have two thumbs left over with which to twiddle, and wait.

Linda Ellerbee started as a local television news reporter in Houston in 1973 and has moved from one local or national show to another ever since. She is not a Twinkie and not a glamor girl. Never hiding her intelligence and feistiness, she did not fit television's female model. When cancer struck, she did not hide that, either, appearing on the air without the requisite camouflage of a wig. In 1986, she wrote *So It Goes*, a sassy book about her life in television.

Censorship, Formal and Informal

Victoria Woodhull was arrested four times for obscenity in her outspoken weekly newspaper. The charges were brought by Anthony Comstock, who later prosecuted Mae West. Woodhull and her sister, Tennessee Clafin, spent long periods in jail, awaiting trial. Finally, on June 26, 1873, a judge declared that the obscenity law did not cover newspapers.

Although the suffrage amendment appeared on the Oregon ballot six times between 1884 and 1912, it got little coverage in the state's largest and most influential newspaper. In 1905, a meeting attended by several prominent Eastern leaders made the movement legitimate for coverage in the *Oregonian*. It was consistently negative.

President Woodrow Wilson attempted to use the wartime Committee on Public Information to censor press coverage of Alice Paul's White House pickets and the jailing of the demonstrators.

There are no reports in the newspaper of record about the 1973 sex discrimination suit filed against the *New York Times* by seven women on the staff, representing all the women at the paper.

The 1992 pro-choice march on Washington, D.C., the largest demonstration in the capital in American history, got less ink or airtime than Macy's Thanksgiving Day parade.

> **"**
> I would give up my life for my
> children, but not myself.
> **"**

Edna, in Kate Chopin's novel
The Awakening, *1899*

CHAPTER 8

Domestic Life

*I*t is not that women are really smaller-minded, weaker-minded, more timid and vacillating; but that whosoever, man or woman, lives always in a small, dark place, is always guarded, protected, directed and restrained, will become inevitably narrowed and weakened by it. The woman is narrowed by the home and the man is narrowed by the woman.

Charlotte Perkins Gilman, The Home, 1903

I sleep in a hammock, which requires no making up; I break an egg for my breakfast and sip it raw from the shell; I make lemonade in a glass and then rinse the glass—and my housework is done for the day.

Sculptor Elizabet Ney describing her Austin, Texas studio, c. 1905

If you write me and wish me conventional happiness, I will never forgive you. Don't wish me happiness—wish me courage and strength and a sense of humor—I will need them all.

Anne Morrow, letter to a friend after deciding to marry Charles Lindbergh, 1928

Cary Grant: Haven't you ever met a man who could make you happy?
Mae West: Sure, lots of times.
She Done Him Wrong, 1933

Once the Right realizes there's a lesbian baby boom, it will try to pass legislation requiring people to have a marriage license to buy a turkey baster.

Donna Red Wing, Gay and Lesbian Alliance Against Defamation, 1994

**Woman with broom,
19th century**

Nurse with her "charge," 1899

*F*ew words are as loaded as *family* and *home*. Few criticisms of what women do carry as much weight as the one claiming that those who work for freedom and equality are destroying family and home. Although many women, but not all, have liked living in families of varying shapes and in homes of one kind or another, both family and home have come in for protest and reinvention, and both are understood to be political concepts.

Narrowly defined in public speech, *family* and *home* actually have different meanings for women at different times in history and among different races and classes. For white women in Colonial America, the home was the means of staying alive. For Native Americans, the tribe was as much a part of family as parents or children were. When industrialization took production—and men—out of the home, white women's lives changed. A slave woman's blood family was often torn apart and the communal family perhaps became more important. Home might be Africa or heaven or freedom, but rarely was it the place the slave owners had brought them to.

In spite of the sentimentality associated with it, marriage has come in for constant criticism from women bent on changing the status quo. Among nineteenth-century feminist pioneers, many dropped the word *obey* from their marriage ceremonies. Lucy Stone retained her name, leading other women who did the same to call themselves "Lucy Stoners." Elizabeth Cady Stanton and Ernestine Rose flouted respectability by advocating divorce reform. Theirs was the revolutionary idea that a woman should be able to end a marriage if it didn't please her.

Questions of sex and marriage were intensely debated throughout the 1850s.

Iron with bell in the handle, used to monitor the work of slave women, c. 1850

Although most feminists wanted to reform laws governing relations between the sexes and the state, a more radical fringe was growing that would advocate banishing all the laws. From abolitionist reformers came a movement of sex radicals promoting open discussion of sexuality, an end to censorship, and abolition of all constraints that turned a wife into her husband's chattel. The free lovers, of whom the most outspoken and controversial was Victoria Woodhull, wanted sexual coupling freed of coercion; they didn't advocate promiscuous sex. By the turn of the century, marriage, divorce, and sex education had become mainstream issues.

> **I**t was possible, sometimes necessary, to be "married" to one's work. Since many professions just opening to women forced them to resign if they married, and because women understood the difficulty of managing both home lives and work, many, especially the activists, remained single or else married late in life.

The relationship between work and home for women was the next frontier. In the heated discussions of the late nineteenth and early twentieth centuries, you can hear some women rattling their cages and others embracing their houses, much as you can today. No conflict was as entirely about middle-class white women as this one was and is. Black women did not have the choice not to work. While settlement house founder Jane Addams could strive for release from "the family claim," black women could strive for time with their families and release from the white women's houses in which they worked. "A comfortable concentration camp," was how Betty Friedan described the home in *The Feminine Mystique* in 1963. She—and the other Smith College graduates whose experience underlay Friedan's book—were reacting to the previous decade's insistence that white women and their suburban houses were merged. They were rebelling against their capitulation to cultural coercion, to a world in which television ads featured women nearly having orgasms over clean ovens.

Yet during those same years, a home could be a sanctuary. In Little Rock, Arkansas, in the mid-1950s, the fight to integrate the public schools began and ended in the home of newspaper publishers Daisy Bates and her husband. Every morning, the nine teenagers who would brave the state's wrath to integrate the high school met at the Bates home to plan the day's confrontations. Every evening, they returned there to strategize and get support.

For all its restriction, home has been a place where radical ideas were aired without the repercussions public space brought. The nineteenth-century women's movement was born and thrived in women's parlors. It might be a convenient place to build a business—as all the Lydia Pinkhams, Sarah Breedlove Walkers, and Martha Chases, women who mixed concoctions at their kitchen stoves or sewed dolls in their workrooms—could attest. In the late twentieth century, women dropping out of corporate life for entrepreneurship are not only frustrated by glass ceilings, but eager to have some relationship to their own ceilings at home.

For most of American history, it was restriction, legal and social, not choice, that kept women at home. It is against the coercion, not the houses, that women's protest has been aimed. Elizabeth Cady Stanton, who knew Indian cultures and white communities like Brook Farm, where women's roles were flexible, always saw the isolation of housewives as a social problem. Nineteenth-century activists kept envisioning collective domestic lives and organized for change, including a campaign for wages for housework, after the Civil War.

Although forced marriages existed on a large scale—either directly forced, as in the case of the Japanese Picture Brides, or indirectly, by a system that made it impossible for a woman to support herself—there were always alternatives to nuclear families. One was communal living. The Shakers, led by Ann Lee, built nineteen settlements between the Revolution and the 1820s. Experimental communes, some associated with free

Nina E. Allender drawing, **The Suffragist,** *June 13, 1914*

love, attracted the interest of some nineteenth-century feminists. A century later, many second-wave feminists had spent parts of the 1960s in communal living, acquiring more critical ideas about the role of women in nuclear families and the institution of heterosexuality.

In the nineteenth century, when women chose to live with other women, their arrangements were called Boston marriages. It was assumed that these were friendships, which, indeed, they were. Whether they were also romantic and sexual marriages is sometimes hard to determine, but many surely were. The growth of women's colleges provided homes for many female couples, as did the settlement movement and women's politics.

The fact that more than half the first women's college graduates did not marry struck terror in the hearts of defenders of the status quo and caused a huge backlash against women's education. But women persisted in getting educations instead of husbands: three-quarters of

Roz Chast cartoon, 1988

the women who went on to get Ph.D.'s in American universities between 1877 and 1924 remained single. In 1960, the situation reversed: around 80 per cent of female graduates married in their twenties.

A wife almost always became a mother. During the years of colonization and expansion, white women's babies had been necessary for the country's survival, and women had as many children as they could bear. After the Revolution, childbearing was still a woman's purpose in life, as well as her patriotic duty. Black women's babies were up for sale. The choice to not have children was more possible for white women as reliable birth control was developed and the right to use it won. "Voluntary motherhood" was part of the nineteenth-century feminist agenda long before there was technology to support it. A mother did not always become a wife, and many a feminist was happy to point out that motherhood was much glorified, but somehow the glory didn't apply if the word *unwed* came before *mother*.

It was hard, but possible, to resist the social and economic pressure to marry and have children. Westward expansion offered, among other things, escape from marriage and motherhood. Some women abandoned families, others just refused and struck out on their own on the prairie or in the mining towns. Iowa homesteader Elizabeth Corey always signed herself "Bachelor Bess."

In Montana, "The Crazy Mountains" still stand as testimony to one possible price of resisting. Originally the "Crazy Woman Mountains," legends say that a woman, overcome by the chores of the wagon train, ran away, only to be found, depressed and incoherent, in the mountains.

Feminist attention shifted to cooperative housekeeping. The first reformers were trying to improve their own lives. Victoria Woodhull wanted apartment hotels and child care services. Later, cooperative domestic schemes were invented by rich women for immigrants and poor women.

Campaigns for day care centers, public kitchens, and cooperative housing for industrial workers went on all through the 1890s. All the media, not just feminist publications, took up the search for better domestic arrangements. The *Ladies' Home Journal* and *The Woman's Journal* regularly reported on cooperative housekeeping for fifty years. "The private kitchen must go the way of the spinning wheel, of which it is the contemporary," snapped Zona Gale, who won a Pulitzer Prize for Drama when she wasn't thinking about kitchens.

Children as a cause occupied much of women's political work. Civil War widows were among the first to get child care help outside their own families. Working, immigrant mothers followed. No issue revealed the country's class and race distinctions more clearly than how children were or were not cared for: from black mammys in Southern households to exploitation of child labor. And no issue has been more emotional as a barricade to women's progress than the welfare of children.

Children have also been an organizing tool. Many women first entered politics working for the "acceptable" goal of child welfare and evolved to other activities. At the turn of the century, Mary Church Terrell, founder and first president of the National Association of Colored Women, whose members were likely to be working mothers, led the group to establish kindergartens and day nurseries. A network of mother clubs provided information on rearing children and running a home. Just as the white world was professionalizing housework and motherhood, training experts to replace what had been "woman's instinct," Terrell joined them by raising money for schools of domestic science.

Depression and war were good for child care. Federally financed day care, created largely to provide employment for teachers, was part of the Works Progress Administration program during the 1930s. In 1941, when mothers' labor was needed for the war effort, Congress appropriated money for day care and nursery schools in a record two weeks. By 1945, 3,100 centers cared for 130,000 children. At the war's end, the funds were withdrawn.

No campaign in history, except, perhaps, the seventy years' attempt to persuade women that they didn't want to vote, equaled the effort to drive women home after the end of World War II. Job layoffs were immediate, suburban houses went up, financing was easy, and every expert and media pundit propagandized wife and mother as the only role for women.

It worked. Between 1945 and 1960, the average marriage age was the lowest in the Western world and the birth rate soared. For the first time, college-educated women had as many children as poor women did.

The white gloves that were so integral to the public image of First Lady Mamie Eisenhower became emblematic—and not only of a ladyhood that defined female middle-class life in the 1950s. Folklore attested to another purpose: Mrs. Eisenhower's gloves were detectives. Brushing along a dining table or bookshelf, they exposed the cardinal sin of female life in that decade: *dust!*

The road was short from white gloves to Betty Friedan's "concentration camp." Along a somewhat longer road, the daughters of fifties housewives became the hippies, antiwar activists, freedom riders, and women's liberationists of the next two decades.

Domestic Goddesses

❮ *Catherine Beecher* imagined a model New England village with a town laundry, town bakery, and cooked food delivery service. With her sister, Harriet Beecher Stowe, she wrote *The*

Marina Gutierrez, photograph, Untitled, *1988*

American Woman's Home (1869), a book that included architectural plans for homes with movable walls and flexible spaces. Catherine Beecher believed that rather than invade male turf, women should use the female sphere as a power base. The superiority of woman in the home versus the need for women to be free of domestic prisons would be debated for decades afterward.

⫷ **Melusina Fay Pierce,** a Massachusetts housewife, rebelled at sacrificing her talents to "the dusty drudgery of house ordering" and demanded pay for housework. Writing in the *Atlantic Monthly* in 1868 and 1869, she pointed out that Colonial American women had been more integral to the system than they had become by the industrialized mid-nineteenth century. Seeing economic cooperation as the road to self-determination, she designed houses without kitchens in blocks with cookhouses and apartment houses with collective kitchens.

⫸ **Abby Fisher** wrote the first African-American cookbook in 1881. Because she could neither read nor write, the former South Carolina slave who moved to San Francisco dictated the book. Karen Hess, a food historian who discovered the book and brought it back into print in 1995, said its importance is in acknowledging the role of African-American women in the creation of Southern cooking: "They brought okra and rice, eggplant and benne seeds from Africa and even when the recipes were English, these women added their genius, their thumbprints, to every dish they cooked."

"The Model Kitchen," designed by Ellen Swallow Richards, the World's Columbian Exposition, Chicago, 1893

✁ **Ellen Swallow Richards,** a Vassar graduate trained as a chemist, devoted her talents to using science and technology to release women from the drudgery of housework. She started the Women's Laboratory at MIT to educate female students interested in science. At the Columbia Exposition in Chicago in 1893, the kitchen she designed showed the world how to get maximum nutrition from food and maximum heat from fuel. *New England Kitchen* magazine put many of her ideas into public circulation. Richards started the American Home Economics Association in 1909 to improve living conditions in homes, institutions, and communities.

✍ **Charlotte Perkins Gilman**'s short story, *The Yellow Wallpaper* (1892) is about a woman driven crazy by confinement in her house. *Women and Economics* (1898), a theoretical work decades ahead of its time, makes the case for redefining household roles. The economic independence of women, she believed, depended on working outside the home for wages. To reconcile this work with motherhood, she called for kitchenless houses or central kitchens for apartment houses and day care centers.

✁ **Fannie Farmer,** crippled in one leg by polio and therefore considered unmarriageable, opened her School of Cookery in Boston in 1902, educating housewives rather than professional chefs, as most cooking schools did. Farmer transformed home cooking, making it more efficient than the oral tradition by which recipes had been handed down, by specifying exact measurements. Years ahead of

Breakfast in tenement, New York City, c. 1905

Betye Saar, The Liberation of Aunt Jemima, *mixed media, 1972*

the professionals of her time, she stressed healthy diets, especially for treating illnesses. In 1896, her publisher, doubting the success of her first cookbook with its precise recipes, insisted she pay the production costs herself. He lived to see how wrong he was. Farmer was one of the earliest women and the first professional nutritionist to lecture at Harvard Medical School, and she wrote a popular monthly magazine column. Her cookbooks have remained in print all these years.

 Aunt Jemima was created in 1890, along with Uncle Ben. She is the prototype of the Southern mammy, warm and nurturing, as white people saw her, a happy provider of sustenance in all forms. At the height of controversies about reforming and simplifying household work, she epitomized a whole set of values associated with preindustrial households, community life, and African-American women happy to take care of white people.

 Betty Crocker was created in 1921 by General Mills, a plain, grandmotherly, white-bread, Midwestern image in great contrast to the emerging modern women of the time, and one of the first icons of the modern advertising industry. Played by a succession of actresses, "she" had a popular cooking school on radio. With each succeeding decade, her picture got younger and younger. In 1995, the Minneapolis-based company that made her announced a plan to accommodate the diversity of real America and "morph" the Betty Crocker image with photos of seventy-five ethnically diverse women to create a new woman for the 1990's.

 Martha Stewart began in the 1980s to sell "taste," "beauty," and domesticity on a huge scale, a living reprimand to working women who barely have time to read a newspaper, much less make new flowerpots look old. In addition to books and television shows, Stewart's home furnishing products now include paint that costs over $100 a gallon. To Maureen Dowd of the *New York Times*, she is "scary, like Big Nurse with a pastry bag."

Marriage Contracts

 Redefining marriage—in writing—was not a new idea. British feminist Mary Wollstonecraft had done it in the eighteenth century. American radicals in the nineteenth century, like Lucy Stone and Henry Blackwell, created their own documents and ceremonies, defying the state's right to define marriage.

 In 1897 Letticie Pruett, a white California woman, married Fong See, a Chinese immigrant salesman. Because interracial marriages were illegal, they signed a formal business contract. She convinced her husband to abandon his lingerie business aimed at prostitutes, move to Los Angeles, and go into the business of Chinese antiques and art. He became the "godfather" of L.A.'s Chinatown.

 In the 1960s and 1970s, many American women and their mates saw writing out contracts as ways of rethinking their arrangement. As Susan Edmiston wrote in *Ms.* magazine in 1972, "Sitting down and working out a contract may seem a cold and formal way of working out

Lily Martin Spenser, **The Young Husband:**
First Marketing, *painting, 1854*

an intimate relationship, but it is often the only way of coping with the ghosts of 2,000 years of tradition lurking in our definition of marriage."

☞ Writer Alix Kates Shulman and her husband drew up an agreement in 1970 that is now taught at Harvard Law School. Their contract divides—with great specificity—household duties and child care—who helps with homework on what nights, who strips the beds, and who makes them.

Scenes from Some Marriages

☞ The first married women's property acts were passed in Mississippi (protecting a married woman's rights over her own slaves) in 1839 and in New York in 1848. In 1860, New York added to its guarantees that every married woman is "the joint guardian of her children, with her husband."

☞ In the 1870s, two out of five Vassar graduates married before age twenty-seven. In 1960, four out of five did.

☞ Julia Ward Howe's grandmother, Sara Mitchell, was married at fourteen to Dr. Hyrne, an officer of Washington's army. Howe always remembered her grandmother saying that after her engagement, she "wept on being told that she must give up her dolls."

☞ The painter Lily Martin Spencer was raised by a feminist mother. When she married, Mr. Spencer did the domestic work, an arrangement reflected in her painting *The Young Husband, First Marketing,* done in 1854.

☞ In 1853, Elizabeth Drake, twenty-six, abolitionist, feminist, temperance fighter, decided she wanted a husband. Her advertisement in the *Water-Cure Journal* brought over sixty replies and she soon married Isaac Slenker in a simple Quaker-style agreement. A proponent of free love, her sex radicalism got her arrested for obscenity in 1887.

☞ Mary Livermore ran the Sanitary Commission during the Civil War and the Chicago suffrage newspaper, *The Agitator,* afterward. When she was appointed editor of *The Woman's Journal,* the official paper of the American Woman's Suffrage Association, in 1870, her husband moved to Boston with her to help with her work.

≫ In the late nineteenth century, especially at the height of the gold rush, a thriving slave trade brought poor young women, sold by their families, from China into the Western states as prostitutes. A woman known generically as China Annie escaped to marry her Chinese lover. Her owner charged her with grand larceny for stealing herself. After four weeks, she was found and hauled into court, but the judge dismissed the case and allowed her to return to her chosen husband.

≪ Ella Knowles of Montana became the state's first female lawyer in 1889. Nominated by the Populists to run for attorney general in 1892, she became known as the Portia of the People's Party. Although she lost the election, the winner named her assistant attorney general and later asked her to marry him. She did.

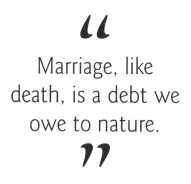

> **"**
> Marriage, like death, is a debt we owe to nature.
> **"**
>
> *Julia Ward Howe*

When Sex Radicals Marry

≪ In 1886, Kansas City sex radicals Lilian Harman and Edwin Walker put their ideas about freedom from government constraint into practice. Their marriage ceremony began with the bride's father reading a statement about the subjection of women in traditional Christian marriage; a woman lost her individuality as a legal person, he said, "even to the surrender of her name, just as chattel slaves were required to take the name of their master." Walker abdicated in advance all his conventional marital rights, repudiating the legal powers husbands had over wives. He acknowledged her right to custody of any children "should any unfortunate fate dissolve this union." Lillian Harman said she entered into the union "of my own free will and choice" and gave her hand "in token of my trust." Her father concluded the ceremony with: "I do not 'give away the bride,' as I wish her to be always the owner of her person."

≫ Sculptor and suffragist Adelaide Johnson married English businessman Alexander Jenkins, fellow vegetarian, twelve

Just before her wedding ceremony in 1931, Amelia Earhart gave her future husband, George Palmer Putnam, a letter containing "things which should be writ before we are married:"

You must know again my reluctancy to marry, my feeling that I shatter thereby chances in work which means so much to me.

In our life together I shall not hold you to any medieval code of faithfulness to me, nor shall I consider myself bound to you similarly.

I may have to keep some place where I can go to be myself now and then, for I cannot guarantee to endure at all times the confinements of even an attractive cage.

I must extract a cruel promise, and that is you will let me go in a year if we find no happiness together.

years younger, in 1896, when she was thirty-seven. The ceremony in her Washington, D.C., home was presided over by a woman minister, with Johnson's sculptures of Susan B. Anthony and Elizabeth Cady Stanton as bridesmaids. Jenkins took her name—as "the tribute love pays to genius."

≪ From 1908 to 1924, more than 20,000 Asian women, most of them Japanese, went, by arrangements their families made with go-betweens, to the American territory of Hawaii to marry Japanese plantation workers settled there. Many were not told what they were about to undertake. Selling daughters into marriage is not unusual in American history.

≫ Crystal Eastman, feminist/socialist/pacifist, described, in 1923, her "marriage under two roofs." She lived with their two children in one home, her husband in another close to his office. They discussed the evening's plans on the telephone every morning. The arrange-

Marriage: The Ongoing Feminist Critique

1820s: Frances Wright, writer and reformer, notorious for daring to speak in public, wore white and carried the Declaration of Independence, which she frequently referred to in her lectures. She spoke to large crowds about women's rights, including equal property rights, fairer divorce laws, and birth control. Her idea that free unions should replace legal marriage was entirely scandalous.

1840s–1860s: Elizabeth Cady Stanton was well acquainted with the lives of the Iroquois Indians, which included collective domestic work and the idea that Spirit-related people were more closely linked than blood-related people. Although married and the mother of seven children, Stanton found spirit-relatedness with Susan B. Anthony and the women's movement:

"Instead of compelling a woman by law to live with a drunkard, they ought to pass laws forbidding drunkards to marry. If, as at present, all can freely and thoughtlessly enter into the married state, they should be allowed to come as freely and thoughtfully out again."
Elizabeth Cady Stanton (under the pseudonym Sunflower) in The Lily, 1850

"I feel, as never before that this whole question of women's rights turns on the pivot of the marriage relation, and mark my word, sooner or later, it will be the topic for discussion."
Elizabeth Cady Stanton, 1853

"The woman has no name. She is Mrs. Richard Roe or Mrs. John Doe. . . . Mrs. Roe has no right to her earnings; she can neither buy nor sell, make contracts nor lay up anything that she can call her own. . . . Mrs. Roe has no legal existence; she has not the best right to her own person. The husband has the power to restrain and administer moderate chastisement."
Elizabeth Cady Stanton to the New York State Legislature, 1860

1868: There was nothing *little* about Louisa May Alcott, who well knew that her popular portrayal of female self-sacrifice in her novel, *Little Women,* was an accommodation to her culture. The novel's first part ended with Meg married, Amy yearning for glamour, Beth for a life in music, and Jo still wanting everything that boys have. In Part Two, in true nineteenth-century fashion, the girls' aspirations were set aside and heterosexual marriage sealed the story.

"Publishers are very perverse & won't let authors have their way early, so my little women must grow up & be married in a very stupid style," Alcott confided to a friend.

1873: In Woodhull and Clafin's Weekly, Victoria Woodhull charged the nation's most celebrated clergyman, Henry Ward Beecher with having a "liaison" with another clergyman's wife. Woodhull "wished to show that 'the foremost minds of the age' had outgrown the institution of marriage, rendering to it only the outward homage of hypocrites, not the adherence of conscience or the practice of life."

ment gave each partner space away from the other. She called her husband's sometimes absence "a refreshment" because "women, more than men, succumb to marriage. They sink so easily into that fatal habit of depending on one person to rescue them from themselves. . . . The two-roof plan encourages a wife to cultivate initiative in rescuing herself, to develop social courage, to look upon her life as an independent adventure and get interested in it."

≪ Rose Pastor had worked in a Cleveland cigar factory as a girl. She came to New York to write for the *Jewish Daily News* and participate in radical politics. The fiery speaker married millionaire socialist Graham Phelps Stokes over the objections of her family. The Bolshevik Revolution of 1917 radicalized her, and she became one of the founders of the Communist Party. News of her death made the front pages of New York newspapers, fascinated by the "uptown meets downtown" marriage.

1912: "It is said that equal say will enable the women to get equal pay and equal pay is dangerous. Why? Because it would keep the women from getting married. Well, then, if long miserable hours and starvation wages are the only means men can find to encourage marriage it is a very poor compliment to themselves." *Mollie Schepps, shirtwaist maker, at working women's suffrage rally*

1920: "The problem of women's freedom is how to arrange the world so that women can be human beings, with a chance to exercise their infinitely varied gifts in infinitely varied ways, instead of being destined by the accident of their sex to one field of activity—housework and child-raising. If and when they choose housework and child-raising, to have that occupation recognized by the world as work, requiring a definite economic reward and not merely entitling the performer to be dependent on some man." *Crystal Eastman*

1969: "Marriage is a dehumanizing institution—legal whoredom for women. . . . Confront the structure which forces men into the dehumanizing roles of our oppressors. Confront the Bridal Fair, which encourages vulnerable young girls to be dutiful, uncomplaining, self-sacrificing, "loving" commodities on the marriage market, and well-packaged, fully automated, brand-conscious consumers." *WITCH protest at The Bridal Fair, New York*

1969: "We are gathered here in the spirit of our passion to affirm love and initiate our freedom from the unholy state of American patriarchal oppression. . . . We promise to love, cherish and groove on each other and on all living things. . . . We promise not to obey. . . . We promise these things until choice do us part." *WITCH un-wedding ceremony*

1969: "If you can't have sex with your husband, he can get a divorce or annulment. If he doesn't love you, that's not grounds for divorce. . . . You have to live with him wherever he pleases. If he decides to move someplace else, either you go with him or he can charge you with desertion, get a divorce and, according to law, you deserve nothing because you're the guilty party." *The Feminists Marriage License Bureau demonstration, New York City*

1970s: The critique of marriage owed a lot to socialist and Marxist ideas, which fueled the politics of women's liberation. Like their predecessors, women in the late twentieth century were divided between wanting to change the institutions of marriage and family so they served women better or abolishing them altogether.

1995: Legislators, most of them women, in Washington State, concerned about domestic abuse, proposed adding this warning to marriage license applications: "Neither you nor your spouse is the property of the other. The laws of this state affirm your right to enter into this marriage and at the same time to live within the marriage free from violence and abuse."

Mary Woolley and Jeannette Marks in Amherst, Massachusetts, 1920s

I am trying for nothing so hard in my own personal life as how not to be respectable when married.
Mary Heaton Vorse

Marriage is a great institution, but I'm not ready for an institution yet.
Mae West

If you want to sacrifice the admiration of many men for the criticism of one, go ahead, get married.
Katharine Houghton Hepburn to her daughter

Devoted Companions, Lovers, and Partners

≪ Mary Woolley and Jeannette Marks met at Wellesley in 1895, when female domestic twosomes on campus were common. Woolley was a history instructor, Marks a freshman. Five years later, they exchanged a ring and a jeweled pin and pledged "ardent and exclusive love." They spent the rest of their lives together at Mount Holyoke College, where Woolley was president and Marks taught English. Wooley worked in the early days of the American Association of University Women and the Women's International League for Peace and Freedom, Marks in the National Woman's Party.

≫ Elsie de Wolfe and Elisabeth Marbury lived in an artistic world where their relationship was entirely accepted. De Wolfe started as an actress, but became an independent and very successful interior decorator. Marbury had gone into business raising poultry, which she abandoned to become a powerful theatrical and literary agent.

≪ Anna Howard Shaw, president of the National American Woman Suffrage Association until 1915, lived with Lucy Anthony, Susan B. Anthony's niece. The house built for them in 1908 outside Philadelphia had a Japanese-style gateway and a grove Shaw planted with small trees brought back from every country she visited on her suffrage speaking tours.

≫ Elizabeth Irwin, educator and founder of the Little Red Schoolhouse, shared her life with Katherine Anthony, feminist writer, whose works include biographies of Susan B. Anthony and Margaret Fuller.

≪ Libby Holman attended Columbia Law School but dropped out to be a jazz singer. In 1924, she made her stage debut as a harlot in *The Fool*. Her lover, Louisa Carpenter, was heiress to the Du Pont fortune. The two often dressed in men's suits to stroll around Harlem.

≽ Lillian Smith and Paula Snelling created *South Today*, a journal that published the work of black writers and white women in the 1940s. Smith and Snelling lived an aggressively antiracist life together, famous for their interracial parties at home and their long-term civil rights activism.

≼ The 1975 obituaries of suffragist Mabel Vernon, one of Alice Paul's closest associates, reflected the changing times by acknowledging Costa Rican peace activist Consuelo Reyes as her "devoted companion."

Free Sharon

Karen Thompson and Sharon Kowalski had been living together in Minnesota for four years when, in November 1983, Kowalski was severely injured in a car accident. Thompson, a physical education professor, spent several hours a day on her lover's rehabilitation. Her attempt to become the legal guardian, with the power to make medical decisions, was blocked by Kowalski's parents, who denied that their daughter was a lesbian. The parents won in court and Thompson was denied the right to see her partner for several years, while Kowalski was moved to a distant nursing home. The lesbian community joined Thompson in campaigning to overturn the decision. In 1990, Thompson was allowed to take her lover home on weekends, but a year later, a judge ruled against legal guardianship.

Marriage Alternative 1: Remaining Single

Harriot K. Hunt, one of the first female physicians, celebrated, in 1835, the twenty-fifth anniversary of her "marriage" to her profession.

> Let it become more respectable to go through life in a single state of blessedness than to marry for the sake of averting the curse, and society would see great improvement in the marriage relation.
>
> Louisa Humphrey, The Sibyl, 1857

> I am the only faithful worshiper of Celibacy and her service becomes more fascinating the longer I remain in it. Even if so inclined, an artist has no business to marry. For a man, it may be well enough, but for a woman on whom matrimonial duties and cares weigh more heavily, it is a moral wrong, I think, for she must neglect her profession or her family, become neither a good wife nor a good artist.
>
> Harriet Hosmer, 1860s

"

I have blessed cats, dogs and mobile homes, but I am not allowed to bless two Christians who love each other.

"

Counsel at 1987 ecclesiastical trial of Methodist minister Rosemary Denman for her lesbianism

Susan B. Anthony at home with wall of photos of friends, 1900

> I put in my list all the busy, useful independent spinsters I know, for liberty is a better husband than love to many of us.
>
> *Louisa May Alcott,* Happy Women, *1868*

On Susan B. Anthony's fiftieth birthday in 1870, *Woodhull and Clafin's Weekly* celebrated, showing the world "that a single woman can have a home and an anniversary as well as married people. It is decidedly encouraging to those who are compelled to remain single 'from choice.'"

> Men? Sure, I've known lots of them. But I never found one I liked well enough to marry. Besides, I've always been busy with my work. Marriage is a career in itself and to make a success of it you've got to keep working at it. So until I can give the proper amount of time to marriage, I'll stay single.
>
> *Mae West*

> Being an old maid is like death by drowning—a really delightful sensation after you have ceased struggling.
>
> *Edna Ferber*

Marriage Alternative 2: Communities

The Woman's Commonwealth, founded in Belton, Texas, began with weekly prayer meetings in 1866 by women gripped not only by religious fervor, but by the frustrations of not owning property and of living with drunken husbands. Ridiculed and often stoned in the streets by the townspeople, the women began to share living space for safety and sympathy. Several moved in with their leader, Martha McWhirter, whose husband moved out. This may have been the country's first battered women's shelter. By 1883, they were building houses of their own, which were often shot at by angry husbands who wanted their wives to come home. In 1886, the Commonwealth opened its doors to the public as the Central Hotel. The town boycotted them for a year, but eventually their communal residence and profit-making venture did thrive. The architecture was original for its time: unpretentious styling, a blend of private and public space, individual bedrooms and large group areas. There were separate areas for dentistry, shoe-mending, rug-weaving, and other self-taught trades. When they moved to a new location outside Washington, D.C., in 1899—having amassed more than $200,000, a quarter of which was in land holdings they had improved themselves—the town of Belton begged them to stay.

Of the 977 women in the 1902 edition of Who's Who, almost half did not marry.

    The first settlement houses—Hull House in Chicago, the College Settlement in New York, and Andover House in Boston—created a new way for women to live. The first women opening settlements, 90 percent of whom were college graduates, were determined to make themselves useful in society. Hull House had the first public playground in Chicago. The settlements' public kitchens provided decent meals for women working long hours in sweatshops and for their families. To make these as modern as possible, Hull House worker Julia Lathrop went to Boston to learn scientific food preparation at Ellen Swallow Richards New England kitchen.

    The settlement workers made a difference by creating clubs and classes, kindergartens, clinics and summer camps. In a culture eager to "Americanize" the new immigrants, they were among the first to appreciate the survival of Old World cultures. They also helped themselves, creating support networks and new structures for living.

    By 1911, there were over 400 settlement houses in the United States.

> **"**
> I don't breed well in captivity.
> **"**
>
> *Gloria Steinem*

Marriage Alternative 3: Friends as Family

    We had often felt the need of such a paper companion as we have endeavored to make *The Sibyl*. Could we have had the visits of such a one when struggling alone, we would have valued it above all price.
    Lydia Sayer Hasbrouck, The Sibyl, *1857*

Black club women meeting at Young Women's Christian Association (YWCA)

> To satisfy my own inner self, I must be surrounded by true friends [who] never for a moment doubt my motives and always understand me thoroughly.
>
> *Fania Cohn, organizer of garment workers, to Theresa Wolfson, economist and expert on working women, 1922*

Homes of Their Own: Working Women

> A man, provided he wears good clothes, or isn't a manual laborer, can get a room anywhere in this city, and no questions asked . . . but my antecedents will be the subject of inquiry and if I say I am a working girl, the door will be shut against me.
>
> *Topeka, Kansas, newspaper interview, 1888*

≫ The Industrial Revolution offered women new opportunities, but also displaced them. Literally. As young, white, female labor was recruited for mills and factories, the question of where they would live—away from home and family—became paramount. Many philanthropic and religious groups came together to "solve" the problem, which often meant providing housing and social control under the same roof, much as women's colleges did.

≪ The Young Women's Christian Association ran a boardinghouse in New York in 1860 and in Boston in 1868. By 1875, there were twenty-eight associations. The first YWCA for American Indian young women opened in Oklahoma in 1890. The Ys offered more than sleeping arrangements. The country's first classes in typewriting were given in 1870. Founded at a time when women's physical condition was considered delicate, the Y offered physical education, some intended for recreation, a need working women rarely found time to attend to, and some intended to strengthen women for work.

≫ In Philadelphia, at the end of the nineteenth century, Viola Richmond started a working woman's club that eventually owned three city houses and a vacation house in the country.

≪ The Jane Club in Chicago was organized by Mary Kenney, a young Irish woman working in the book trade who became a union organizer. This cooperative housing for young, single, women factory workers, managed by the residents, with no fussy rules, was named after Jane Addams. In the 1960s, when Chicago women formed a network to provide safe abortions for women who couldn't get them legally, they called themselves The Janes.

≫ The White Rose Mission in Harlem was organized by Victoria Earle Matthews, a woman born into slavery. The Mission met black women migrants from the South at the docks in Norfolk, Virginia, and New York, offering them a place to live, help finding jobs, training, and courses in black history.

≪ In 1911, The Junior League in New York City raised $340,000 for a hotel that housed over 300 women. Their $4-$7 weekly rent included use of the laundry and pressing rooms, sewing machines, typewriters, library, gymnasium, ballroom, and small private parlors called "courting rooms."

Divorce

In the nineteenth century, divorce was possible, but it carried an enormous social stigma. In spite of pressure from supporters of Elizabeth Cady Stanton and Ernestine Rose, incompatibility was never sufficient in the eyes of the law. Bigamy, desertion, and extreme cruelty were legitimate grounds; adultery was the most common. Most courts granted custody of children to the father.

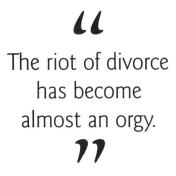

> **"**
> ## The riot of divorce has become almost an orgy.
> **"**
>
> Atlantic Monthly
> *magazine, 1920*

Walking Out on Brigham Young

Anna Webb married Mormon leader Brigham Young in 1869 when she was twenty-four and he was sixty-eight. Under Mormon law, which sanctioned polygamy, she became wife number twenty-seven and she didn't like it. Anna had been married before and was counseled by her peers that the charismatic leader had done her a favor because no one else would have married a divorced woman.

But criticism of the practice of taking multiple wives was growing. Women objected to being all but abandoned for younger and younger wives. Many critics pointed out the economic bias of a system where women did all the domestic work and it was cheaper for men to marry them than to pay them wages. Anna left her husband and the community, living in fear of reprisals. Six years later, however, she spoke up. On the rising tide of objections to polygamy, she gave interviews to newspapers and went on a lecture tour. In 1882, her speeches helped pass federal legislation banning polygamy in the territories.

THE "Y"

The Y has supported sex education and birth control and stood behind liberalizing abortion laws. Its antiracist history is strong. The first YWCA in the South evolved from a working woman's home in Columbia, South Carolina, started by former slave Celia Saxon, who became a pioneer black educator. Almost a decade later, in 1960, the opening of the YWCA cafeteria to black people in Atlanta marked the first desegregated public dining facility in that city. The Y has been foremost among women's organizations in having black women in leadership positions.

While in most states the divorce laws are the same for men and women, they can never bear equally upon both while all the property earned during a marriage belongs to the husband.

Susan B. Anthony, 1897

✎ When Nina Otero-Warren of Santa Fe left her husband after two years, in the early years of the twentieth century, she declared herself widowed, which allowed her to run for public office and homestead land.

✎ By 1922, there were 131 divorces for every 1,000 marriages. The rate climbed steadily afterward until the 1960s, when it skyrocketed, hitting 50 percent in the 1970s and remaining there ever since.

✎ California passed the first no-fault divorce law in 1970. Most states followed. Alimony has been drastically limited, half of all divorced mothers with custody of their children have been awarded no child support, and many more fathers have won custody of their children. Some experts blame "the feminization of poverty" on new divorce laws and attitudes. One study found that a man's living standard generally rose 42 percent after a divorce, while his ex-wife's and children's standard of living fell 73 percent.

Divorce is the one human tragedy that reduces everything to cash.
Rita Mae Brown, 1983

⋙ The term *displaced homemakers*, coined in the 1970s, describes women with no job skills outside the home who find themselves cast out of economic security after divorce. In 1990, there were 16 million such women in America, three out of five living below the poverty level. The motto of the Displaced Homemakers Network, a service agency in Washington, D.C., is, "Just a man away from poverty."

The Motherhood Choice

Not all women are intended for mothers. Some of us have not the temperament for family life. . . . Clubs will make women think seriously of their future lives, and not make girls think their only alternative is to marry.
The Woman's Era, 1894

Until 'mothers' earn their livings, 'women' will not.
Charlotte Perkins Gilman, 1916

There is no evidence that suggests women are naturally better at caring for children . . . with the fact of child-bearing out of the center of attention, there is even more reason for treating girls first as human beings, then as women.
Margaret Mead, 1939

When we think of the institution of motherhood, no symbolic architecture comes to mind, no visible embodiment of authority, power or of potential or actual violence. Motherhood calls to mind the home, and we like to believe that the home is a private place.
Adrienne Rich, Of Woman Born, 1976

Ask your child what he wants for dinner only if he's buying.
Fran Leibowitz, 1977

Who Minds the Children?

⋙ The Shakers cared for children in large cradles that held six children at a time. They were the first to build child-sized furniture.

⋙ In 1854, a Nursery for Children of the Poor opened in New York City. Some others followed, all under the umbrella of philanthropy. The next were for children of Civil War widows, then immigrants whose mothers worked in factories or domestic service and who, without child care, were often left locked in tenement rooms. The settlements helped them. In 1891, Jane Addams and Jenny Dow organized a day nursery at Hull House.

❧ Margarethe Meyer Schurz, wife of statesman Carl Schurz, had studied progressive infant education in Germany. In 1856, she started a small kindergarten in a vacant store in Watertown, Wisconsin. Elizabeth Peabody came to visit and, inspired, opened the first American kindergarten in Boston in 1860.

❧ In 1864, the Philadelphia YWCA offered day care. Other Y's followed. In Cleveland, almost 700 families used the service.

❧ Susan Blow opened the first public kindergarten in St. Louis in 1873.

❧ Kate Douglas Wiggin, author of *Rebecca of Sunnybrook Farm* (1903), founded a pioneering kindergarten, where care was more than custodial.

❧ Women coming of age in the 1920s were the largest childless group in any decade. A quarter of those born in the first decade of the twentieth century had no children.

> Diana Trilling, writer and critic, married to Lionel Trilling, said that the subject of whether or not to have children "never came up" among her friends.

Perhaps in some cases the father, in his youth, was fit to be a father. But in his knock-kneed fifties, he is too hard headed for anything spiritual to spring from him. Then let his wife rotate the children crop just as sensible farmers rotate the crop of potatoes. Let her look about for a young father, fit to be perpetuated in a child. After all, I should think the baby crop is quite as important as the potato crop.
Isadora Duncan, 1923

❧ In the 1930s, federally financed day care (welfare) and nursery schools operated under the Works Progress Administration as a way of creating jobs for unemployed teachers and child development experts. They were generally open ten to twelve hours a day, six days a week.

❧ In 1941, in a record time of two weeks, Congress authorized federal funds for child care. Women's labor was needed for the war. Rich children got educational care, poor children got therapeutic services. The funds were withdrawn at the end of the war. By March 1, 1946, there was no federal support for child-care centers.

❧ During the Depression, marriage and birthrates declined. But from 1940 to 1945, the birthrate climbed from 19.4 to 24.5 per thousand, the age of first marriage dropped, and the marriage rate accelerated. This rush into marriage and parenthood continued for two more decades. The sharpest rise in the birthrate was among the most highly educated women.

❧ The National Organization for Women's Bill of Rights in 1967 called for child-care facilities established by federal law on the same basis as parks, libraries, and public schools.

Most American children suffer too much mother and too little father.
Gloria Steinem, 1971

⤜ The Family and Medical Leave Act, drafted in 1984, passed by Congress and signed by President Clinton in 1993, provides workers in businesses with more than fifty employees up to twelve weeks of unpaid leave yearly to care for a newborn or a newly adopted child.

⤛ In 1995, 75 percent of women with children over six years old have jobs.

Lesbian Motherhood: Heather's Mommies

Court rulings that bar a woman from raising her child because she's lesbian are the result of hysteria and prejudice. I'd rather see a child with a good lesbian mother than a bad heterosexual mother.
Dr. Judd Marmor, USC Professor of Psychiatry, 1973

⤜ In 1990, *Time* magazine said an estimated 1.5 million U.S. lesbians were mothers.

⤛ In September 1993, the Massachusetts Supreme Court granted joint parental rights to Dr. Susan Love and Dr. Helen Cooksey, surgeons in their mid-forties and former faculty members at Harvard Medical School. Their five-year-old daughter was conceived by Love through artificial insemination.

⤜ In June 1994, a Virginia court overturned a lower court ruling that homosexuality made someone an unfit parent. The case had become a rallying point in the lesbian community. Sharon Bottoms, a divorced woman, had lost custody of her three-year-old son to her mother because she had a live-in relationship with another woman. "I'm not a hero," Bottoms said, when her son was returned to her, "I'm just a mother trying to get her son back."

Dr. Spock Sees the Light

Earlier editions referred to the child of indeterminate sex as he. Though this in one sense is only a literary tradition, it, like many other traditions, implies that the masculine sex has some kind of priority.

The "Bible" of mothering from the 1940s on was Dr. Benjamin Spock's *Baby and Child Care*. Spock, who became a prominent activist in the movement against the Vietnam War, was capable of change, as demonstrated by his 1976 revision of the "Bible," in which he sought to "eliminate the sexist biases of the sort that help to create and perpetuate discrimination against girls and women."

Spock's revision also says that early childhood distinctions in clothes and playthings between boys and girls "begins in a small way the discriminatory sex stereotyping that ends up in women so often getting the humdrum, subordinate, poorly paid jobs . . . and being treated as the second-class sex."

Mother's Day demonstration, Women's Action Coalition in Grand Central Station, New York City, 1992

Home Life

My address is like my shoes. It travels with me. I abide where there is a fight against wrong.
Mother Jones

I hereby make my solemn oath that I shall never in future years expect of my wife any culinary or housekeeping proficiency. She shall never be required, whatever the emergency, to DUST!
Charles W. Stetson, engaged to Charlotte Perkins, 1882

⤞ In the summer of 1915, when most of her money was spent supporting her magazine, *The Little Review*, Margaret Anderson, with her sister's family and two friends, pitched five tents and squatted by the lake north of Chicago. Her only disappointment was her inability to have her grand piano delivered to the beach.

⤞ After 1920, housewives' hours of work increased—in spite of labor-saving devices. Home was not seen as a workplace, but a retreat.

Today's woman gets what she wants. The vote. Slim sheaths of silk to replace voluminous petticoats. Glassware in sapphire blue or glowing amber. The right to a career. Soap to match her bathroom's color scheme.
Chicago Tribune ad, 1930

✑ A 1966 study in New York estimated that the average homemaker worked 99.6 hours a week. In the 1970s, a woman who worked outside the home also did thirty-four hours of housework a week. The market value of women's unpaid labor, not included in the Gross National Product, is billions of dollars.

The Politics of Housework

Don't fall for any line about the death of everything if men take a turn at the dishes. They will imply that you are holding back the Revolution (their Revolution). But you are advancing it (your Revolution). . . .

Keep checking up. Periodically consider who's actually doing the jobs. These things have a way of backsliding so that a year later once again the woman is doing everything. After a year make a list of the jobs the man has rarely if ever done. You will find cleaning pots, toilets, refrigerators and ovens high on the list. He will accuse you of being petty. . . .

Also make sure that you don't have the responsibility for the housework with occasional help from him. "I'll cook dinner for you tonight" implies it's really your job and isn't he a nice guy to do some of it for you.

Pat Mainardi, The Politics of Housework, 1970

Help Wanted: Homemakers. Requirements: Intelligence, good health, energy, patience, sociability, skills: at least 12 different occupations. Hours: 99.6 a week. Salary: None. Opportunities for advancement: None. Job Security: None.

Ms. magazine, July 1972

More than ever, the job of full-time homemaker may be the riskiest profession to choose.

Time magazine, 1990

Growing Up Female: The Dolls

Girls play house and learn something about being women and mothers from their dolls. But only middle-class girls have a solid history as doll consumers. Before the Civil War, girls' play was outdoor play. The doll industry grew along with department stores like R. H. Macy, Jordan Marsh, and Marshall Field, spectacular palaces of consumption, after the Civil War. The waves of immigrant girls coming with their families in the early twentieth century did not participate, already saddled, as children, with domestic chores.

Both women and men made the earliest dolls, but they made them differently. The dolls women produced appealed to the senses, were soft to the touch, cloth dolls stuffed with cloth

BARBIE

Barbie was born in 1959, created by a woman for women, derived from a three-dimensional pinup sold in Germany, full of contradictions. Partly, she was a revolt against motherhood. The doll was not a baby, and the girl who played with her did not play house. She had breasts and clothes and makeup. She became not only the best-selling doll in the world—the average American girl, it is said, owns eight—but the most probed, analyzed, and deconstructed object in popular culture. Concerned women charge that her slim body promotes unnatural role models and anorexia in girls. Lesbians say she features in their experiences of coming out. Feminists who have cared to comment over the years found her too white, too femme, too silly, or "empowering" and "the eternal feminine."

> To first generation Barbie owners, of which I was one, Barbie was a revelation. She didn't teach us to nurture, like our clinging, dependent Betsy Wetsys and Chatty Cathys. She taught us independence. Barbie was her own woman. She could invent herself with a costume change: sing a solo in the spotlight one minute, pilot a starship the next. She was Grace Slick and Sally Ride, Marie Osmond and Marie Curie.
>
> M. G. Lord, Forever Barbie, 1994

> Virtually every consumer seems to have queered Mattel's artistic intention to some extent. . . . My friends told me about how they had loved or hated Barbie and about what they had done—turned her punk, set her on fire, made her fuck Midge or Ken or G.I. Joe.
>
> Erica Rand, Barbie's Queer Accessories, 1995

> Lesbian Barbie: Invisible, Native American Barbie: No longer available, since white Barbies have pushed her to the floor, stolen her belongings and killed her. Offensive white Barbies celebrate holiday in honor of this.
>
> P.C. Casualties comics, 1995

> Maybe we were taking out our anger on Barbie. The boys could make fun of us, but we could make fun of her. And so we looked up her skirt, made fun of her huge boobs and laid Big Jim on top of her and then had her slap him while the other dolls laughed.
>
> Celina Hex, "Doll Parts" in Bust ('zine), 1995

fibers, using women's knowledge of textiles. Julia Beecher, Catherine's sister, made dolls like these. Male doll makers produced more mechanized, realistic products. Thomas A. Edison made a talking doll. Mothers used dolls to teach daughters to sew, to teach them about relationships; men said dolls were meant to entertain and amuse. Black female dolls were always softer and cuddlier than white dolls.

While men produced dolls as a business, often a sideline to bonnet and carriage-making, women made them at home. Doll-making, in a time when women had limited operating capital and little hope of bank loans, was a home industry, done with sisters and other female kin, stretching the boundaries of the home and creating new roles for women.

Mrs. Chase

The mother of all dollmakers was Martha Jenks Wheaton Chase. Elizabeth (Bess) Chase, her daughter, graduate of the Rhode Island School of Design, whose job was painting faces on the dolls, lived at home and became her mother's business partner. Another daughter, Anna, married the boy next door and helped manage the business. As the business grew and other women workers were hired, Mrs. Chase insisted on a family atmosphere, calling the place where the dolls were made "the dolls house," never "the shop."

She was among the first to make boy dolls as well as girls and eventually to make dolls in five different sizes, from newborns to four-year-olds. Since motherhood was understood to require expertise and techniques, the dolls were useful in teaching child care. Chase dolls were endorsed by the settlement house movement.

In 1911, Chase developed "Miss Demon Strator," an adult-size woman doll, five feet, four inches tall, based on her own proportions, wearing a dress and hat, that was used in burgeoning nursing schools to train students to handle patients. The teaching mannequin became known as "Mrs. Chase."

A sharp businesswoman, she was among the first to advertise in magazines. By the 1920s, over 100,000 Chase dolls had been sold worldwide, despite their high price.

Girls' Games On-Line

At the end of 1995, a company best known for arcade shoot-em-ups produced McKenzie and Company for girls on CD-ROM. The aim of the game is for the girl to win her man. All the objects of desire are handsome and more guys to pursue are available on additional discs. The girl player can also shop at a virtual mall and try on makeup.

The New F Word

The family is a human institution: humans made it and humans can change it.
Shere Hite, The Hite Report on the Family, 1994

≪ Since 1970, the proportion of traditional families—Mom, Dad and their 2.2 biological kids—has decreased by 35 percent.

≪ A quarter of the children born in the 1980s and 1990s are being raised by single parents.

≪ There are more households composed of people living alone or childless couples than there are households of married parents living with children.

≪ After 1980, the number of couples choosing to live together rather than marry climbed 80 percent. The greatest increase is among couples over thirty-five, many of those people previously divorced. One in four Americans over eighteen today has never married. In 1970, it was one in six.

≪ In 1994, Shere Hite argued that the traditional nuclear family is often inferior to

Harriet Beecher
Stowe, 1852

Charlotte Perkins Gilman, niece
of Harriet Beecher Stowe, 1915

Artist Faith Ringgold
and daughter, writer
Michelle Wallace

alternative arrangements. In *The Hite Report on the Family*, she found that men raised by single mothers have better relationships with women than those in two-parent families, and that children's respect for their mothers has increased with the rise in single and employed mothers.

✃ As a result of the modern women's movement, words like *spinster* and *Old Maid* have nearly disappeared from our vocabulary. The family is understood to be capable of harboring abuse of women: incest, sexual abuse, battering and other forms of domestic violence. Agencies and refuges built to cope with what happens to women in some families are the product of the women's activism in the last twenty years. The female members of the family have emerged from the shadows, honoring bonds between mothers, sisters, and other female kin, attacking the cultural propensity for mother-bashing and, in poet Alice Walker's words, "thinking back through our mothers."

Family Trees: "Thinking Back Through Our Mothers" (and Sisters)

✃ Sarah Miriam Peale, eighteenth-century painter, never married. She lived with her sisters, all of whom were artists.

✄ Sisters Elizabeth and Emily Blackwell practiced medicine together in the nineteenth century. Elizabeth said, "When I determined to study medicine, although none of us realized what the study might involve, it was with the entire approbation of all the dear brothers and sisters that I prepared for my studies."

✃ Lucy Stone, feminist, married Henry Blackwell, brother of Elizabeth and Emily. Their daughter, Alice Stone Blackwell, edited the *Women's Journal* for thirty-five years. She was instrumental in healing the split in the women's movement between Lucy Stone and Susan B. Anthony. After her mother's death, she became more radical, working against government repression of free speech and deportation of radicals.

✄ Frank Baum, author of *The Wizard of Oz*, was the son-in-law of Matilda Joselyn Gage, one of Susan B. Anthony's closest associates and an editor of three volumes of the *History of Woman Suffrage*.

✃ Margaret Mitchell's mother was a leading Southern suffragist.

✄ Suffrage cartoonist Nina Allender's grandniece was novelist Kay Boyle.

✃ Edith Hamilton, classical scholar, and Alice Hamilton, doctor and suffragist, were sisters.

✄ Anna Lord Strauss, head of the League of Women Voters, was the great-granddaughter of Lucretia Mott.

✃ Charlotte Perkins Gilman was the niece of Harriet Beecher Stowe and Catherine Beecher.

✄ Katharine Hepburn's mother, Katharine Houghton Hepburn, was a feminist and birth control activist.

✃ Writer Michele Wallace, author of *Black Macho* (1979), is the daughter of artist and activist Faith Ringgold.

When I was in my mid-twenties and she in her sixties, she apparently decided it was important that I should know that she had some continuing love life, lest I fall into the assumption that constrains many Americans in all their intimacy after early middle age, that sexual activity does not mix with gray hair.

    Mary Catherine Bateson on her mother, Margaret Mead, 1984

Cleaning Up the World: The Domestic Life of Politics

Men are universally afraid of a broomstick and a woman's tongue. If not other weapons are allowed us, let these be freely used, together with bars and bolts to keep the tax-gatherer at bay.

    The Lily, urging women with property not to pay taxes, 1851

It is the presence of filth which so outrages us. We have waited long for our brothers, who have made the filth, to arise in their boasted might and cleanse and purify their politics. . . . The reeking political slime in which they daily writhe calls aloud to us for purification. Woman, with her scrubbing brushes, her dustpan, her soap suds, . . . is baring her arms and fortifying her constitution to come to the rescue.

    Abigail Scott Duniway, New Northwest, *1871*

In 1900, Carry Nation began her "hatchetation drive" to rid the world of saloons. In Kansas, legally a dry state, she and her female troops attacked the illegal liquor business. Newspapers loved the stories. Saloonkeepers hung signs in their windows that said: "All Nations Welcome but Carry."

Lou Rogers, "Rushing the Growlers," Judge, October 25, 1913

*PTA members protesting local government
corruption, Garfield, New Jersey, 1957*

I told them to take their babies and tiny children along with them when their case came up in court. . . . While the judge was sentencing them to pay thirty dollars or serve thirty days in jail, the babies set up a terrible wail so that you could hardly hear the old judge. . . . [In jail] I said, "You sing the whole night long. Say you're singing to the babies." . . . Complaints came in by the dozens. "Those women howl like cats," said a hotel keeper to me. . . . Finally, after five days, the judge ordered their release.

Mother Jones, labor organizer, on miners wives in Pennsylvania, in her Autobiography, 1925

Things to Do in a Woman's House

Revolutionize Agriculture

Eliza Lucas Pinckney was the only person who successfully grew indigo, flax, silk, and hemp on her South Carolina plantation in the mid-eighteenth century. Her secret: "I love the vegitable world extreamly."

Contact Spirits in the Cause of Matriarchy

Isabella Beecher Hooker, lifelong nineteenth-century woman's rights activist, was introduced to Spiritualism by Victoria Woodhull. The upstairs bedroom of Hooker's Hartford, Connecticut, home was once the setting of a séance during which the city's most prominent mediums waited for a spirit to announce that her divine mission was to lead a matriarchal government of the world.

Watch Yourself in Bed

Mae West's apartment was done in white and gold, with mirrored walls. When she showed the bedroom, with mirrors above the circular bed, she explained, "I like to see how I'm doing."

Break Down Barriers by Talking

Members of Daughters of Bilitis, the first national lesbian organization, started in San Francisco in 1955, had informal "gab 'n' java" meetings in members' houses, precursors of the consciousness-raising groups in the late 1960s. One such meeting introduced members of the Mattachine Society—the gay male group also founded in San Francisco—to the women, the first time many of the lesbians had ever talked to a gay man. Eventually, there was considerable coordination between the two groups.

Host a Renaissance

The Harlem Renaissance in the 1920s thrived on connections made among people who might otherwise not have met, the exchange of both patronage and ideas. Women generally made this happen. Jesse Fauset, literary editor of *The Crisis*, held intellectual evenings that functioned as stages for intellectual happenings. Regina Anderson, librarian at the Harlem public library and Ethel Ray Nance, who worked at *Opportunity* magazine, sheltered new arrivals like Zora Neale Hurston when they came to New York. In Washington, D.C., Georgia Douglas Johnson held a "freewheeling jumble" on Saturday nights, introducing Edna Millay or Rebecca West to Angelina Grimké or Jean Toomer.

Invent Something

Gertrude Muller marketed the portable child's toilet seat she invented in 1924. In addition to "the toidy," Muller designed the first safety auto seat and folding booster seat for children. She was neither married nor a mother.

Marion Donovan invented disposable diapers in 1951, originally made out of a shower curtain and absorbent padding. Since manufacturers thought it too expensive to produce, Donovan financed the product herself. Long before the diapers became supermarket staples, she sold her company and moved on to inventing a multiple skirt hanger and an elasticized zipper pull.

Ann Moore patented the Snugli in 1977. As a Peace Corps worker in West Africa, she admired the local baby carriers that allowed women to bring their children to work. After the birth of her first child, Moore made a pouch from an old sheet, opened for the baby's hands and feet, with straps crisscrossed in the back. The Snugli, she believes, is not only efficient, but promotes close parent/baby bonding.

> **"**
> Don't iron while the strike is hot.
> **"**
>
> *Women's Equality Day Slogan, 1970*

Last Words

"Why should women waste half their lives cleaning the house?" Frances Gabe of Oregon asked the *Los Angeles Times* in 1981. They shouldn't. She designed and built a self-cleaning house, with no carpets ("carpets are dust collectors"), floors sloping in all corners, and a rotating ceiling fixture to spray the rooms, composition furniture, resin-covered walls, a blower system, and a dishwasher installed in a cupboard.

United Mine Workers,
Varsant, Virginia, 1976

Ⓦe would have every arbitrary barrier thrown down. We would have every path laid open to women as freely as to men. If you ask me what offices they may fill, I reply—any. I do not care what case you put; let them be sea captains, if you will.

Margaret Fuller, Woman in the Nineteenth Century, *1845*

A woman should be able to feel when she lies down at night that she is really thanking her maker, and not her husband, for having given her this daily bread.

Olive Logan, actor and suffragist, 1870

I do not claim that all women, or a large portion of them, should enter into independent business relations with the world, but I do claim that all women should cultivate and respect in themselves an ability to make money.

Ellen Demorest, cofounder of The Woman's Tea Company, 1872

"Well, Sarah, how do you like your work?" her former mistress asked in calling on her one day. "I never thought of it before, but now that you speak," she replied, "I think the reason I like it so well is because everybody calls me Miss Clark."

Former household servant who has gone to work in a bakery, in Domestic Service, *by Lucy Maynard Salmon, 1897*

The ladies who employ domestics came to Washington to speak about higher wages, shorter hours, and better working conditions for their help. The domestics, of course, or their representatives were not invited.

Justice, Garment Workers Union journal, 1923

Women would ask questions and the men would just stand back. I guess they'd say to themselves, "I'll wait for someone to say something before I do." The women were more aggressive than the men.

Jessie Lopez de la Cruz, organizer for the United Farm Workers, 1962

The cartoon character "Super Domestica" created by Chirla, immigrant activist group in Los Angeles. She tells domestic workers: "There are ways to come to an agreement with your employer. Use the relationship you have with her, especially if she likes you. This can work to your advantage." 1996

Women loggers during World War I

*I*n early America, everyone's work kept both the colonists and the Native Americans alive. Women did whatever it took: laundry, butter churning, clothesmaking, herb growing, logging, mill grinding, and carpentry. Their work supported every war. At Valley Forge, women cooked, laundered, and scavenged food from the countryside. Still, in the first decades of the new republic, only seven professions were available to women who needed or wanted money: teacher, seamstress, tailor, milliner, dressmaker, household servant, and factory operative.

Female slaves worked, unpaid, full-time, from age 9 or 10 until death. During the Civil War, women nursed and doctored, clothed and fed troops on both sides. While the war, like all subsequent wars, brought new opportunities for some women, it devastated others. The catastrophic loss of male lives left large numbers of women who had been economic consumers suddenly needing work. The fight for women's education was a direct result of the need to earn money. In spite of an ideology that said tender "ladies" would be "coarsened"

Be lazy, go crazy.

Motto of anthropologist Margaret Mead

by labor, nearly a million women were wage earners in the post–Civil War period, many in a constant fight with starvation and pauperism. The available work was limited in a culture whose favorite proverb was, "Every man to his trade, but every woman to the washtub."

The West could not have been settled without the Native American women who acted as guides and the white women who hitched, drove, and shod oxen and horses, mined for California gold and Colorado silver, rode the range, broke and trained horses, and worked homesteads and ranches. In the professions—among actresses, authors, lawyers, doctors, and journalists—women from the West are represented out of all proportion to the population.

The 1900 census showed that most women earned money doing domestic work. Of 1.5 million domestic workers, almost all were female. But the fringes are as interesting as the majority: There were also 1,365 female miners and quarriers; 8,246 hunters, trappers, guides, and scouts; and 3,000 women in the Chicago stockyards. The labor of farmers' wives and miners' wives, of poor women taking in boarders, sewing, and washing, was not counted by the census-takers. Nor, often, by women themselves. As one textile worker said in 1929, "Some girls think that as long as mother takes in washings, keeps ten or twelve boarders or perhaps takes in sewing, she isn't working."

The insistence that motherhood was a woman's real job persisted in spite of reality. While marriage and motherhood might offer an escape from wage-earning for some white women, it offered nothing of the kind for everyone else. Nursing and teaching were acceptable jobs because they extended cultural definitions of woman's nurturing role. Choosing work over mothering was perverse; doing both, unthinkable.

The motherhood issue faded when women's labor was needed—usually in wartime—but out it came when the economy contracted. Antagonism to working wives was strong during the Depression. Between 1932 and 1937, the federal government prohibited more than one member of a family from working in the civil service, which amounted to full-scale discrimination against women. In a 1936 survey, 82 percent of those polled said no when asked if women with employed husbands should work.

But women had always fought the rules and public opinion, defying, at the same time, employers, male workers, and cultural norms of acceptable female behavior. In the 1830s, female militancy hit the Lowell, Massachusetts, textile factory. In the 1840s, "lady shoe-binders" formed a union and marched. The early twentieth century saw a large-scale struggle for decency, democracy, and safety in the workplace, a struggle thrown center stage by the gruesome Triangle factory fire in 1911.

Garment workers, mostly Italian and Jewish immigrants, were among the most heroic women in American history. Beaten on picket lines and thrown in jail, their courage inspired other workers beyond the sweatshops. Years later, activist Pauline Newman would say she could still see the brave strikers, "young people, mostly women, walking down and not caring what might happen. The spirit, I think, the sprit of a conqueror led them on."

More heroines emerged from the bloody labor battles of the 1920s and 1930s in Appalachia. In the agricultural work of the Southwest, Mexicanas laid the groundwork for a history of labor militancy that reached full flower in the United Farm Worker's movement in the 1960s.

Less violently, somewhat less dramatically, women pushed their way into medicine and law in the last half of the nineteenth century and built institutions to enable other women to follow them. The women's movement won women's right to keep their earnings, criticized the exclusion of females from ministry and the law, the country's most important professions, and supported the pioneers in those and other fields. Many movement newspapers carried free classified ads for poor women looking for work.

Stanton, Anthony, and their peers were the first flashpoint for the erratic history of cooperaton across class lines. By the 1890s and into the twentieth century, some women with access to power and money used it on behalf of working women. "Society ladies" not only fought for the vote but also joined picket lines and handed out leaflets about the conditions of women workers. Josephine Shaw Lowell and her friends in the Consumers' League used their status and buying power to create a "white list" of shops that actually allowed vendors to sit down in the course of a day or spend more than five minutes on rest room breaks. Garment workers, initially mistrustful of the "helpful" ladies in the Women's Trade Union League, called them "the mink brigade." At Hull House in Chicago, Jane Addams provided meeting space for working-class women trying to organize, no small provision in a time when most male unions met in smoky rooms above saloons at dinnertime.

Male unions of a different kind were keeping women out of medicine. Male medical students and doctors actively discouraged a growing number of women who wanted medical educations all through the 1850s. The Civil War made nursing a serious profession and raised the possibility of female doctors. In 1860, there were fewer than 200; by 1900, more than 7,000. The rise paralleled the rise of obstetrics and gynecology. Medicine was something a married woman could do and something women knew they needed. In the throes of Victorian modesty, one woman with an ulcerated breast had described it to her male doctor as a pain in the stomach.

Even with training, women doctors had a hard time. Landlords refused to rent office space to them, fearing the stigma it would bring. Hazing and undermining by male peers was relentless: one doctor was persuaded that it was her duty to extract hospital patients' teeth; another's first lecture as a professor at a medical college was boycotted.

The American Medical Association finally admitted women in 1876. The early black women doctors went to practice in the South, to "help the race," like the schoolmarms a generation before. The number of female doctors peaked in 1910, then declined. Women's medical colleges closed, since coeducational schools took women. But there were limitations; most had a quota system, often as low as 5 percent.

Women were first admitted to law schools at the same time as medical schools, but resistance to them was stronger. It was impossible to contrive law as a nurturing thing or pretend that female lawyers were not going entirely against the cultural grain by intruding on the public sphere. By 1910, there were 9,000 woman doctors and 1,500 female lawyers. By 1920, although 47 percent of college students were female, only 3 percent of lawyers were.

In 1896, Ellen Spenser Mussey and Emma M. Gillet tutored six young women in law, but when the local college refused their students admission because "women did not have the mentality for law," the two opened their own law school in Washington, D.C.

The 1920s and 1930s were dominated by something new, women in aviation, small in number, but very visible. Amelia Earhart wasn't the most accomplished, only the most famous of the women in the air. Aviation jobs were offered to women after World War I because airplane manufacturers were eager to demolish the macho association lingering from the reputations of Flying Aces during the war. What better way to reassure the public of the safety and simplicity of flying than to recruit women? By the 1930s, jobs for women in the air were shifting to newly hired stewardesses, attractive women with nursing training who were recruited to care for passengers. By 1940, the female aviators were gone.

Second-wave feminists addressed head-on all the arbitrary and superstitious ideas about working women inherited from history. Old battles over mothers in the workforce reignited in the late 1960s. The question of women's capabilities returned. In factories, women's jobs fit what employers determined to be "feminine skills": manual dexterity and the ability to stand repetition. Modern feminists proved that women had or could develop the "masculine skills" of physical strength and problem-solving. This perhaps accounts for the defiant machisma of the period.

The separation of women's work and men's work was abolished in theory by civil rights legislation. In 1963, when Congress passed the Equal Pay Act, working women earned 59 percent of the average male income. Title VII of the 1964 Civil Rights Act made race and sex discrimination by employers and labor unions illegal. Want ads were no longer classified by gender after 1970. But ending gender discrimination in practice is a different task, one that has occupied lawyers, activists, and other groups for the past two and a half decades.

It is clear that women have worked because they were told to, asked to, or wanted to. To support parents, siblings, children, lovers, husbands, and themselves. When a man made money or not, died, was drunk, walked out, or when the woman preferred his absence. For independence. To buy extras like clothes, radios, movie tickets, educations, visits to Paris. To be socially useful. To grow. To escape oppressive families. To meet challenges. "When a great adventure is offered," said Amelia Earhart, "you don't refuse it."

While the reasons make sense, the rules have had Alice in Wonderland logic. Married women couldn't be teachers, but single women were distracting. Looking attractive was important for some jobs, but looking too attractive was dangerous. Act like a lady, women were told, work harder, speak up, keep quiet. Don't talk to other women.

Working women encountered men's rules and defied them, overthrew them, altered them, bent them, or ignored them, as they did in all other areas of American life.

> Like doctors, many of the first lawyers learned their profession as apprentices. The first women with official law degrees were Ada H. Kepley at the Union College of Law in Chicago in 1870 and Charlotte E. Ray, a black woman, who graduated from Howard University Law School and went into practice.

The Tools of Women's Work

The Cotton Gin

The claim that a woman invented the machine that made cotton a valuable commercial product has been around a long time. In the 1870s, the feminist newspaper *Revolution* said that

Katherine Green of Rhode Island had dreamed it up in the 1700s while visiting her Georgia plantations. She allegedly let Eli Whitney claim the patent "through fear of the ridicule of her friends and loss of social position recognition of her work might have entailed." Whoever invented it, the cotton gin, which could clean 300 pounds of cotton a day, reinvigorated the dying institution of slavery and gave women wage-earning work in cotton factories in the North.

The Circular Saw

Invented by an anonymous Shaker woman in a community near Boston, the new saw revolutionized the nineteenth-century building industry. Before that, lumber was sawed and hewn by hand.

Liquid Paper

Bette Graham, high school dropout, had worked her way up to an executive secretary's job. Always a messy typist, she was frustrated by the new IBM electric typewriters, whose carbon ribbons smeared when she tried to erase mistakes. Inspired by watching an artist paint over his errors as he lettered office windows, she started using white paint and a watercolor brush at her desk. When coworkers asked for the magic formula, she bottled it, labelling it Mistake Out. In 1956, she offered her cover-up fluid to IBM. They declined. She marketed it herself, at home, and it took more than a decade to become profitable. Eventually, the Gilette Company bought Liquid Paper for $47.5 million, plus a royalty. When she died in 1980, Graham's fortune went to her son, Michael, a member of the singing group The Monkees, who used it to produce some of the first music videos.

Factories

> In vain do I try to soar in fancy and imagination above the dull reality around me but beyond the roof of the factory I cannot rise.
> *Letter from a Lowell factory worker, 1826*

The sewing machine was invented in 1846, but was not used commercially on a large scale until 1860. Because each machine did the work of six girls, 73,000 women workers were displaced by its proliferation. Women who had made money with their needles had to look elsewhere.

By 1900, one-fifth of America's 25 million women were in the workforce, a quarter of them, mostly young and unmarried, worked in factories. Thirty-seven percent of all cigar workers were women.

Taxidermist Mrs. Martha Maxwell of Boulder, Colorado, 1870s

Lowell: A Corporation with a Soul?

In 1839, there were 12,507 operatives in the cotton mills of Lowell, Massachusetts, mostly white women from the agricultural class, for whom factory work was only a temporary episode, not their whole lives. Although workers boasted of being "sure of good wages and of being treated like human beings," Lowell was the site of one of the first important efforts to organize workers, a protest by the Lowell Female Labor Reform League in 1845 and 1846.

Lucy Larcom, who started work at ten and became a famous poet, said she resented being touted as a "factory-girl of the olden-time," comparing it to "politicians boasting of carrying their dinners in a tin pail in their youth." The model corporation in Lowell—"a corporation with a soul," one mill worker said—featured safe, clean dormitories, classes and lectures, and amenities unknown elsewhere, including plants shading the light in the windows.

The mill workers' magazine, *The Lowell Offering*, was internationally praised. Among the "graduates" of Lowell were Harriet Hanson Robinson, who worked from the age of ten until she married, wrote a memoir of factory life, and became active in abolition and women's suffrage. Margaret F. Foley spent a year in the mills and became a sculptor, joining other expatriates studying in Rome.

Sweatshop, circa 1905

Hours are from 7:30 A.M. to 6:30 P.M., but in the busy season, until 9 P.M. Many workers are eight, nine, or ten years old. There is no overtime pay. Signs say, "If you don't come in on Sunday, don't come in on Monday." When inspectors come, the children hide in big crates. Lack of sanitary and safety precautions mean little to the inspectors. The dangerous locked doors, preventing a fast exit, are everywhere. Extra time in the bathroom is deducted from your pay, but the facilities are down in the yard, far away. You may not talk during working

Lewis Hines photograph, **Making Old-Fashioned Stogies,**
Pittsburgh, Pennsylvania, 1800s

hours. You are always under surveillance: male managers wear rubber heels and sneak up on you. There is no heat, no ventilation. You pay for your needles, for the electricity to run your machine, and for the box you sit on. (Chairs with backs will be provided after 1910.) You go home to a tenement no better than the factory. At home, many rooms have no windows. Your life expectancy is less than forty-eight years.

The Uprising of the 20,000, 1909

In New York, shirtwaist factory workers went on strike for more sanitary conditions and more safety precautions in their factories. Triangle factory workers struck first. The companies hired female thugs, prostitutes, some said, to beat workers on the picket lines. Women's Trade Union League members, including J. P. Morgan's daughter, stood on the lines, witnessing illegal arrests and going to court with strikers.

When employers tried hiring black women to scab, Mary White Ovington, one of the founders of the NAACP, brought this to the attention of black and white leaders.

Shirtwaist strikers, New York, 1909

On November 22, 1909, a meeting to consider an industry-wide strike was held at Cooper Union Hall. While male leaders urged moderation, teenager Clara Lemlich, who had been arrested seventeen times and was recovering from a beating on the picket line two days before, interrupted. In Yiddish, she demanded a strike. The joyous pandemonium lasted five minutes.

Strike meetings were conducted in Italian, English, and Yiddish. Arrests and beatings continued. Women were sentenced to two weeks at Blackwells Island, scrubbing floors.

On December 3, ten thousand men and women, led by three women strikers and three Women's Trade Union League "allies," marched to City Hall. Seven hundred twenty-three women and girls were arrested before Christmas. At the end of three months, the strike was settled, with concessions, but no recognition for the union. The Triangle Company still had locked doors and fifty-nine-hour weeks. The following year, a Newark factory fire in which twenty-five workers died would be investigated by activist Ida Rauh, whose warnings were ignored by the city bureaucracy.

But the uprising had given women their place in the Garment Workers Union, which had been male-dominated since its founding in 1900. It also made organizers out of many of the participants and established the value of cooperation among working women and "the mink brigade."

The Triangle Fire

The Triangle Shirtwaist Factory was the largest of its kind, occupying the top three floors of a building in Greenwich Village. It had wooden trim, wooden window frames, and wooden floors. The 500 workers were mostly young girls. All the doors were locked, to prevent the workers from stealing.

On March 25, 1911, there was an explosion. The fire alarm was turned in at 4:45 P.M. Horse-drawn trucks came promptly, but because the ladders only reached seven floors, workers on three remaining floors were stranded. Girls started jumping right away, arms entwined, three or four together. The force of a body hitting the net was estimated at 11,000 pounds. Bodies buried the hoses, and horses panicked from the smell of blood. One hundred forty-six young women died in full view of friends and families.

After the fire, organizing crossed class lines, as it had done in 1909. Leonora O'Reilly headed the Women's Trade Union League committee to investigate factory conditions and propose legislation. In spite of the huge public outcry, state legislators took years to pass watered-down versions of laws to protect workers.

Elizabethton: Sparking the Southern Textile Strikes

In 1929, a rayon plant in Elizabethton, in eastern Tennessee, made the material for the new flapper style of short skirts and exposed legs. More than 300 women walked off their jobs and gathered at the factory gate, refusing to work but ready to negotiate. The plant closed

SACAJAWEA

The good relationships with native peoples that Lewis and Clark enjoyed on their 1804 expedition across the Great Plains to the Pacific Coast were due to the only woman traveling with them. Their guide was a seventeen-year-old Shoshone, captured as a young girl and sold to a French guide. During the expedition, her son was born, and the group waited while she regained her strength. Baby on her back, she was interpreter and guide, laundress and cook, food gatherer, nurse, and doctor. At the end of the journey, her husband was paid, but she got nothing.

During the 1905 women's rights convention in Oregon, white feminists began constructing a feminist hero from the scant references to Sacajawea in Clark's journals. They dedicated a monument to her, Susan B. Anthony urging Oregon's women to be modern Sacajaweas, leading the way to liberty. Abigail Scott Duniway called her a symbol of "thousands of uncrowned heroines whose quiet endurance and patient efforts have made possible the efforts of the world's great men."

Contemporary Native American writer Paula Gunn Allen points out that the idealized statues of Sacajawea can be interpreted to suggest that the right to be on the lands of the West was given to white people by her. The real Sacajawea led a long life, living among the Commanches for more than twenty years and in her old age used her skill at manipulating white bureacracy to help assure her people decent reservation holdings.

down. The spirit spread to mills in nearby Gastonia, Marion, and Danville. The strikers, mostly girls in their teens, ignored a court order to return to work. The government sent in the National Guard. The strike was peacefully settled with promises never kept. Two weeks later, they struck again. Women demonstrated, blocking the roads. Tear gassed and arrested, they returned to walk along the road draped in the American flag, forcing guardsmen to present arms every time they passed.

Work in the West

✐ Marie Dorion of the Iowa tribe helped lead a 3,500-mile overland expedition into Oregon to the fur trading area on the Columbia River founded by John Jacob Astor and known as Astoria.

✐ Arizona Mary, a white woman, drove a sixteen-yoke oxen team carrying freight in the Southwest.

✐ Doña Candelaria Mestas, born in northern New Mexico in 1858, carried mail on horseback in the 1890s, the only known Hispana to do so.

✐ In the 1870s, *The Women's Journal* column, "Notes Concerning Women," carried ideas about the kinds of work women "can do and undertake" in the West.

✐ May Arkright Hutton, Idaho cook and boardinghouse keeper, bought shares in a mine and struck it rich. In her overalls, weighing over 250 pounds, she entertained President Teddy Roosevelt in her mansion and worked for woman's suffrage.

She hauled her own water, chopped her own wood, did the washing . . . by the time us kids got up, she'd have ironed our clothes, fixed our lunches, and cooked our breakfast. And she'd have her bread already punched down. What hour of the morning that little woman got up, I don't know.

Alice Greenough Orr, legendary rodeo star, remembering her mother in Montana in the early twentieth century

Madams and Prostitutes: A House May Not Be a Home, but It's a Darn Good Business

From 1850 to 1900, tens of thousands of women of all races and classes worked as prostitutes, particularly in the mining towns, where men far outnumbered women. They were the second largest group of wage-earning women, after domestic servants. Sometimes they acted collectively, forming organized voting blocs or protective associations.

The Everleigh Sisters: Tiffany Windows and Gold-Plated Pianos

Inexperienced girls and young widows are too prone to accept offers of marriage and leave. If a girl is addicted to drugs or drink, we don't want her.
Ada Everleigh, 1899

The Everleigh sisters became the most famous madams in America when they opened their house in Omaha, Nebraska, in the 1890s, with Tiffany windows and a gold-plated piano. They expanded to Chicago, where three tuxedo-clad orchestras entertained clients and the "girls" wore house jewels estimated to be worth $1 million. Closed down in 1911, Ada and Minna Everleigh grew old together in the New York mansion they bought.

Matty Silks was a notorious madam in the West whose dresses had two pockets, one for money, one for a gun.

Mammy Pleasant: A Stop on the Underground Railroad

Mary Ann ("Mammy") Pleasant, a Georgia slave, had been sent by her master to Boston to be educated, but instead of returning to the plantation, she married a wealthy black Bostonian. After he died, in the 1850s, she moved to San Francisco and set up "boarding houses for bachelors." A woman with one brown eye and one blue one, she was rumored to practice voodoo. Her houses featured legendary cooking and "girls of beauty and class," many of whom married into the elite. "Mammy" used the information gleaned from powerful male customers to invest in the stock market. Her fortune helped thousands of slaves escape to Canada and her house was known as the western end of the Underground Railroad.

Nineteenth-century prostitutes in front of their "cribs" in "Lousetown," the Klondike, Alaska

Calamity Jane: A Legend in Her Own Mind

Martha Jane Canary supposedly got her name because she warned men not to risk calamity by insulting her. Her flamboyant mother, Charlotte, had come, it was said, from an Ohio bawdy house. By 1867, the teenage Jane was in Salt Lake City, a mining town. She turned up with the Union Pacific railroad construction gangs at Piedmont in Wyoming and then, in 1869, was photographed in Cheyenne, drinking at men's bars.

Wherever she was, Jane renounced respectability. She had a child, abandoned women's society, wore men's clothes, rode and cursed, brawled, was a cowpoke, and a pony express rider. She went with a military expedition against the Sioux in the Black Hills with her soldier lover. In 1876, she met Wild Bill Hickock and toured with him and four other men in a road show until he was killed a year later.

She went from being a celebrity to being a character, telling tall tales, hoaxing tenderfeet by claiming that she had killed Crazy Horse and been with General Custer at Little Big

Horn. In her forties, she turned herself into a one-woman show, wearing buckskin and two guns on her hips. She died on the twenty-seventh anniversary of the death of Wild Bill Hickock, who she claimed was the father of her child.

In August 1993, the first women were sworn in as Texas Rangers. One left a year later because of harassment.

Nursing as Radical Action

Lillian Wald, from a middle-class German-Jewish family in Rochester, New York, graduated from the New York Hospital School of Nursing in 1891 and started studying medicine with the pioneering Blackwell sisters. Quitting, she moved to the immigrant Lower East Side, establishing The Nurse's Settlement House in 1893. She sent nurses into poverty-stricken

Nurses, c. 1900

homes where people were dying of tuberculosis and diphtheria. Wald's philanthropic "uptown" peers said she was either a genius or totally crazy.

The Nurse's Settlement became the Henry Street Settlement in 1899, attracting progressives like lawyer Florence Kelley who had won an eight-hour workday and a ban on child labor in Illinois. Kelley, a founding member of the NAACP and secretary of the National Consumers League, was known as "a guerrilla warrior in the wilderness of industrial wrongs." Wald's other friends included reformers Jacob Riis and Jane Addams. Working for the visiting nurse service, Margaret Sanger watched many women die of self-inflicted abortions, which motivated her crusade for birth control.

Unlike other institutions that "helped" immigrants by teaching them to assimilate, Henry Street celebrated immigrants' cultures. In 1909, when the NAACP wanted to have a founding dinner and nobody would let an interracial group onto their premises, Henry Street did.

Offices

Before 1870, office workers were all male, but clerical work soon became the fastest-growing segment of female labor. By 1900, 80 percent of stenographers and typists were female, and in 1930, women made up more than half the entire clerical workforce. Office machines, including the typewriter, required literacy and therefore women, since female high school graduates far outnumbered men. By 1870, the first class of female Western Union telegraph operators were trained and working, earning half what men did. Cooper Union gave classes in telegraphy, typewriting, and stenography, and the YWCA taught free classes in commercial math, bookkeeping, and typewriting.

Alexander Graham Bell demonstrated the telephone at the Philadelphia Centennial Exposition in 1876 and its commercial use caught on fast. Although switchboard operators were originally males, the job fast became the province of young, single, white females. No immigrants, blacks, or Jews were allowed.

A Switchboard, circa 1890
You spend long days seated at a switchboard full of jacks, into which you reach and stretch to fit the proper plugs. You take 250 to 300 calls an hour. Supervision is rigid: a spy system maintains discipline, which includes no talking among operators and strict control of time away from the board to use the bathroom.

Dressing for Success
The "uniform" for office workers was a long dark skirt and a white bodice garment made of flimsy materials, called a shirtwaist, introduced in 1895. Charles Dana Gibson made this

Women working at a switchboard, early twentieth century

the sartorial style of American womanhood. The increasing numbers of women needing these costumes led to the expansion of shirtwaist factories, employing Jewish, Italian and Irish immigrants, which became scenes of fierce labor battles after the turn of the century.

"Race Business"

After 1900, financial industries were prominent in African-American communities, especially insurance and banking, critical to the new black middle class. Mutual benefit societies provided death benefits and investment capital. By the 1920s, workers in these "race businesses" came from the best-educated ranks. Black women were hired as bookkeepers, a job done by men in white businesses.

> Professional services instead of "companionship" in business offices is one of the main matters that should receive our attention.
> *Elsie Diehl, Stenographers and Typewriters Union, 1904*

Mary Farrell sued the Navy Clubs for insisting she wear that silly little skirt at work.

Shopgirls and Salesclerks

One hundred thousand women worked in stores in 1890, especially the growing department stores. They had sixty- to- eighty-hour weeks, low wages, could be fired at will, and were required to stand ten to twelve hours a day. A pass from a male supervisor was required for bathroom visits. Kidney ailments were common. Breaks lasted five minutes.

The Consumers' League: Uptown Meets Downtown

In 1890, philanthropists, settlement house workers, and reformers formed the Consumers League of New York to mobilize consumers as a force against the saleswomen's conditions. Their "white list" educated the public, drawing support to stores offering decent working conditions and wages. They wanted a ten-hour day, a six-day week.

In 1913, the Consumers League supported a drive to unionize New York stores. Socially prominent members distributed leaflets on the busiest streetcorners, blocking traffic and getting arrested.

The Supreme Court affirmed a ten-hour workday for women in 1918.

> **"**
> Jews are never ever permitted to work here. They are all troublemakers.
> **"**
>
> *Prospective employer to Jewish female job applicant sent by Remington Typewriter Agency, 1912*

Race and Work

Black women worked in fields and white people's houses before and after the Civil War, first as slave labor, then as slaves to a racist economy. Few voices rose to defend the "femininity" of black women that might be compromised by working.

Although black women in significant numbers became teachers and nurses, the first occupations outside the home women were allowed into, the majority still did the country's dirty work. The South was considered a housewife's Utopia until the 1930s because of the women who formed a permanent service caste, allowing even low-income white families to hire mammys.

In the cities, to which they were "free" to go, most black women worked as laundresses, seamstresses, scrubwomen, and cooks. From 1900 until well into the 1960s, black female wage earners were mostly barred from peacetime factory work and white occupations of secretarial and sales work.

Did You Know?

In 1996, one in five of all working women held a secretarial or clerical job. Seventy-five percent of working women earned less than $25,000 a year.

War Work

During World War II, 3 million women worked outside the home for the first time. Women with low-paying work got better-paying factory jobs.

Rosie the Riveter, symbol of the thousands of women working in factories to sustain the war effort, was most likely Rosina B. Bonavita, who set industrial records riveting fighter planes.

Welders at Connecticut plant

The need for nurses was constant, but the government and the Armed Forces behaved as though all nurses were white. Mabel K. Staupers, leader of the National Association of Colored Graduate Nurses, changed that. Through most of the war, the Army and Navy had minuscule quotas for black nurses, who were assigned to care for German prison-

Nurses stationed at Fort Clark, Texas, 1943.

ers of war, not white Americans. Staupers boldly said that black nurses entered the armed services "with the high hopes that they will be used to nurse sick and wounded soldiers who are fighting our country's enemies and not primarily to care for these enemies." Eventually, with added pressure from First Lady Eleanor Roosevelt, the quotas and exclusion ended in 1945.

Despite the shortage of physicians, the Army didn't commission female doctors until 1943.

Under the direction of champion aviator Jacqueline Cochran, more than a thousand women flew planes as WASPs (Women's Airforce Service Pilots). They received six months of training at the all-female base, Avenger Field, in Sweetwater, Texas. Among them were golf pro Helen Dettweiler; Marion Florsheim, heiress to the shoe company for-tune; and Helen Richey, the first airline pilot. The women flew longer hours with a lower accident rate than their male peers. Thirty-eight WASPs died for their country. In December 1944, as war seemed to be com-ing to an end, the WASPs were disbanded, and Congress defeated a bill to allow the female pilots to become members of the Armed Forces.

Attention, Women!

JOIN THE WAAC
WOMEN'S ARMY AUXILIARY CORPS ★ U.S. ARMY
APPLY AT ANY U. S. ARMY RECRUITING AND INDUCTION STATION

Women's Army Corps recruiting poster, World War II

Post War Work

Massive layoffs of female workers began in 1945. Protective labor laws were reintroduced. Federal support for child care centers ended March 1, 1946.

In a 1946 *Fortune* magazine survey, 53 percent said women handled people less well than men and were less able to make decisions.

Women didn't stay out of work. By 1947, female employment reached wartime levels, but had been driven back to low-paying jobs.

Agitators on the Road to Progress

In the late 1860s, the New York Working Women's Association, which Susan B. Anthony helped organize, was formed to confront a situation where ragpicking was the only business in which women had equal opportunities with men. Out of the Association came a "Protection Union" for dealing with grievances like contract-breaking and fraud.

In 1886, the Working Women's Society was organized by garment worker Leonora O'Reilly, a collar sewer at thirteen, and society lady Josephine Shaw Lowell.

The Cigar Makers Union admitted female and black workers in 1867.

The Daughters of Saint Crispin, an organization of 800 female shoemakers, met in Lynn, Massachusetts, in 1869, elected a president, and the following year, joined male shoemakers in a demonstration over wages.

Lucy Gonzalez moved from Texas to Chicago in the 1880s, where she wrote for a local labor newspaper and organized female garment workers. After the Haymarket riots in 1886 and the execution of her husband, radical Albert Parsons, by the government, she became one of the founders of the Wobblies (The International Workers of the World) in 1905.

We work eight days in the week. This may seem strange to you who know that there are only seven days in the week. But we work from seven in the morning till very late at night, when there's a rush, and sometimes we work a week and a half in one week.

Striking shirtwaist worker addressing the Colony Club in New York, 1909

⚒ Pauline Newman worked at the Triangle factory. In 1907, the teenager had organized an unsuccessful rent strike to get a toilet on every floor in her tenement building. After the uprising of 1909, she became the first female organizer for the Garment Workers Union. Although she had never been out of town and didn't have a suitcase, the union sent her to upstate New York to raise money for the strikers and she came back with $6,000 from rich women's groups and unions. When Margaret Dreier Robins of the Trade Union League gave Saturday-afternoon teas and gave "the girls" folk dancing lessons, Newman always alert to class tensions, said, "That is the instinct of charity rather than unionism." Newman was a suffrage speaker and a socialist candidate for Congress in 1918.

> **"**
> **Mrs. Treish left her husband, a scab; the union was dearer to her than her family. Brave woman!**
> **"**
>
> Cigar Maker's Journal, *1878*

⚒ Rose Schneiderman fled Russia in 1891. One of nine children, she worked as a cash girl in a department store, then sewed cap linings, for which she had to buy her own sewing machine. The first English words she learned were "Hands off, please." She organized the cap makers into a union and, after 1909, worked with the Women's Trade Union League all her life, eventually becoming its president.

⚒ Leonora O'Reilly's childhood poverty on the Lower East Side left her sensitive to charity, patronage, and patronizing behavior. She disliked do-gooders. In 1909, Mary Dreier gave her a lifetime annuity so she could devote all her time to League work.

⚒ After World War I, women streetcar conductors demonstrated in several cities to keep their jobs, but were forced out of the transportation industry.

⚒ Luisa Moreno had won admission of women to the universities in her native Guatemala. In America after 1928, she sewed in a Spanish Harlem sweatshop and started a Latina garment workers' union. In 1935, leaving her abusive husband, taking her daughter, she began organizing black and Latina cigar rollers in Florida, Mexican farm and food processing workers in the Southwest, and cannery workers in California. She encouraged people of color to run for local union offices and became the first Latina vice president of a major U.S. trade union. Although she had always been a political leftist, it was her refusal to testify against accused Communists in the labor movement—"I will not be a free woman with a mortgaged soul"—that led to her deportation in 1950.

Women's Building mural by Maestrapeace Muralists, San Francisco, shows from left to right former surgeon general Jocelyn Elders, United Farm Workers organizer Dolores Huerta, Mexican healer Maria Sabrina, and (above: partially visible) Puerto Rican nationalist Lolita Lebron

In 1938, at least 80 percent of the pecan shellers in San Antonio, Texas, who walked off their jobs because of wage reductions were Chicanas. Twenty-year-old Emma Tenayuca, a legendary orator working for the agricultural workers' union, was fired. In the largest and most militant strike of a turbulent decade, up to thirty-three women at a time were stuffed in jail cells meant for ten. Although the strike was decided in favor of the workers, the companies mechanized their production soon afterward and thousands lost their jobs.

In 1939, hundreds of Mexican female workers at the Cal San cannery in Los Angeles walked out for better wages and working conditions and union recognition. Their picket line outside the plant stood twenty-four hours a day, seven days a week. Boycott teams kept local groceries from carrying the company's products. In the affluent neighborhood where company owners lived, workers' children marched, carrying signs that read: "I'm underfed because my mother is underpaid." A settlement was reached.

The biggest labor unrest in the seventies was a strike at the Farah Manufacturing Company in 1972. Four thousand workers, mostly Chicanas, walked out and stayed out for two years, while a nationwide boycott of Farah pants eventually forced recognition of the union.

Labor and the ERA

Legislation limiting the numbers of hours women could be forced to work or regulating their working conditions was the pride of the labor movement. When the Equal Rights Amendment was introduced for the first time in December 1923, the potential loss of these protections led women in the labor movement to oppose it.

In 1975, The Coalition of Labor Union Women endorsed the ERA.

Hard Hats: Moving into Blue-Collar Jobs

By the early 1970s, women were demanding access to blue-collar jobs. Federal regulations passed in 1978 set up goals and timetables for women in the construction industry, only asking a "good faith effort." No contractor has ever lost a con-

> The position we ought to take is that of the girl whose boss remarked to her: "Now that she has got cake, she wants ice cream." The girl's response was: "I never thought of ice cream before. But now that you remind me, I shall not stop until I get it."
>
> *Leonora O'Reilly, National Women's Trade Union League Convention, 1909*

" I haven't forgotten how to use a hoe. "

Striking rayon plant worker in Tennessee, 1929, on what would happen if she didn't get her job back

Dolores Huerta, Bella Abzug and Gloria Steinem at United Farm Workers rally, New York City, 1975

DOLORES HUERTA: VIVA LA HUELGA!

In 1968, Dolores Huerta, known as Dolores *Huelga* (strike) for the numbers of strikes she organized, led a boycott of table grapes on behalf of the United Farm Workers union. Later, lettuce and Gallo wines were added to the boycott. Because of Huerta's activism with the United Farm Workers, from the founding of the union in 1962 and continuing through the years as second in command to founder Cesar Chavez, the workers finally won the right to collective bargaining. Huerta, the mother of eleven children, was arrested more than twenty times. She brought the use of a boycott and other nonviolent tactics to the labor struggle.

tract or money for failure to hire women. Trade jobs pay two or three times what traditional female jobs pay.

> He said: Well, we do heavy work.
> She said: I lift weights.
> He said: We work up high.
> She said: I've been skydiving.
> He said: The men are crude.
> She said: I've been in the army.
> He said: They swear every other word.
> She said: So do I. Damnit.
> *Job interview with Sheet Metal Workers Union official, 1979*

⊰ A female contractor working for Sonoma County, California, in 1982 found a cache of pornography left out by the male workers. It was "the worst, most violent stuff, the sleaze of the sleaze. I talked to the superintendent and the magazines disappeared for a while, but then they reappeared. . . . I took all the magazines and cut them up with the table saw into two-inch squares, then put them back in the drawer. They never appeared again—at least not while I worked there."

Entrepreneurs

> I got my start by giving myself a start.
> *Madam C. J. Walker*

⚞ Betsy Metcalf of Massachusetts discovered the secret of bleaching and braiding straw to make bonnets in 1789. She taught others the process and started a business making hats for summer. The straw industry didn't become popular until 1880.

⚞ The widow Mrs. George Benjamin Miller took over her husband's tobacco business in 1790 and became famous as a leading manufacturer of chewing and smoking tobacco. Until 1848, she had the field almost exclusively to herself.

⚞ Grandma Biddy Mason, as a slave in 1854, walked behind her master's 300-wagon train to California, tending livestock. Having sued for her freedom, she settled in the new community of Los Angeles, which had eight white families and two black ones. Accumulating valuable real estate, she built churches, established schools for nurses, and worked as a maternity nurse.

⚞ Victoria Woodhull and her sister Tennessee Clafin founded a bank in 1869 and published a weekly newspaper. "When the doors of her office on Broad Street were first thrown open to the public," a contemporary wrote, "the Lady Brokers were besieged."

⚞ Mary Fields, born a slave in Tennessee, was six feet tall, fast on the draw, strong as a man, smoked cigars, and drank with the men. She hauled freight in Cascade, Montana, then ran a restaurant, which failed because "Black Mary" could never turn away a hungry visitor. She became a stage-

HETTY GREEN: THE WITCH OF WALL STREET

Hetty Green, The Witch of Wall Street, the nineteenth century's leading female financier and most legendary miser, was the only child of two rich New England whaling families. Instead of buying clothes with her clothes allowance, she invested it. With her inherited fortune, she speculated in government bonds and railroads, investing heavily in real estate. Refusing to behave in traditional feminine ways—she bought falling stocks, foreclosed on mortgages, lent money, and had a remarkable sense of timing that lead her to liquidate assets before panics—she was accused of thriving on others' misfortune. She scorned fashion and saved money by having only the bottom flounce of her petticoats laundered. She married Edward Green, who had a million in his own right, when she was thirty-three and he was forty-six. They had two children, but she dropped him when he made bad business deals and lost money.

MILLINERY AND MAGAZINES

Ellen Demorest owned a millinery shop before she married a bankrupt dry goods merchant. She invented mass-produced patterns for home dressmaking, inspired by her black maid's brown paper bag drawings. In 1860, her husband started a fashion magazine featuring colored fashion plates with patterns attached to each picture. Ellen Demorest opened a private dressmaking and millinery business, becoming "the unchallenged dictator of American fashion." In all their businesses, the Demorests employed black women on the same terms as white. In 1868, she and Jane Croly, chief writer for the magazine, founded Sorosis, the first woman's club. In 1872, with Susan King, who had made a fortune in New York real estate, Ellen Demorest launched the Woman's Tea Company, which sent a clipper ship to the Orient for tea to be sold by needy gentlewomen.

coach driver carrying the U.S. mails when she was in her sixties. In her seventies she opened her own laundry business.

⤐ Gertrudis Barcelo, one of the best monte dealers in Taos and Santa Fe, New Mexico, owned and operated the largest gambling hall in the area and was a respected member of the community.

⤐ In 1899, Maggie Lena Walker, a black woman, rescued a cooperative insurance venture that had been started by ex-slave Mary Prout in 1867. Walker enlarged the business and became the first woman bank president.

⤐ Mary Foot Seymour, a white schoolteacher, saw the potential in the newly invented typewriter and shorthand system. In 1879, she started the Union School of Stenography in New York, growing it to four schools and an employment bureau. In 1889, she launched the *Business Woman's Journal*; in 1892, the *American Woman's Journal*. She was active in women's groups and the suffrage movement.

⤐ Jennie Grossinger, the best-known hotel keeper in the world, worked as a buttonhole maker as a child and went to school at night. She helped turn her father's small Catskill Mountain farm into a boardinghouse catering to urban Jewish immigrants. As hostess and business manager of what became a huge resort by 1919, she helped assure the survival of Yiddish culture by featuring, for her guests' entertainment, vaudeville's struggling Jewish singers and comics and, later, the stars of radio.

⤐ Susan Pringle Frost, a white woman whose personal motto was, "With the help of God I will leap over the wall," became the first woman on the Real Estate Exchange in Charleston, South Carolina, and the first to drive her own automobile. As a developer, her major interest was historic preservation. She headed her city's Equal Suffrage League, was a member of the National Woman's Party, and stood on the picket line outside the White House in 1917.

MADAM C. J. WALKER: THERE'S MONEY IN HAIR

The country's first black female millionaire, daughter of ex-slaves, worked in cotton fields and at washtubs until she invented a formula to stop her own hair from falling out because of the harsh chemicals she had been using to straighten it. She moved North in the 1880s, setting up a hair care and cosmetics business that eventually included beauty schools. Long before anyone else, she had a door-to-door sales force. Hers numbered over a thousand. Politically active in the black women's club movement, she worked against lynching and for black women's economic equality and empowerment through employment. Her company charter required that the operation always be headed by a woman. Her daughter, A'Leila, lived in a custom-built mansion on the Hudson River and became a flamboyant hostess and critical financial supporter of the Harlem Renaissance.

Madam C .J. Walker

Doctors

> We have too long been subjected to the impositions of Quacks and quack medicine, and the sooner we learn enough of physiology to take care of ourselves instead of trusting to them, the better will it be. . . .
> *The Lily, 1849*

The Doctor Is a Lady

Doctors were not exempt from the familiar charge that accomplishment destroyed femininity. The father of pioneer Mary Putnam Jacobi wrote to her, soon after she had left home for the Women's Medical School in Philadelphia, "Don't let yourself be absorbed and gobbled up into that branch of the animal kingdom ordinarily called strong-minded women! . . . Be a lady from the dotting of your i's to the color of your ribbons."

In 1903, the University of Oregon Medical School graduated ten doctors—five men and five women. In 1970, the school graduated eighty doctors—seventy-four men and six women.

Elizabeth Blackwell

Elizabeth and Emily Blackwell studied medicine for political reasons. Elizabeth was a self-taught Cincinnati schoolteacher urged to study medicine by a female family friend who "asked me whether, as I had health, leisure and cultivated intelligence, it was not a positive duty to devote them to the service of suffering women."

One of the first obstacles to overcome was her own "repugnance to the physical side of human nature." She had spent her childhood trying to "subdue my body," going without food for days, sleeping on bare floors. Resolved, finally, she wrote to six well-known physicians about her reluctant ambition. They replied that a qualified woman doctor would be a boon to society, but that "it was impossible for a woman to become an equally educated physician."

After Elizabeth Blackwell got a medical degree in 1849, the problems of practicing were more apparent. Female doctors had no way of getting clinical experience. She tried to get women privileges at the Pennsylvania Hospital, a charity hospital that allowed male medical students to observe surgical operations for a ten dollar fee, but they refused. In response, the sisters founded the New York Infirmary for Women and Children in 1857, entirely staffed by women. Eight months later, they opened a nurses' training school, supported by Lady Byron, wealthy widow of the poet. Their ally, Marie Zakrzewska, a German midwife, went to Boston to build the New England Hospital with Dr. Lucy Sewall and Dr. Helen Morton in 1862. In 1874, Elizabeth Blackwell opened the Women's Infirmary medical school.

Anatomy class dissecting cadavers, Women's Medical College of Pennsylvania, Philadelphia, 1900

ALICE HAMILTON

The pioneer of industrial toxicology, Alice Hamilton wanted to be a doctor from the time she was a teenager, partly because she wouldn't have to "work under a superior, as a nurse must do." After medical school at the University of Michigan, she worked at the New England Women's Hospital and did the unthinkable thing for a woman: she became a research scientist. Champion of victims of industrial disease, she worked all her life to discover and stop the use of poisons in manufacturing. She also worked with Jane Addams in the peace movement and was at her side when Addams died. The first woman on the faculty at Harvard, she retired before female medical students were admitted there.

Money for Medicine

Reporting on an 1857 fair held to raise money for Blackwell's New York Infirmary, Lydia Hasbrouck, editor of *The Sibyl*, wrote, "Why is it that women must always connive to raise money, when needed, by getting up paltry displays of trinkets at fairs, which they usually sell for four times their value?"

In 1881, eight doctors, including Lucy Sewall, Emily Blackwell, Mary Putnam Jacobi, and Marie Zakrzewska, offered Harvard $50,000 to open its medical school to women. Harvard declined.

M. Carey Thomas, president of Bryn Mawr College, and other feminists raised $100,000 for a new medical school at Johns Hopkins University contingent on their acceptance of female students. Caroline Harrison, wife of President Benjamin Harrison, considered one of the most domestically oriented First Ladies, told Hopkins officials she would help raise money only if they would admit women.

Harriot Hunt

Hunt and her sister Sarah studied medicine with an English couple in Boston who had cured Sarah of what was thought to be an incurable illness. In 1835, without credentials, they set up a practice, emphasizing good nursing, diet, bathing, exercise, and sanitation, specializing in cases given up by other doctors as incurable. When Sarah gave up medicine for marriage in 1847, Harriot practiced alone. She applied for permission to attend lectures at Harvard Medical College, but the governing board said no. After Elizabeth Blackwell got a medical degree in Geneva in 1849, Harvard relented. But Hunt was convinced to withdraw when the medical students rioted because three black men among the new students, plus a woman, was too much.

Mary Frame Thomas

Mary Thomas, a Quaker, studied privately with a local doctor in Fort Wayne, Indiana, and then at medical school at the University of Pennsylvania, where her stepsister was a lecturer. Before she left for Philadelphia, she prepared months worth of food and clothing for her husband and three children. She got her degree in 1856 and combined a medical practice with work on Amelia Bloomer's magazine, *The Lily*.

In 1869, the University of Michigan opened the first coeducational medical school, with duplicate lectures for subjects likely to cause embarrassment. These included obstetrics and gynecology.

Susan Smith

Valedictorian of her class at New York Medical College, Dr. Smith founded the Woman's Loyal Union, black New York's leading women's club, and the Equal Suffrage League of Brooklyn. In 1895, widowed once, she married an Army chaplain and practiced medicine at Army posts in Montana and Nebraska.

Susan La Flesche

Daughter of an Omaha chief and sister of one of the first Indian anthropologists, La Flesche graduated from the Hampton Institute in 1886 and, supported by the Women's National Indian Association, went to the Women's Medical College in Philadelphia. As a medical missionary to the Omaha, she treated cholera, dysentery, and influenza and spent much of her lifetime trying to call attention to the alcoholism destroying her people, which she attributed to the slaughter of the buffalo and destruction of the native economy. Realizing that liquor was used to get Indians to sign over land to whites, she became an ardent prohibitionist and advocate of banning alcohol on reservations. With her sister, Suzette, also Eastern-educated and fluent in French, she lectured about the theft of Indian lands and the corruption of Indian agents across the United States and through Europe.

Luella Day, a Chicago doctor, went in 1898 to seek gold in the Alaskan Klondike, America's last frontier. There, she fought for honest government and, after four attempts to murder her, escaped in 1904. She wrote *The Tragedy of the Klondike*, a book about corruption, in 1906.

Dr. Caroline McGill got her medical degree from Johns Hopkins University in 1914 and went to Butte, Montana, the toughest mining camp in the West, where she treated victims of stabbings, shoot-outs, and mine explosions.

Dr. Marie Equi, a West Coast Wobbly and open lesbian, distributed contraceptive information to workers in the Pacific Northwest. Charging that the "ruling class owns the army and navy," she was arrested for treason. The prosecuting attorney called her "an unsexed woman." She spent a year in San Quentin.

Margaret Chung, the first Chinese-American woman physician, in 1916 supported herself through medical school by washing dishes and lecturing on China. She helped to support her ten younger siblings after both of her parents died.

CRYSTAL EASTMAN

Crystal Eastman had been a settlement house worker and graduate student in sociology before she got her law degree in 1907. She applied herself to labor law and industrial safety, investigating and writing a pioneering book on the subject, which led to major progressive reform. In the forefront of the suffrage, peace and radical movements, she co-founded what became the American Civil Liberties Union to protect the rights of conscientious objectors in World War I; presided over the Women's Peace Party of New York, joined Alice Paul in the militant fight for suffrage and continually wrote progressive journalism and visionary feminist theory until her death in 1928.

Lawyers

Alas, that no woman learned in the law could be found then to plead her sister's case.
The Lily, November 1856, after Annie Linden disguised as Charlie Linden to get a job, was exposed and taken to court

That pedestal can be a cage.
Justice William Brennan, 1973, in one of the first Supreme Court cases dismantling laws designed to shelter women

◁ Margaret Brent, the first woman to try a case, a spinster and gentlewoman with "masculine abilities," came to Maryland in 1638. The colony's governor died in 1647, leaving her his executor and executor of all Lord Baltimore's property, which he had represented. But the legal system denied such positions to women. Brent convinced the court to affirm her position as "administrator." After some years, she petitioned for a vote in the General Assembly, but was denied.

▷ Lucy Terry, a Massachusetts slave, the first black woman to publish her poetry, married a free man and farmed in Vermont. When Williams College refused to admit her son as a student, she argued his case before the college trustees, to no avail. In 1785, when a neighbor tried to seize some of her land, she argued before the state Supreme Court. This time, she won.

◁ Myra Bradwell, the first woman lawyer in Illinois, studied with her husband, an ex-judge, in Chicago. In 1869, the Bradwells, Elizabeth Cady Stanton, and Mary Livermore won married women's right to control their own earnings, but Bradwell's application for a license to practice law was denied. She appealed to the U.S. Supreme Court, which also refused, although Arabella A. Mansfield had been admitted to the Iowa bar without opposition. Bradwell was not to win standing at the bar until 1890, but she used her time well. She published a weekly legal newspaper, joined the Illinois women's suffrage association, and got Mary Todd Lincoln released from the mental sanitarium in which her son had placed her.

▷ Belva Lockwood, graduate of the National University Law School, was the first woman admitted to practice before the Supreme Court (1873), after a seven-year struggle. Her first case was a divorce, which she won, and she managed to find a legal way to compel the man to pay alimony, something that never happened before. She got a bill passed that allowed women who had been members of the bar for three years to practice before the high court, and six women followed in her footsteps almost immediately. In 1906, she was one of the attorneys for the Eastern Cherokee Indians, for whom she won a $5 million settlement from the United States government.

≪ Lavinia Goodell, daughter of abolitionist William Goodell, was admitted to the Wisconsin bar in 1873 and the Supreme Court two years later. Famous for her numbers of female clients, Goodell worked for temperance and woman's suffrage.

≫ Sisters Annie and Florence Cronise of Ohio were admitted to the Supreme Court bar in 1873. Annie married a lawyer in 1874. Eventually, Annie's husband became deaf, but their lucrative law practice continued. She sat beside him in court, silently repeating every word said by the judge, jury, and opposing counsel so that he could read her lips.

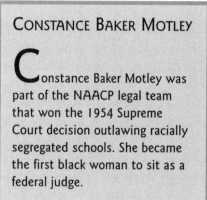

CONSTANCE BAKER MOTLEY

Constance Baker Motley was part of the NAACP legal team that won the 1954 Supreme Court decision outlawing racially segregated schools. She became the first black woman to sit as a federal judge.

Clara Foltz

Clara S. Foltz was a dressmaker, milliner, voice teacher, and landlady. When her husband refused to support her and her five children, she went to study in a law office. She divorced, won child custody, and began practicing in 1878. In San Francisco, Hastings Law College turned her away, but Foltz convinced the state Supreme Court that the law college, as a branch of the university, was compelled to take women.

The day the Supreme Court admitted her, a man asked her to represent him in a land claim suit. Knowing nothing about that legal area, she took the case. To pay the court's ten dollar fee, she pawned her breastpin. The next morning, she grabbed a pamphlet about land office law from the Surveyor General's office and had the scheduled case put off from 10 A.M. to 1 P.M. After winning the case, she retrieved her pin.

Banding Together: Lawyers in Groups

The first association of women lawyers was The Equity Club, founded in 1886 by women students and graduates of the law department at Michigan University. Two years later, the Women's International Bar Association was organized to open law schools to women, get them to the bar and bench, and disseminate knowledge concerning women's legal status.

Second Wave Feminism and Lawyers

≪ The National Organization for Women was the first modern feminist group to concentrate on litigation. Beginning in 1966, cases of sex discrimination were handled by volunteer lawyers at NOW's national office. In 1971, thirty-five feminist attorneys started the

Women's Legal Defense Fund. Future Supreme Court Justice Ruth Bader Ginsburg and others not only litigated, but conducted a public relations campaign to "guard against the tendency some might have who don't know and haven't thought about it, to see these cases almost as a joke."

For the first time in history, the litigators and strategists in the fight for women's legal rights were almost all female. Drawn by the excitement and success of these legal challenges, more women went to law school than ever before. Twenty-five percent of law students during the 1970s were female and are now 26 percent of the practicing lawyers.

In the 1990s, nearly 50 percent of law students are female, but 90 percent of the judges, partners in law firms, and tenured professors on law faculties are still male. Because of women's work in the law, not only has the country been changed, but the law itself. Feminist jurisprudence sees the unequal power of men and women in society as a question of legal significance.

On August 10, 1995, Roberta Cooper Ramo, a New Mexico lawyer who once could not find work because of her gender, became the first female president of the American Bar Association.

RACHEL CARSON: TROUBLEMAKER

Rachel Carson, zoologist and environmentalist, published *The Sea Around Us*, a study of ocean life, in 1951. Its success made her the country's most famous female naturalist. But *Silent Spring*, published in 1962, a clarion call about the dangers of chemical pesticides, provoked critics to call her a hysterical female, out of her depth among professional scientists. She was defended and supported by a network of women's groups, especially women in garden clubs, who had provided some of the data for her book. Carson is in part responsible for mobilizing the numbers of women who became active in all aspects of the environmental movement.

Scientists, Hard and Soft

We need to expand who's observing, broaden who can become a scientist. We call some knowledge superstition. The problem with modern science is that it separates knowledge from experience, downgrading experience and the kind of people who rely on experience.

Biologist Ruth Hubbard, 1994

Maria Mitchell, a largely self-taught astronomer, discovered a comet in 1847. Disowned by her Quaker church for having doubts, she taught science at Vassar College for twenty-three years and was a consistent advocate of science education for women.

Alice Cunningham Fletcher, ethnologist and friend of the La Flesche family, lived among the Omaha Indians in the 1880s and wrote some of the earliest studies of the Plains Indians.

Lilien Jane Martin, psychologist, dissatisfied with retirement, began studying gerontology and set up the first counseling center for the elderly in 1929.

❮ Florence Sabin, anatomist, discovered how the human lymphatic system works. Active in the suffrage movement, Sabin became the first female professor at Johns Hopkins in 1917. After retirement, she became an activist for public health reform in Denver.

❮ Ellen Semple, geographer, valedictorian at Vassar in 1882, lived in rural Kentucky to study the influence of geographic isolation on a population and spent the rest of her career writing about the geographic influences on culture.

❮ Nettie Stevens, cytogeneticist, a carpenter's daughter, worked as a teacher and librarian, finally entering Stanford University in 1897, and eventually finding support for her work at Bryn Mawr College. In 1905, she discovered chromosomes as sex determinants.

> " If girls have such keen eyes and patience, why can't it be applied to science? "
>
> *Astronomer Maria Mitchell*

> The naming of the sex hormones is also sexist. The eggs sit around waiting for a sperm to come along and if it doesn't, they fall to pieces. Sperm is always fresh, but eggs sit on the shelf getting older every day. The truth is, it takes the active participation of both. We say sperms fertilize (active) and eggs are fertilized (passive). The grammar compels us. Sperm cells are probably more prone to environmental damage. The old eggs idea is usually used to keep women out of the workplace.
> *Dr. Ruth Hubbard, 1994*

Architects

Among Native Americans, women constructed houses for their people: hogans for the Navajo, wickiups for the Apache, tipis for the Plains, chickees for the Seminoles. In Pueblo society, women made mud into bricks and built adobes, replastering every year.

> One of the greatest reforms that could be, in these reforming days . . . would be to have women architects. The mischief with the houses built to rent is that they are all male contrivances.
> *Harriet Beecher Stowe, mid-nineteenth century*

❮ Louise Blanchard Bethune, the first professional woman architect in America, was

A Blackfeet woman raises a tipi pole, northern plains, North Dakota, 1900

educated at home and as an apprentice. At the age of twenty-five, she had her own office in Buffalo, New York, the nation's second busiest railway center. While building houses was considered most suitable for women, Bethune found it "the most pottering and worst paid work an architect ever does," and was known for some of her city's best schools and hotels. In 1891, she refused to compete for the design of the Woman's Building at the World's Columbian Exposition in Chicago because male architects were paid $10,000 to design buildings at the fair while women had to compete, provide all construction drawings, and receive only a $1,000 prize.

➤ Margaret Hicks, the first woman graduate of Cornell University's architecture school in 1878, unlike most of her peers, refused to let her skills be the private property of rich people. She designed tenements for immigrants in New York City in the 1880s, giving them innovative touches like light and air, closets, and bedrooms.

➤ Sophia G. Hayden, the first woman graduate of the regular architectural course at Massachusetts Institute of Technology, won the design competition for the Woman's Building at the World's Columbian Exposition, held in Chicago in 1893.

✦ Julia Morgan, the first woman to receive an engineering degree at the University of California at Berkeley in 1894, was from a well-connected family. Her most famous client was Phoebe Apperson Hearst, whose son, William Randolph Hearst, was so impressed by his mother's architect that he hired her to build his extravagant showplace at San Simeon. Most of Morgan's work, however, was for women's organizations, building clubhouses, retirement houses, and a number of YWCAs. She was passionate about hiring and encouraging younger women. In her fifty years of practice, she designed 800 buildings.

✦ Eleanor Raymond designed one of the first solar heated houses, for Dr. Maria Tekles, in Massachusetts in 1948.

✦ The Cambridge School of Architecture and Landscape Architecture, founded in 1915 to train women, lasted twenty-seven years and was taken over in 1942 by the Harvard School of Design.

✦ In 1974, the Women's School of Planning and Architecture, created by feminists, held the first American conference on women in architecture.

Kiowa woman Good Eye completing her arbor roof, outside Andarko, Oklahoma, 1899

Dr. Mae Jamison, NASA astronaut

Aviators

Flying seems easier than voting.
Harriet Quimby, first woman to request a pilot's license, 1911

⊰ Amelia Earhart kept a notebook of news items about women's achievements as they took over jobs reserved for men. In 1919, she enrolled as a premed student at Columbia University, but she left after a year. She worked as a social worker while taking flying lessons. As the first woman to fly the Atlantic (as a passenger, in 1928), she became America's First Lady of the Air, partly because she looked so much like national hero Charles Lindbergh. She also lectured, worked as an editor at *Cosmopolitan* and *McCalls* magazines, and supported the most aggressively feminist organization of the period, the National Woman's Party. On June 30, 1937, she took off from New Guinea and her plane disappeared.

⊱ Jacqueline Cochran, a succesful beautician who attended nursing school, had her own line of cosmetics and became an accomplished, competitive flier. She ran the all-female military flying school during the Second World War.

⊰ Kathryn Cheung of Los Angeles was the first Chinese-American to earn a pilot's license. A member of Amelia Earhart's 99 club, she was known for her daring feats and worked as a commercial pilot.

⊱ When Mae Jemison told her teachers she wanted to be a scientist, they suggested she think about nursing. Undaunted, she went to medical school and studied engineering at night. In 1987, she was selected as one of fifteen astronaut candidates. In 1992, she became a mission specialist on the shuttle *Endeavor*, staying in space for eight days.

THE GLASS CEILING IN SPACE

The Mercury Astronaut program in the 1960s included twenty-six women, including veteran fliers Jackie Cochran, Jerrie Cobb, and Bernice Steadman. Thirteen passed the preliminary tests. It was whispered that women might be better astronauts, since they lasted three times longer than the male pilots in the isolation tanks.

It never happened. Women pilots, who were not allowed to fly commercial jets or military aircraft, were required to wear high heels and hose, to look like ladies, while NASA tested them. In September 1961, the final phase of testing was canceled. The women charged discrimination. At a special Congressional subcommittee hearing on the selection of astronauts, Scott Carpenter and John Glen testified against them. So did Jackie Cochran.

On June 15, 1963, the Russians sent a woman into space.

In 1983, astrophysicist Sally Ride, traveling as a mission specialist aboard the Challenger, became the first American woman in space.

In 1995, Air Force Lt. Col. Eileen Collins took the helm of the shuttle Discovery as the first woman to pilot an American spaceship. She invited the eleven surviving members of the "Fellow Lady Astronaut Trainees" program to the launch.

Last Words

Muriel Siebert, the first female member of the New York Stock Exchange, lobbied in 1987 to get a ladies' room installed on the seventh floor of the Big Board, the site of the luncheon club she frequented. She warned the Exchange's chairman that if the ladies' room was not installed in time, she would have a Port-o-San delivered to the board of directors. She got what she wanted.

The Last Word
Staying Alive

25 Things Women Have Done for Each Other

> Men say we are ever cruel to each other. Let us end this ignoble record and hence-forth stand by womanhood. If Victoria Woodhull must be crucified, let men drive the spikes and plait the crown of thorns.
> *Elizabeth Cady Stanton, 1872*

✖ Susan B. Anthony stormed out of the Sons of Temperance convention in 1852 because women were not allowed to speak. Intent on organizing women for temperance, she was buoyed then and in the fifty years of their friendship by Elizabeth Cady Stanton, who advised her on public speaking ("If attacked, be cool and good-natured"), pushed the connection between temperance and women's rights to its limits (women should be allowed to divorce their husbands for drunkenness), and provided those elusive, critical elements called faith and support.

✖ Dr. Elizabeth Blackwell's New York Infirmary for Women and Children in the 1850s was financially supported by Lady Byron, wealthy widow of the poet.

✖ Sophia Smith, born in 1796 into a rich Massachusetts family, became deaf at forty. She intended to leave her money for a school for the deaf, but Harriet Rogers started the Clarke School in 1868. Smith's will endowed, instead, the first women's college, which she helped plan before she died in 1870. Smith College, boasting the same entrance standards as the best men's colleges, opened in 1875.

✖ Elizabeth Peabody of Boston supported the school for Native Americans started by activist Sara Winnemucca.

✖ When flamboyant Victoria Woodhull declared her candidacy for the presidency in 1872, many suffragists disdained her. Woodhull, free love advocate, offended many of the "respectable" upper-class women. Elizabeth Cady Stanton, however, defended her: "I have thought much of our dear Woodhull and all the gossip about her and have come to the conclusion that it is a great impertinence in any of us to pry into her affairs."

➤ Caroline Harrison, wife of President Benjamin Harrison, considered one of the most domestically oriented First Ladies, was asked to help raise money for a new medical school, Johns Hopkins. She said she would do so only if women were admitted on an equal basis with male students.

➤ The development of women's sports at UCLA was largely due to pressure and money from Phoebe Appleton Hearst, mother of William Randolph Hearst. Her son also met architect Julia Morgan, who designed his San Simeon, California, palace, through his mother.

➤ In 1914, her will revealed that Mrs. Frank Leslie, journalist and publisher, who had never overtly embraced the woman's movement, left nearly $2 million to Carrie Chapman Catt for suffrage work. Catt used what was left after the Leslie family fought the will—nearly $1 million—to start *The Woman Citizen* in 1917. The newspaper was the official organ of the National Woman Suffrage Association until the vote was won.

➤ Jeannette Rankin was adrift after college until she heard Emma Smith DeVoe and Abigail Scott Duniway speak at a suffrage meeting in Washington state in 1910. Rankin returned home to work for the women's vote in Montana, which was won in 1914, and went on to become the first woman elected to the U.S. Congress.

➤ Painter Georgia O'Keeffe was persuaded to visit the Southwest, which became the inspiration for her major work, by Dorothy Brett and Mabel Dodge.

➤ Katherine McCormick, heiress to the McCormick farm machinery fortune, gave Margaret Sanger a check for $40,000 at a dinner one night, to be used for birth control pill research.

➤ Susan Glaspell's plays were produced by Eva Le Galienne at her Civic Repertory Theater. In the 1930s, Glaspell worked with Hallie Flanagan on the Federal Theater Project as head of the Midwest Playreading Department.

➤ Mrs. Alva Belmont kept the militant National Woman's Party of Alice Paul afloat with Vanderbilt money. Her 1933 will left the party $100,000. Bryn Mawr President M. Carey Thomas left $50,000 in 1935.

➤ Madam C. J. Walker, beauty industry millionaire, left $5,000 to Mary McLeod Bethune's school for Negro girls in Florida, $5,000 to Lucy Laney's institute in Georgia, and paid a teacher's salary at Charlotte Hawkins Brown's preparatory school in North Carolina.

➤ Heiress Peggy Guggenheim bought photographer Berenice Abbott a camera she couldn't afford and opened a shop in Paris selling handmade lampshades with the struggling poet Mina Loy in 1926. Guggenheim sold Loy's collages, in their flea market frames, to New York art buyers. In 1939, as Occupation Forces advanced on Paris, Peggy Guggenheim and writer Emily Coleman rescued an alcoholic, disintegrating Djuna Barnes from a nursing home, sending her home to America.

➤ In 1939, because she was a member of "the Negro race," the Daughters of the American Revolution refused the great contralto Marian Anderson permission to sing at Constitution Hall, which they owned. First Lady Eleanor Roosevelt stepped in, resigning her membership in the DAR and helping to arrange a concert at the Lincoln Memorial to which 7,500 people came.

⤜ In the late 1940s, Lucille Ball's friend Marcella Rabwin was lying in the hospital, depressed after her second miscarriage. The door to her room opened and in came Ball, humming burlesque music. She took off her hat, then her coat, and did a striptease down to her underwear. Then, without a word, she dressed and left. The screaming, laughing Rabwin said she was "a different person after that."

⤜ In Hollywood, Rita Hayworth took young Shelley Winters under her wing, encouraged her, and found film parts for her.

⤜ In 1951, the campaign to force the United States Lawn Tennis Association to invite Althea Gibson to play in the national championships was led by white champion Alice Marble, whose influence broke the color line in tennis.

⤜ Janis Joplin, appalled at the neglect, created a gravestone for the great blues singer Bessie Smith.

⤜ On March 25, 1961, on the fiftieth anniversary of the fire at the Triangle Shirtwaist Factory that killed scores of women workers, fourteen survivors of the fire shared the platform at a commemoration ceremony with former First Lady Eleanor Roosevelt, former cabinet member Frances Perkins, and union organizer Rose Schneiderman.

⤜ In the early 1970s, poet Alice Walker, having discovered Zora Neale Hurston's work, written forty years before, made a personal pilgrimage to Hurston's hometown of Eatonville, Florida. Horrified by Hurston's unmarked grave, Walker purchased a headstone and had it inscribed "Genius of the South," from a poem by Jean Toomer.

⤜ As a Random House editor, Toni Morrison was influential in getting work by women of color into print. In 1975, she published *Corregidora* by Gayl Jones, a novel about the horrifying ramifications of interracial rape.

⤜ In 1976, Beverly Sills, set to sing the role of Violetta in *La Traviata* at the Metropolitan Opera, campaigned vigorously to get Sarah Caldwell to conduct. Sills succeeded, but it would be another twenty years before another woman would lift a baton in the Met pit.

⤜ In 1995, Zina Garrison, who had played professional tennis for more than a decade, was tormented about retiring. She announced her withdrawal, then suffered second thoughts. Billie Jean King advised her not to "go with what other people want" or worry about the media or worry about her husband and family. Garrison stayed in the game, calling King, otherwise considered tough and feisty, a "little angel."

Author's Note

A book praising buried connections among women depends, obviously, on personal connections too. I salute the feminist scholars, writers, librarians, conference-givers and journal editors whose work changes history. In particular, the members of the Columbia University Seminar on Women and Society and the Women Writing Women's Lives group at the City University of New York Graduate Center, where this book's contents were often discovered and discussed. The Barnard Center for Research on Women has treasures in its archives and in Leslie Kalman, Director and Isabel Ochoa, Assistant Director. I am grateful to The University Seminars at Columbia University for assistance in preparing the manuscript for publication.

Thanks to Philip Lief for inventing and sustaining this extravaganza; to Debra Elfenbein for editorial wisdom and Hillary Cige for her taste and Amazonian support; to picture editor Sabra Moore for finding buried treasures and being a pleasure to work with; to indexer Sondra Audin Armer, who has made the book truly useful; Flora Davis for her smarts and eagle eyes; Mary Ruthsdotter of the National Women's History Project for "getting it" all; to Andrea Denny-Brown, Linda Barnes, Laura Brezel and Erica Rose for labor above and beyond; to Roz Greenberg for keeping my hands functional and, for their camaraderie, sanity, and help: Peter Breger, Mary Kay Blakely, Janet Kelly, Honor Moore, Carol Overby, Arlene Kramer Richards, and Sue Shapiro.

Space limitations have caused hand-wringing omissions, woefully, but I welcome suggestions for a second edition.

Suggested Readings

General

Paula Gunn Allen, *The Sacred Hoop: Recovering the Feminine in American Indian Traditions*, Beacon Press, 1986.

——, ed., *Spider Woman's Grandaughters: Traditional Tales amd Contemporary Writing by Native American Women*, Beacon Press, 1989.

Karlyn Kohrs Campbell, ed., *Women Public Speakers in the United States, 1925–1993*, Greenwood Press, 1994.

Ellen Carol DuBois and Vicki L. Ruiz, eds., *Unequal Sisters: A Multicultural Reader in U.S. Women's History*, Routledge, 1990.

Sara M. Evans, *Born for Liberty*, Free Press, 1980.

Paula Giddings, *When and Where I Enter: The Impact of Black Women on Race and Sex in America*, Bantam Books, 1988.

Sue Heinemann, *Timelines of American Women's History*, Perigee, 1996.

Darlene Clark Hine, Elsa Barkley Brown, and Rosalyn Terbog-Penn, eds., *Black Women in America*, Indiana University Press, 1994.

Linda K. Kerber, Alice Kessler-Harris, and Kathryn Kish Sklar, eds. *U.S. History as Women's History: New Feminist Essays*, University of North Carolina Press, 1995.

Linda K. Kerber and Jane Sherron De Hart, eds., *Women's America: Refocusing the Past*, Fourth Edition, Oxford University Press, 1995.

Gerda Lerner, ed., *Black Women in White America*, Vintage Books, 1973.

Mei T. Nakano, *Japanese American Women: Three Generations, 1890–1990*, Mina Press, 1990.

Vera Norwood, *Made from This Earths American Women and Nature*, University of North Carolina Press, 1993.

Rosaura Sanchez and Rosa Martinez Cruz, eds., *Essays on La Mujer*, Chicano Studies Center, University of California, Los Angeles.

Lynn Sherr and Jurate Kazickas, *Susan B. Anthony Slept Here: A Guide to American Women's Landmarks*, Times Books, 1994.

Carmen Delgado Votaw, *Puerto Rican Women*, Lisboa Associates, 1995.

Sydney Stahl Weinberg, *The World of Our Mothers: The Lives of Jewish Immigrant Women*, Schocken Books, 1990.

Judy Yung, *Chinese Women of America*, University of Washington Press, 1986.

1. Politics

Harriet Hyman Alonso, *Peace as a Women's Issue: A History of the U.S. Movement for World Peace and Women's Rights*, Syracuse University Press, 1993.

Kathleen Barry, *Susan B. Anthony: A Biography of a Singular Feminist*, Ballantine Books, 1988.

Catherine Clinton and Nina Silber, eds., *Divided Houses: Women and the Civil War*, Oxford University Press, 1992.

Nancy Cott, *The Grounding of Modern Feminism*, Yale University Press, 1987.

Angela Davis, *Women, Culture and Politics*, Random House, 1989.

Flora Davis, *Moving the Mountain: The Women's Movement in America since 1960*, Simon & Schuster, 1991.

Elisabeth Griffith, *In Her Own Right: The Life of Elizabeth Cady Stanton*, Oxford University Press, 1984.

Miriam Gurko, *The Ladies of Seneca Falls: The Birth of the Woman's Rights Movement*, Schocken Books, 1974.

Adrienne Harris and Ynestra King, eds., *Rocking the Ship of State: Toward a Feminist Peace Politics*, Westview Press, 1989.

Stanlie M. James and Abena P. A. Busia, eds., *Theorizing Black Feminisms*, Routledge, 1993.

Christine A. Lunardini, *From Equal Suffrage to Equal Rights: Alice Paul and the National Woman's Party*, New York University Press, 1986.

Mary E. Massey, *The Bonnet Brigades*, Knopf, 1966.

Peter Nabokov, ed., *Native American Testimony*, Viking, 1991.

Leila J. Rupp and Verta Taylor, *Survival in the Doldrums: The American Women's Rights Movement, 1945 to the 1960s*, Oxford University Press, 1987.

Miriam Schneir, ed., *Feminism in Our Time*, Vintage Books, 1994.

Doris Stevens, *Jailed for Freedom: American Women Win the Vote*, revised edition edited by Carol O'Hare, NewSage Press, 1995.

Amy Swerdlow, *Women Strike for Peace: Traditional Motherhood and Radical Politics in the 1960s*, University of Chicago Press, 1994.

Susan Ware, *Holding Their Own: American Women in the 1930s*, Twayne Publishers, 1982.

——*Still Missing: Amelia Earhart and the Search for Modern Feminism*, Norton, 1993.

Jean Fagan Yellin, *Women and Sisters: The Antislavery Feminists in American Culture*, Yale University Press, 1989.

2. The Female Body

The Boston Women's Health Book Collective, *The New Our Bodies, Ourselves*, Touchstone Books, 1984.

J. Delaney, M. J. Lupton and E. Toth, *The Curse: A Cultural History of Menstruation*, University of Chicago Press, 1976, 1988.

Debra Evans, *Without Moral Limits: Women, Reproduction and the New Medical Technology,* Crossway Books, 1989.

Lillian Faderman, *Odd Girls and Twilight Lovers: A History of Lesbian Life in Twentieth-Century America*, Columbia University Press, 1991.

Linda Gordon, *Woman's Body, Woman's Right: Birth Control in America,* Penguin Books, 1990.

bell hooks, *Black Looks: Race and Representation*, South End Press, 1992.

J. W. Leavitt, ed., *Women and Health in America: Historical Readings,* University of Wisconsin Press, 1984.

Shirley A. Leckie, *Elizabeth Bacon Custer and the Making of a Myth,* University of Oklahoma Press, 1993.

Joan Nestle, ed., *The Persistent Desire: A Femme-Butch Reader*, Alyson Publications, 1992.

Hal D. Sears, *The Sex Radicals: Free Love in High Victorian America,* Regents Press of Kansas, 1977.

Ann Snitow, Christine Stansell and Sharon Thompson, eds., *Powers of Desire: The Politics of Sexuality,* New Feminist Library, 1983.

3. The Female Body in Motion

Susan K. Cahn, *Coming On Strong: Gender and Sexuality in Twentieth-Century Women's Sport,* Harvard University Press, 1994.

Ellen W. Goellner and Jacqueline Shea Murphy, eds., *Bodies of the Text: Dance as Theory, Literature as Dance,* Rutgers University Press, 1995.

Allen Guttmann, *Women's Sports: A History,* Columbia University Press, 1991.

Sue Macy, *Winning Ways: A Photohistory of American Women in Sports,* Henry Holt, 1996.

Gay Morris, ed. *Moving Words: Re-writing Dance,* Routledge, 1996.

Mariah Burton Nelson, *Are We Winning Yet? How Women Are Changing Sports and Sports Are Changing Women,* Random House, 1991.

Joan Ryan, *Little Girls in Pretty Boxes: The Making and Breaking of Elite Gymnasts and Figure Skaters,* Doubleday, 1995.

4. The Female Mind

Minna Carson, *Settlement Folk: Social Thought and the American Settlement Movement, 1885–1930, University of Chicago Press.*

Joseph L. Geller and Maxine Harris, eds., *Women of the Asylum: Voices from Behind the Walls, 1840–1945,* Doubleday, 1995.

Nancy Hoffman, ed., *Woman's "True" Profession: Voices from the History of Teaching,* Feminist Press, 1981.

Helen Lefkowitz Horowitz, *Alma Mater: Design and Experience in the Women's Colleges*, University of Massachusetts Press, 1993.

Peggy Orenstein, *School Girls: Young Women, Self-Esteem, and the Confidence Gap*, Doubleday, 1994.

Barbara Miller Solomon, *In the Company of Educated Women: A History of Women and Higher Education in America*, Yale University Press, 1985.

5. Writers and Artists

Gloria Anzaldua, *Borderlands: La Frontera*, Auntie Lute Books, 1987.

Hazel Carby, *Reconstructing Womanhood: The Emergence of the Afro-American Woman Novelist*, Oxford University Press, 1987.

Elaine Hedges and Ingrid Wendt, eds., *In Her Own Image: Women Working in the Arts*, Feminist Press, 1980.

Audre Lorde, *Sister Outsider*, The Crossing Press, 1984.

Cherrie Moraga and Gloria Anzaldua, eds., *This Bridge Called My Back: Writings by Radical Women of Color*, Persephone Press, 1988.

Toni Morrison, *Playing in the Dark: Whiteness and the Literary Imagination*, Harvard University Press, 1992.

Peter E. Palmquist, *Camera Fiends and Kodak Girls*, Midmarch Arts Press, 1989.

Naomi Rosenblum, *A History of Women Photographers*, Abbeville Press, 1994.

Charlotte Streifer Rubenstein, *American Women Artists: From Early Indian Times to the Present*, C.K. Hau, 1982.

6. Entertainers

Ally Acker, *Reel Women: Pioneers of the Cinema 1896 to the Present*, Continuum, 1993.

Jeanine Basinger, *A Woman's View: How Hollywood Spoke to Women, 1930–1960*, Knopf, 1993.

Joanne Bentley, *Hallie Flanagan: A Life in the American Theatre*, Knopf, 1988.

Linda Dahl, *Stormy Weather: The Music and Lives of a Century of Jazzwomen*, Pantheon.

Gillian G. Gaar, *She's A Rebel: The History of Women in Rock and Roll*, Seal Press, 1992.

Rosamund Gilder, *Enter the Actress*, Ayer, 1977.

Daphne Duval Harrison, *Black Pearls: Blues Queens of the 1920s*, Rutgers University Press, 1988.

Sally Placksin, *American Women in Jazz*, Wideview Books, 1982.

7. Media

Alexander Alland, Sr., *Jessie Tarbox Beals: First Woman News Photographer,* Camera Graphic Press, 1978.

Barbara Belford, *Brilliant Bylines,* Columbia University Press, 1986.

Susan J. Douglas, *Where the Girls Are: Growing Up Female with the Mass Media,* Times Books, 1994.

Julia Edwards, *Women of the World: The Great Foreign Correspondents,* Houghton Mifflin, 1988.

Kay Mills, *A Place in the News: From the Women's Pages to the Front Page,* Columbia University Press, 1990.

Nan Robertson, *The Girls in the Balcony: Women, Men and The New York Times,* Ballantine Books, 1993.

Ann Russo and Cheris Kramarae, eds., *The Radical Women's Press of the 1850s,* Routledge, 1990.

Alice Sheppard, *Cartooning for Suffrage,* University of New Mexico Press, 1994.

Martha M. Solomon, ed. *A Voice of Their Own: The Woman Suffrage Press,* University of Alabama Press, 1991.

8. Domestic Life

Miriam Formanek Brunell, *Made to Play House: Dolls and the Commercialization of American Girlhood, 1830–1930,* Yale University Press, 1993.

Dolores Hayden, *The Grand Domestic Revolution: A History of Feminist Designs for American Homes, Neighborhoods and Cities,* MIT Press, 1981.

Maxine L. Margolis, *Mothers and Such,* University of California Press, 1984.

Glenna Matthews, *Just a Housewife: The Rise and Fall of Domesticity in America,* Oxford University Press, 1987.

Elaine Tyler May, *Barren in the Promised Land: Childless Americans and the Pursuit of Happiness,* Basic Books, 1995.

9. Work

S. Armitage and E. Jameson, eds., *The Women's West,* University of Oklahoma Press, 1987.

Doris Cole, *From Tipi to Skyscraper: A History of Women in Architecture,* Brazillier, 1973.

Mona Harrington, *Women Lawyers: Rewriting the Rules,* Knopf, 1994.

Barbara J. Harris, *Beyond Her Sphere: Women and the Professions in American History,* Greenwood Press, 1978.

Jacqueline Jones, *Labor of Love, Labor of Sorrow: Black Women, Work, and the Family from Slavery to the Present,* Vintage Books, 1986.

G. Kass-Simon and Patricia Farnes, eds., *Women of Science: Righting the Record,* Indiana University Press, 1990.

Angel Kwolek-Folland, *Engendering Business: Men and Women in the Corporate Office, 1870–1930,* Johns Hopkins University Press, 1994.

Molly Martin, ed., *Hard-Hatted Women: Stories of Struggle and Success in the Trades,* Seal Press, 1988.

Annie Nathan Meyer, *Women's Work in America,* Holt, 1891. Reprinted 1972 by Arno Press.

Sara Ruddick and Pamela Daniels, eds., *Working It Out: 23 Women Writers, Scientists and Scholars Talk about Their Lives and Work,* Pantheon, 1977.

Deborah Gray White, *Ar'n't I a Woman? Female Slaves in the Plantation South,* Norton, 1985.

Permissions

Grateful acknowledgment is given for permission to reprint photographs and illustrations from the following sources:

Index